ETHICS

BENEDICT DE SPINOZA was born in Amsterdam in 1632, where his orthodox Jewish family had fled from persecution in Portugal. Spinoza was expelled from the synagogue because of his heterodox philosophy, and earned his living as an optical-lens grinder, to be at liberty to pursue his ideal of truth. He identified God with nature and he denied the possibility of an Act of Creation. Spinoza's *Ethics*, published after his death in 1677, elaborates his attempt to portray God and nature, body and soul, as one, a doctrine which inspired the Romantic poets, particularly Coleridge and Shelley. His influence spread to the nineteenth century and George Eliot, who began a translation of his works, admired him as the enemy of superstition and the hero of scientific rationalism. Spinoza also won the respect of Flaubert and Matthew Arnold, and many writers since then have been moved by the beauty and serenity of his thought.

EDWIN CURLEY, Professor of Philosophy at the University of Michigan, is the editor and translator of *The Collected Works of Spinoza* (Princeton, vol I, 1985; vol II forthcoming), editor (and translator to the extent the edition incorporates material from the Latin version) of Hobbes's *Leviathan* (Hackett, 1994), and the author of the following books on Descartes and Spinoza: *Spinoza's Metaphysics* (Harvard, 1969), *Descartes Against the Sceptics* (Harvard, 1978) and *Behind the Geometrical Method* (Princeton, 1988). He is a Fellow of the American Academy of Arts and Sciences and for eleven years held research positions at the Australian National University, where much of his work on Spinoza was done.

STUART HAMPSHIRE was elected a Fellow of All Souls College in 1936 and was a tutor in philosophy until the war, when he served in the Army. After a short period in the Foreign Office, he returned to the teaching of philosophy at University College London. In 1950 he became a Fellow of New College, Oxford, and in 1963 was appointed Professor of Philosophy at Princeton University. After being Warden of Wadham College, Oxford, from 1970 to 1984, he was then appointed Professor of Philosophy at Stanford University, California. He is the author of *Thought and Action, Freedom and the*

Individual, Freedom of Mind and Other Essays, Modern Writers and Other Essays, Morality and Conflict and *Justice is Conflict*. He has also written *Spinoza* (1951) and *Innocence and Experience* (1989), both of which have been published by Penguin.

BENEDICT DE SPINOZA

Ethics

Edited and Translated by
EDWIN CURLEY
with an Introduction by
STUART HAMPSHIRE

PENGUIN BOOKS

PENGUIN BOOKS

Published by the Penguin Group
Penguin Books Ltd, 80 Strand, London WC2R 0RL, England
Penguin Putnam Inc., 375 Hudson Street, New York, New York 10014, USA
Penguin Books Australia Ltd, 250 Camberwell Road, Camberwell, Victoria 3124, Australia
Penguin Books Canada Ltd, 10 Alcorn Avenue, Toronto, Ontario, Canada M4V 3B2
Penguin Books India (P) Ltd, 11 Community Centre, Panchsheel Park, New Delhi – 110 017, India
Penguin Books (NZ) Ltd, Cnr Rosedale and Airborne Roads, Albany, Auckland, New Zealand
Penguin Books (South Africa) (Pty) Ltd, 24 Sturdee Avenue, Rosebank 2196, South Africa

Penguin Books Ltd, Registered Offices: 80 Strand, London WC2R 0RL, England

www.penguin.com

This translation first published in the USA in *A Spinza Reader* by
Princeton University Press 1994
This edition published in Penguin Books 1996

040

Translation copyright © Princeton University Press, 1994
Introduction copyright © Stuart Hampshire, 1996
All rights reserved

The moral right of the translator and editor has been asserted.

Set in Adobe Janson
Typeset by Datix International Limited, Bungay, Suffolk

Printed and bound in Great Britain by Clays Ltd, Elcograf S.p.A.

ISBN-13: 978-0-140-43571-9

www.greenpenguin.co.uk

CONTENTS

Ethics

INTRODUCTION

It is a feature of the history of philosophy that any great thinker presents a different face to the public in response to changing philosophical and political interests. Since 1951, when Penguin published my study of Spinoza, there have been large changes in the interests of English-speaking philosophers, and in expounding Spinoza's *Ethics* emphasis will now tend to fall in different places to meet these contemporary concerns. In 1951 all metaphysical speculation was apt to be dismissed by many anglophone philosophers as without content or value, and particularly if the metaphysics claimed to rest upon purely logical demonstrations in the style of Euclid's *Elements*. Kant had given reasons for rejecting the claims of rationalist metaphysics, and the radical scepticism of the 1950s was more drastic, asserting that any claim by a philosopher to have arrived at genuine knowledge, unless by observation and experiment, was a false claim. Spinoza's *Ethics* makes no appeal to sense experience and experiment in support of its conclusions, and its geometrical style flaunts the deductive and non-observational structure of its arguments.

To build a bridge to contemporary interests, and hence to understanding, it seemed necessary in the 1950s to suggest that Spinoza's metaphysics envisaged the possibility of a unified knowledge of the natural order, and that it exhibited the consequences of such unified knowledge in the areas of morality and politics. This interpretative approach to the *Ethics* seems to me entirely valid and still relevant, but it is one among several possible approaches.

Spinoza begins the *Ethics* with arguments to prove that there must be a single self-subsistent substance, to be identified as '*Deus sive Natura*', 'God or Nature', which is the cause, directly or indirectly, of all things, and which is self-created. This statement is a denial of the possibility of a transcendent creator, distinct from his creation, and a denial of the first principles of Judaism and of Christianity. God must be immanent in the natural order, the creator in its creation, if we are to avoid the incoherence of thinking of two substances in reality: a creator distinct from his creation. There could not have been an act of creation, as Jews and Christians claim that there has been; this would imply that God had reason to choose to create the actual world rather than other possible worlds. But what reason could there be other than the creator's nature which made the actual world the only possible world? We must think of the natural order as the unfolding of God's nature in accordance with eternal laws which constitute his essential nature. The origin of things is not to be found in an act of will, but rather in the rational order which constitutes God or Nature. These arguments for God's immanence undermine the orthodox tradition of Western morality and metaphysics, and they remove the need for any intermediary between God and man in the form of a Church and of a priesthood. We do not need any privileged revelation of God's intentions and we must not apply to God any part of the vocabulary that is applicable to finite human minds.

Using his natural powers of reasoning, a free person, free from superstitions and illusions, can work out for himself what is the necessary framework of human knowledge. He will discriminate in his own thinking different levels of human knowledge, with logically necessary truths on the highest level and knowledge of events in the common order of nature, derived from sense perception, on the lower levels. The *Ethics* itself consists of propositions which, with their attached proofs, claim to be necessary truths, successively defining the nature of God, the mind, the emotions, human bondage to the emotions, and the power of understanding to foster human freedom. Divided into five parts, the argument of the book moves from the eternal natural order to humanity's place within the natural order and to the consequences for a true conception of human freedom and of attainable happiness.

God or Nature, the one substance, is infinite and includes within itself everything that exists. But human beings, who are a composite unity of body and mind, necessarily think of reality as divided into two distinct categories of existents: material objects in space and thoughts. Nature as a whole, and every living and persisting individual within it, must be thought of as a composite unity of body and mind, of Extension and Thought. Descartes' Christian God had created two orders of being: Extension, including all objects in space, and Thought, which is a separate domain. Descartes found himself unable to account adequately for the relation between the two domains. Therefore, he could give no clear account of the unity of a person. For Spinoza Thought and Extension (bodies in space) are two aspects of a single reality, as reality presents itself to human beings. We can switch from considering reality under one heading to considering things under the other, always recognizing that thoughts can only be explained by other thoughts and the movements of bodies by the movements of other bodies. We can study an animal's behaviour as explained by its appetites and expectations ('It wants its mate and expects to find it here') or as explained by physical causes ('There was a chemical reaction which started the movement of muscles . . .'). The same tract of behaviour can be described and explained in both ways, and neither type of explanation is to be preferred to the other as being more fundamental. They each equally represent the common order of nature, but we must not in our minds mix and confuse the two necessarily distinct orders of causes. A thought, or a state of mind, does not really explain the movement of a body, which can only be adequately explained by physical laws of motion: equally a thought or a mental state is not to be adequately explained by the movement of the person's body, but rather by the laws of thought which give sense to the thought. When I smile, a thought explains the pleasure which the smile conveys; the movement of the lips is properly explained by events in the brain and nervous system.

Reality is inexhaustible, and there must be infinite ways in which it can be thought of. But human beings conceive, not only of themselves, but of everything in nature either as a configuration of thoughts (desires and perceptions) or as a configuration of compound objects and of simple objects within them (e.g. atoms and molecules).

In its application to human beings, embodied minds and animated bodies, this double-aspect theory of the mind seems intelligible, and it can be applied to animal behaviour without too much strain. The difficulty comes when the theory is applied to inanimate things, to which appetites and perceptions are not normally attributed, at least in ordinary unphilosophical speech. In Spinoza's metaphysical vision all things are in a sense, and in different degrees, animated. The important qualification is 'in different degrees'. Orthodox Aristotelianism had recognized a scale of being in the universe with human beings, possessing reason, at the head of the scale. Spinoza's supposed scale of being has a less abrupt discontinuity: human beings have a greater power of thought than other creatures, but all creatures have perceptions which to some degree reflect reality. Under both attributes, Thought and Extension, reality is to be understood in terms of a scale of complexity within which individual things are ranged from the most simple, which are elementary particles under the attribute of Extension, up to the most complex physical systems; similarly, thoughts, including desires and perceptions, range from the most rudimentary appetites for nourishment or sex (desires) and specific reactions to the environment (perception) up to the fully articulate desires and beliefs of human beings. There is a scale of complexity in the mental domain of desires and perceptions matching the scale of complexity among physical objects. A human body, and particularly a brain, is an extraordinarily complex thing, and Spinoza remarks that its powers are still unknown. We do know that a person's appetites, unlike the appetites of animals, can become conscious and articulate desires and can become also the objects of thoughtful reflection.

It is of the nature of thought to be reflexive and our independence and freedom reside in this native power, which is a reflection of the complex structures and powers of the human body and brain. All individual things, from top to bottom of the scale, strive to preserve themselves and to protect and extend their independence of the environment as far as they can. Their individual nature, whether as persons or as animals, or as (in the ordinary sense) inanimate objects, is a function of their power of self-maintenance in the face of external influences. In their political and social conflicts and in their struggles for power and for liberty, human beings are only conforming to a universal law of nature. The prescriptions of morality must be understood as guides to social harmony and peace, which is the common interest of all reasonable persons, as they strive to survive.

Spinoza clearly believed that he had solved the problem of the relation between mind and body which had baffled Descartes and which is still baffling philosophers in our time. He insisted that any cause operating in nature considered as a system of thought is identical with a cause operating in nature considered as a physical system. This entails that, for every change in a human mind, which can be explained in psychological terms, there must be a replica in the body which is a change to be explained in the terms of physical laws. The identity claimed for the two orders of causes has always puzzled Spinoza's correspondents and modern commentators alike. I have an interpretation to suggest which is speculative but possible. First, nature is not divided into just two domains, Thought and Extension, but human beings have two ways of thinking of objects in nature, including themselves. God or Nature has no limits and must be characterized by an infinity of attributes, not just two. Human beings are finite things and limited, and for us everything presents itself either as a body in space, governed by laws of motion, or as a thinking, knowing thing, governed by laws of thought. We may think of a particular thing (animal or person) as having an aim and appetite of its own, which explains its behaviour teleologically, and as a desiring and perceiving creature; or we may explain the thing's behaviour as the effect of external causes, and this is the model of a mechanical explanation. As a person, an embodied thinker, I have to think of my actions and movements as arising from my desires and perceptions; but I also have to think of my bodily actions and bodily movements as effects of changes in my brain and sense organs which in turn are themselves the effects of external causes. So thoughout nature, considering individual objects, I may alternate between considering them as comparatively active agents, partly self-determined by their desires and perceptions, and considering their behaviour as entirely the effects of external bodily causes. Evidently it will be useless in our present state of knowledge to consider a piece of machinery as if it were a thoughtful agent or to consider a thoughtful person as if he or she were a piece of machinery: useless, given that our knowledge of one is of something passive and knowledge of the other mainly knowledge of something active. Human knowledge is evidently very limited, and reflects only some aspects of nature. But we have an *a priori* assurance that these two aspects of Nature are well founded in reality, and that both forms of explanation are valid within the limits of our knowledge.

The active–passive distinction, which I suggest is parallel to the Thought–Extension distinction, is focused in the *Ethics* on human passions. The argument is that, by reflecting on our passions, and on the rudimentary and uncritical thought associated with them, we convert them into thoughtful sentiments and reasonable attitudes. Emotions that have begun as mere pathological states, independent of the subject's reasoning, may be re-directed towards objects that are intelligible objects of emotion in the light of reason. Human beings are governed by their passions, by their loves and hates, their pleasures and pains, their hopes and fears, and the requirement of morality is that by thoughtful reflection they should change the direction of these sentiments so that they contribute to the person's survival and to his or her happiness. Reason by itself cannot move to action without the motive force of passion, but we can become passionately reasonable (as implied by the phrase 'the intellectual love of God') and reasonably passionate in pursuit of our freedom and self-governance.

All our emotions are either pleasures or pains conjoined with the thought of an object as the cause of pleasure or pain. The accompanying thought is normally confused and inadequate, arising only from the association of ideas in our experience. When on reflection a person perceives the inadequacy, the emotion is immediately changed. If we stay with our common-sense views of the world, founded on our day-to-day experiences, we shall still believe that the earth is flat and that the sun is a small object in the sky above us. We can be equally thoughtless and immature in our emotions and therefore foolish in the conduct of our affairs, moving from one objective to another without rational control and direction. Through systematic knowledge of the workings of the mind, matching systematic knowledge of physics, we can gain control of our sentiments and follow a consistent path towards tranquillity and happiness. Applying the revolutionary insights of Galileo's new physics to the mind, Spinoza comes to agree with Epicurus and Lucretius: use the native power of the mind ('*vivida vis animi*' in Lucretius), which is a mechanism for understanding causes, and you will be emotionally at ease with yourself.

Spinoza was always denounced during his life, and for a century afterwards, as not only an atheist, but also as a materialist and a determinist: that is, he claimed that all things, including persons, are determined in their actions by the laws of physics. The phrase 'God or Nature' gives a sense in which he was an atheist, but he was a materialist with a difference and also a determinist with a difference. Human beings do not have supernatural souls and their processes of thought are inseparably linked to bodily processes. This seems a form of materialism. Our mental powers and our physical powers are indissolubly linked – but we can learn to understand the natural order, at least in part, *sub specie aeternitatis*, under its aspect as an eternal framework and system of natural laws. Our knowledge of the intellectual order of things will always be fragmentary, because our powers of mind are limited and the intellectual order is unlimited and infinite. This is materialism with a difference, because God or Nature is as much an intelligible system of thought as a system of material objects. Spinoza's so-called determinism is the belief that all behaviour, whether of human beings or of other natural creatures, is to be explained by causes, but by causes of two contrasting kinds: causes that are eternally valid as explanations of their effects, and causes that are valid as explanations at a particular time and in particular circumstances. Any living thing's desire to avoid pain and death is an example of a cause of the first kind: my desire to avoid my particular neighbour provides a cause of my behaviour which explains it within the common order of causes in nature and *sub specie durationis*. The first kind of explanation is a complete explanation and the statement of it is a necessary truth. The second kind of explanation is incomplete, because the chains of causes stretch back in time without limit and stopping-point in the common order of nature. Our knowledge of this second kind of cause must always be comparatively unreliable because imperfect. There is an absolute distinction in Spinoza's philosophy between understanding some part of the intellectual order of things, which is knowledge of eternal truths, and the contrasting knowledge of things as they exist at a particular time in the common order of nature. Mathematics and the fundamental laws of physics (laws of motion) and laws of psychology (laws of thoughts) belong to the first category; the useful truths of medicine and of statecraft belong to the second category.

Having repudiated a transcendent creator and the morality founded on God's rewards and penalties, the *Ethics* still directs the reader to an overriding interest in things that are eternal at the expense of our transient interests in the things that happen around us. This is a freethinker's idea of redemption along the path that leads to freedom of mind and to happiness through intense thought and reflection and through detachment from accidental worldly ambitions and conflicts. The tone of the *Ethics* is self-consciously the tone of a book of prophecy. Spinoza stands in the tradition of the Jewish prophets and draws upon Maimonides, author of *The Guide of the Perplexed* (1190). The Euclidean format of theorem and proof was designed to stress the impartiality and impersonality of the arguments, which are intended to be free from rhetoric and to appeal only to reason. The appeal to reason, and to an understanding, as far as possible, of the fundamental laws of physics and of thought, is not a call to withdrawal from the world and to substitute the enjoyment of theory for the enjoyment of living. On the contrary both in the *Ethics*, and in his *Theological-Political Treatise* and in *The Political Treatise*, Spinoza presents theory as the necessary guide to action and particularly to political prudence which can save men and women from tyranny, war and destruction. It is known that Spinoza played a part in Dutch politics and he consistently argued that everyone should try to create the conditions for security, peace of mind and for the active enjoyment of one's own powers, physical and mental.

Every individual thing, and consequently every individual person, strives to preserve and to increase his or her individuality, against the threat of being overcome and absorbed by external forces. The drive to self-assertion, and to an aggressive sense of my own power and distinctiveness as a person, is always present, and some of this sense of unity and this aggressiveness is transferred to communities of persons. Nothing is more useful to a person, he claims, than the added strength that comes from the union with other persons in a community, which then becomes itself an individual thing, with its own drive to self-preservation. The aggressive manœuvres of Churches and sects in the seventeenth century, and of nation states in the nineteenth and twentieth centuries, are intelligible within Spinoza's natural philosophy and his idea of history. It is natural that every composite entity, whether a nation or a religious sect, should hold itself together by trying to extend its freedom of action and its power as far as they will go, exactly as an individual person does.

This picture of an inevitable and unceasing struggle for power between nations and Churches is, taken by itself, a depressing one, and in line with the suggestions of Machiavelli and of Hobbes. But the *Ethics* points to the way out of the insecurity and unfreedom which the competition and conflict involve, both for individual citizens and for statesmen. When we reflect on the composite nature of all individuals, except elementary particles and including persons, and on their two-sidedness (Thought and Extension), the path of escape into freedom, or into relative freedom, becomes clear. A person, two-sided, is both comparatively free, in so far as he is following a coherent line of thought, and unfree, in so far as he is conceived as an organism responding to physical forces in the environment. All material things, including living organisms, have a Chinese-box structure, being composed of bodies within bodies up to ever higher levels of complexity, with elementary particles (*corpora simplicissima*) as the bottom level. In a person as a thinking subject, the levels of complexity are levels of reflexiveness, of thoughts about thoughts, Chinese boxes of self-monitoring thought.

One naturally begins by hating the sectarians of a religion which is not one's own, or the nationalist citizens of a nation which is in conflict with one's own. Those are natural reactions easily understood within the common order of nature and within the laws of psychology which govern the emotions. But they are only reactions, not actions, and it is within my power to do something about my reactions, namely, to reflect and to evaluate the source and the quality of the thought that enters into them. As soon as I reflect, I can see that clinging to these hatreds will contribute nothing either to my security or to my happiness, and that I must re-think my attitude to these potential enemies rather than be the victim of immediate and thoughtless reactions, which are likely to lead to violence and misery. I will see the advantages for me of a prudent strategy of conciliation, negotiation and tolerance, as soon as I am free to think clearly.

The *Tractatus Theologico-Politicus*, which is an argument for toleration in matters of religion and faith, was published in Spinoza's lifetime, unlike the *Ethics*, and unlike the *Political Treatise*, which was left unfinished. In his philosophy of mind he had proposed a strictly philosophical foundation for his advocacy of toleration. Belief could not of its very nature be enforced, and the state was only responsible for the protection of public order. The great majority of citizens, untouched by philosophy, will always be restrained by the imagination of divine rewards and divine punishments rather than by a perception of rational self-interest. It is a principle of statecraft, therefore, not to subvert the superstitious beliefs of established religions when religious scepticism is likely to lead to disorder and violence. A rational and enlightened morality, public and private, is likely at all times to be the possession of a minority, of those who have the habit of reflection and of self-consciousness and of detachment from their thoughtless passions.

Parts IV and V of the *Ethics* – 'Of Human Bondage' and 'Of the Power of the Intellect' – establish the foundations of morality and of human freedom. Spinoza did not follow the Stoics in arguing that the wise person is altogether free of emotion. The path of wisdom and happiness is the enjoyment of intellectual activity and resides in the pleasure taken in the deployment of physical and mental powers. Activity, self-direction, freedom in all its forms: these are the supreme values, and the elements of happiness. It makes no sense to require, as Manichean Christians did require, that the mind should suppress the bodily passions, and should cultivate only spiritual powers. Persons must be mind–bodies, an indissoluble unity which can be considered from two points of view, and with two distinct vocabularies and two distinct kinds of causation. That the mind or soul should survive by itself when the life of the body has ended is, for Spinoza, an unintelligible supposition: it suggests that the soul or mind is an individual, or quasi-substance, rather than a distinguishable aspect of the activity of an individual, who is a person. But in a famously obscure passage (Book V, Proposition 23) Spinoza asserts that 'The human mind cannot be absolutely destroyed with the body, but something of it remains which is eternal.' He adds 'we feel and know by experience that we are eternal'. The claim is that, in so far as our thought is disconnected from memory and imagination, and is knowledge of eternal and necessary truths, our thought is disconnected from the limitations of time, and in this thinking we are united with the eternal aspect of Reality (God or Nature) as thought. We make the transition from thinking of ourselves as particular things in the constantly changing face of Nature, each with a particular standpoint and location in time, to thinking of ourselves as being, in our thinking, parts of the eternal framework of Reality.

It is often asked why the *Ethics* is set out 'in geometrical manner' in imitation of Euclid's *Elements*. Readers will easily see that the proofs are very far from being rigorous and that the definitions and other premises within the argument often presuppose the propositions allegedly deduced from them. This circularity in reasoning is not a weakness peculiar to Spinoza among philosophers, nor is it to be seen as a weakness when metaphysics, and not formal logic, is in question. Metaphysics is an attempt to present a coherent picture of reality as a whole, including a speculative account of the origin of things and of the place of human beings within the imagined scheme. The words to be stressed are 'coherent' and 'speculative'. Spinoza is open to criticism in so far as the *Ethics* seems to contain inconsistencies, which need to be interpreted and clarified. Even if all apparent inconsistencies had been cleared up, the vision of Reality which the *Ethics* conveys would still be only a speculation, one possible scheme of things among others. There is no universally agreed, or self-evident test, which might prove that this scheme is superior to all others in its credibility. But here I am stating my own opinion, and not the opinion of Spinoza, who lived long before Hume and Kant had questioned the claims of pure reason to reveal the plan of the universe. In the *Ethics*, and in his correspondence with other thinkers, Spinoza represents the propositions of this system as self-evident truths, or as directly deducible from self-evident truths. There is no way round them, if one is determined to be consistent and determined also to make no appeal to faith or to the mysteries of the unknown.

While making these claims for the power of reason in investigating reality, Spinoza at the same time represents God or Nature as vastly and immeasurably outstripping human powers of cognition and of understanding. Nature is characterized by infinite attributes unknown to us and for ever beyond our reach. Part of the grandeur of the *Ethics* is its calm rejection of any idea of humanity's special election and of its privileged dominance in the universe. In mathematics we have some insight into the structure of things, and we should extend this insight until it amounts to an 'intellectual love of God'. This power of mind will be its own reward.

In addition to his two political treatises already mentioned, Spinoza's mature works include *On the Correction of the Understanding*, which ought to be read in conjunction with the *Ethics*.

Stuart Hampshire

FURTHER READING

Much of the Spinoza legend is based on the earliest biographical accounts:

Pierre Bayle, *Historical and Critical Dictionary*, Rotterdam, 1696, article on Spinoza.

John Colerus, *The Life of Benedictus de Spinoza*, tr. in Frederick Pollock's *Spinoza, His life and philosophy*, London, 1899.

Jean Lucas, *The Oldest Biography of Spinoza*, tr. A. Wolf, London, 1927.

But there is now a more up-to-date and reliable account in Wim Klever's 'Spinoza's Life and Works', in:

Don Garrett (ed.), *The Cambridge Companion to Spinoza*, Cambridge University Press, 1995.

This is a valuable compendium of contemporary scholarship, with an excellent bibliography. For general introductions to Spinoza's works, readers should consult:

Henry Allison, *Benedict de Spinoza: An Introduction*, Yale University Press, 1987.

Alan Donagan, *Spinoza*, University of Chicago Press, 1988.

Stuart Hampshire, *Spinoza*, Penguin, 1951.

For commentary on the *Ethics* read:

Jonathan Bennett, *A Study of Spinoza's ETHICS*, Hackett, 1984.

Edwin Curley, *Behind the Geometrical Method*, Princeton University Press, 1988.

NOTE ON THE TEXT

We know from Spinoza's correspondence that he was at work early in the 1660s on a draft of his philosophy, written in geometric form, and that the early portions of this work were sufficiently well-advanced that he was prepared to circulate them among friends. From the correspondence we can infer some things about the work at that stage: some of the definitions took a different form; some claims which Spinoza then treated as axioms, and which his friends resisted, became propositions in the final version of the *Ethics*, theses he argued for, rather than assuming them without argument.

By 1665 Spinoza seems to have been near completion of the work as he then conceived it. He speaks of the work as if publication were not far off, and he is beginning to think about who might translate his Latin text into Dutch, to permit it to reach a wider audience. At that point the *Ethics* would have been a three-part work, in which the third part contained material which subsequently appeared in Part IV.

But in 1665 he lay this project aside to write his *Theological–Political Treatise*. One of his aims in that work, it seems, was to pave the way for the *Ethics* by attacking, in more conventional prose, the religious prejudices which he thought would be an obstacle to acceptance of the *Ethics*, particularly the prejudice (as he saw it) that Scripture provides an authoritative conception of God's nature. He also appended to that work an extended argument, based on a rather Hobbesian political theory, for freedom of thought and expression.

When the *Theological–Political Treatise* was published in 1670, it created such a storm of protest that it made publication of the *Ethics* more, rather than less, difficult. Spinoza came close to publishing the *Ethics* in 1675, by which time it was a five-part work; but opposition from the theologians caused him to desist. Before he died in 1677, however, he did arrange for its posthumous publication, along with some other, unfinished works (an epistemological treatise, a political treatise, and a Hebrew grammar) and the bulk of his surviving correspondence. Simultaneously with the publication of the *Opera posthuma* (OP) there appeared a Dutch translation of most of its works, known as the *Nagelate Schriften* (or NS). Because of the timing of the two editions we can infer that the NS translations were done from manuscripts, and not from the printed text of the OP.

The translation presented in this volume is done from what is still the standard edition of Spinoza's works, edited by Carl Gebhardt (Heidelberg: Carl Winter Verlag, 1925, 4 vols). The volume and page numbers given in the margins refer to this edition, as an aid to checking the translation and to tracking references in secondary sources. Gebhardt was the first editor to systematically use the NS translations as a control on the proof-reading of the editors of the OP. Frequently he introduces variant texts from the NS in his edition of the text, in brackets. I have translated these, but the reader should be aware that the status of the NS variants is controversial. Some of what Gebhardt took to be variant versions of Spinoza's text may be the consequence of the translator's licence or error. (Perhaps the most interesting case, philosophically, is the variant reading of Axiom 2 of Part II.) Two Dutch scholars, Fokke Akkerman and Piet Steenbakkers, are currently preparing a new critical edition of the *Ethics*, which will no doubt revise many of Gebhardt's conclusions. Some of their results, particularly as regards cross-references from one part of the *Ethics* to another, are already incorporated in this edition.

In this translation, when '*or*' is in italics it translates the Latin *sive* or *seu*, which normally indicates an equivalence rather than an alternative. Roman numerals refer to parts of the *Ethics*. Arabic numerals are used for axioms, definitions, propositions, etc. The following abbreviations are used:

A = axiom
P = proposition
D (following a roman numeral) = definition
D (following P + an arabic numeral) = demonstration
C = corollary
S = scholium
Exp = explanation
L = lemma (cf. the excursus on physics after IIP13)
Post = postulate
Pref = preface
App = appendix (at the end of Part I and of Part IV)
Def Aff = the definitions of the affects at the end of Part III

So 'ID1' refers to Definition 1 of Part I. 'IIIP15C' refers to the corollary to Proposition 15 of Part III, etc.

The Ethics

DEMONSTRATED IN GEOMETRIC ORDER
AND DIVIDED INTO FIVE PARTS,
WHICH TREAT

I. Of God
II. Of the Nature and Origin of the Mind
III. Of the Origin and Nature of the Affects
IV. Of Human Bondage, *or* the Powers of the Affects
V. Of the Power of the Intellect, *or* on Human Freedom

FIRST PART OF THE ETHICS
OF GOD

DEFINITIONS

D1: By cause of itself I understand that whose essence involves existence, *or* that whose nature cannot be conceived except as existing.

D2: That thing is said to be finite in its own kind that can be limited by another of the same nature.

For example, a body is called finite because we always conceive another that is greater. Thus a thought is limited by another thought. But a body is not limited by a thought nor a thought by a body.

D3: By substance I understand what is in itself and is conceived through itself, that is, that whose concept does not require the concept of another thing, from which it must be formed.

D4: By attribute I understand what the intellect perceives of a substance, as constituting its essence.

D5: By mode I understand the affections of a substance, *or* that which is in another through which it is also conceived.

D6: By God I understand a being absolutely infinite, that is, a substance consisting of an infinity of attributes, of which each one expresses an eternal and infinite essence.

1

II/46   Exp.: I say absolutely infinite, not infinite in its own kind; for if something is only infinite in its own kind, we can deny infinite attributes of it [NS: (i.e., we can conceive infinite attributes which do not pertain to its nature)]; but if something is absolutely infinite, whatever expresses essence and involves no negation pertains to its essence.

D7: That thing is called free which exists from the necessity of its nature alone, and is determined to act by itself alone. But a thing is called necessary, or rather compelled, which is determined by another to exist and to produce an effect in a certain and determinate manner.

D8: By eternity I understand existence itself, insofar as it is conceived to follow necessarily from the definition alone of the eternal thing.

    Exp.: For such existence, like the essence of a thing, is conceived as an eternal truth, and on that account cannot be explained by duration or time, even if the duration is conceived to be without beginning or end.

AXIOMS

A1: Whatever is, is either in itself or in another.

A2: What cannot be conceived through another, must be conceived through itself.

A3: From a given determinate cause the effect follows necessarily; and conversely, if there is no determinate cause, it is impossible for an effect to follow.

A4: The knowledge of an effect depends on, and involves, the knowledge of its cause.

A5: Things that have nothing in common with one another also cannot be understood through one another, *or* the concept of the one does not involve the concept of the other.

II/47   A6: A true idea must agree with its object.

A7: If a thing can be conceived as not existing, its essence does not involve existence.

P1: *A substance is prior in nature to its affections.*
    Dem.: This is evident from D3 and D5.

P2: *Two substances having different attributes have nothing in common with one another.*
    Dem.: This is also evident from D3. For each must be in itself and be

conceived through itself, *or* the concept of the one does not involve the concept of the other.

P3: *If things have nothing in common with one another, one of them cannot be the cause of the other.*

Dem.: If they have nothing in common with one another, then (by A5) they cannot be understood through one another, and so (by A4) one cannot be the cause of the other, q.e.d.

P4: *Two or more distinct things are distinguished from one another, either by a difference in the attributes of the substances or by a difference in their affections.*

Dem.: Whatever is, is either in itself or in another (by A1), that is (by D3 and D5), outside the intellect there is nothing except substances and their affections. Therefore, there is nothing outside the intellect through which a number of things can be distinguished from one another except substances, *or* what is the same (by D4), their attributes, and their affections, q.e.d.

II/48

P5: *In Nature there cannot be two or more substances of the same nature* or *attribute.*

Dem.: If there were two or more distinct substances, they would have to be distinguished from one another either by a difference in their attributes, or by a difference in their affections (by P4). If only by a difference in their attributes, then it will be conceded that there is only one of the same attribute. But if by a difference in their affections, then since a substance is prior in nature to its affections (by P1), if the affections are put to one side and [the substance] is considered in itself, that is (by D3 and A6), considered truly, one cannot be conceived to be distinguished from another, that is (by P4), there cannot be many, but only one [of the same nature *or* attribute], q.e.d.

P6: *One substance cannot be produced by another substance.*

Dem.: In Nature there cannot be two substances of the same attribute (by P5), that is (by P2), which have something in common with each other. Therefore (by P3) one cannot be the cause of the other, *or* cannot be produced by the other, q.e.d.

Cor.: From this it follows that a substance cannot be produced by anything else. For in Nature there is nothing except substances and their affections, as is evident from A1, D3, and D5. But it cannot be produced by a substance (by P6). Therefore, substance absolutely cannot be produced by anything else, q.e.d.

Alternatively: This is demonstrated even more easily from the absurdity of its contradictory. For if a substance could be produced by something else, the knowledge of it would have to depend on the knowledge of its cause (by A4). And so (by D3) it would not be a substance.

II/49   P7: *It pertains to the nature of a substance to exist.*

Dem.: A substance cannot be produced by anything else (by P6C); therefore it will be the cause of itself, that is (by D1), its essence necessarily involves existence, *or* it pertains to its nature to exist, q.e.d.

P8: *Every substance is necessarily infinite.*

Dem.: A substance of one attribute does not exist unless it is unique (P5), and it pertains to its nature to exist (P7). Of its nature, therefore, it will exist either as finite or as infinite. But not as finite. For then (by D2) it would have to be limited by something else of the same nature, which would also have to exist necessarily (by P7), and so there would be two substances of the same attribute, which is absurd (by P5). Therefore, it exists as infinite, q.e.d.

Schol. 1: Since being finite is really, in part, a negation, and being infinite is an absolute affirmation of the existence of some nature, it follows from P7 alone that every substance must be infinite. [NS: For if we assumed a finite substance, we would, in part, deny existence to its nature, which (by P7) is absurd.]

Schol. 2: I do not doubt that the demonstration of P7 will be difficult to conceive for all who judge things confusedly, and have not been accustomed to know things through their first causes—because they do not distinguish between the modifications of substances and the substances themselves, nor do they know how things are produced. So it happens that they fictitiously ascribe to substances the beginning which they see that natural things have; for those who do not know the true causes of things confuse everything and without any conflict of mind feign that both trees and men speak, imagine that men are formed both from stones and from seed, and that any form whatever is changed into any other. So also, those who confuse the divine nature with the human easily ascribe human affects to God, particularly so long as they are also ignorant of how those affects are produced in the mind.

II/50   But if men would attend to the nature of substance, they would have no doubt at all of the truth of P7. Indeed, this proposition would be an axiom for everyone, and would be numbered among the common notions. For by substance they would understand what is in itself and is conceived through itself, that is, that the knowledge of which does not require the knowledge of any other thing. But by modifications they would understand what is in another, those things whose concept is formed from the concept of the thing in which they are.

4

This is how we can have true ideas of modifications which do not exist; for though they do not actually exist outside the intellect, nevertheless their essences are comprehended in another in such a way that they can be conceived through it. But the truth of substances is not outside the intellect unless it is in them themselves, because they are conceived through themselves.

Hence, if someone were to say that he had a clear and distinct, that is, true, idea of a substance, and nevertheless doubted whether such a substance existed, that would indeed be the same as if he were to say that he had a true idea, and nevertheless doubted whether it was false (as is evident to anyone who is sufficiently attentive). Or if someone maintains that a substance is created, he maintains at the same time that a false idea has become true. Of course nothing more absurd can be conceived. So it must be confessed that the existence of a substance, like its essence, is an eternal truth.

And from this we can infer in another way that there is only one [substance] of the same nature, which I have considered it worth the trouble of showing here. But to do this in order, it must be noted,

I. that the true definition of each thing neither involves nor expresses anything except the nature of the thing defined.

From which it follows,

II. that no definition involves or expresses any certain number of individuals,

since it expresses nothing other than the nature of the thing defined. For example, the definition of the triangle expresses nothing but the simple nature of the triangle, but not any certain number of triangles. It is to be noted,

III. that there must be, for each existing thing, a certain cause on account of which it exists.

Finally, it is to be noted,

IV. that this cause, on account of which a thing exists, either must be contained in the very nature and definition of the existing thing (*viz. that it pertains to its nature to exist*) or must be outside it.

From these propositions it follows that if, in Nature, a certain number of individuals exists, there must be a cause why those individuals, and why neither more nor fewer, exist.

For example, if twenty men exist in Nature (*to make the matter clearer, I assume that they exist at the same time, and that no others previously existed* II/51

5

in Nature), it will not be enough (i.e., *to give a reason why twenty men exist*) to show the cause of human nature in general; but it will be necessary in addition to show the cause why not more and not fewer than twenty exist. For (by III) there must necessarily be a cause why each [NS: particular man] exists. But this cause (by II and III) cannot be contained in human nature itself, since the true definition of man does not involve the number 20. So (by IV) the cause why these twenty men exist, and consequently, why each of them exists, must necessarily be outside each of them.

For that reason it is to be inferred absolutely that whatever is of such a nature that there can be many individuals [of that nature] must, to exist, have an external cause to exist. Now since it pertains to the nature of a substance to exist (by what we have already shown in this scholium), its definition must involve necessary existence, and consequently its existence must be inferred from its definition alone. But from its definition (as we have shown from II and III) the existence of a number of substances cannot follow. Therefore it follows necessarily from this, that there exists only one of the same nature, as was proposed.

P9: *The more reality or being each thing has, the more attributes belong to it.*
   Dem.: This is evident from D4.

P10: *Each attribute of a substance must be conceived through itself.*
   Dem.: For an attribute is what the intellect perceives concerning a substance, as constituting its essence (by D4); so (by D3) it must be conceived through itself, q.e.d.

II/52   Schol.: From these propositions it is evident that although two attributes may be conceived to be really distinct (i.e., one may be conceived without the aid of the other), we still cannot infer from that that they constitute two beings, *or* two different substances. For it is of the nature of a substance that each of its attributes is conceived through itself, since all the attributes it has have always been in it together, and one could not be produced by another, but each expresses the reality, *or* being of substance.

So it is far from absurd to attribute many attributes to one substance. Indeed, nothing in Nature is clearer than that each being must be conceived under some attribute, and the more reality, or being it has, the more it has attributes which express necessity, *or* eternity, and infinity. And consequently there is also nothing clearer than that a being absolutely infinite must be defined (as we taught in D6) as a being that consists of infinite attributes, each of which expresses a certain eternal and infinite essence.

But if someone now asks by what sign we shall be able to distinguish the diversity of substances, let him read the following propositions, which show that in Nature there exists only one substance, and that it is absolutely infinite. So that sign would be sought in vain.

P11: *God,* or *a substance consisting of infinite attributes, each of which expresses eternal and infinite essence, necessarily exists.*

Dem.: If you deny this, conceive, if you can, that God does not exist. Therefore (by A7) his essence does not involve existence. But this (by P7) is absurd. Therefore God necessarily exists, q.e.d.

Alternatively: For each thing there must be assigned a cause, *or* reason, both for its existence and for its nonexistence. For example, if a triangle exists, there must be a reason *or* cause why it exists; but if it does not exist, there must also be a reason *or* cause which prevents it from existing, *or* which takes its existence away.

II/53

But this reason, *or* cause, must either be contained in the nature of the thing, or be outside it. For example, the very nature of a square circle indicates the reason why it does not exist, namely, because it involves a contradiction. On the other hand, the reason why a substance exists also follows from its nature alone, because it involves existence (see P7). But the reason why a circle or triangle exists, or why it does not exist, does not follow from the nature of these things, but from the order of the whole of corporeal Nature. For from this [order] it must follow either that the triangle necessarily exists now or that it is impossible for it to exist now. These things are evident through themselves; from them it follows that a thing necessarily exists if there is no reason or cause which prevents it from existing. Therefore, if there can be no reason or cause which prevents God from existing, or which takes his existence away, it must certainly be inferred that he necessarily exists.

But if there were such a reason, *or* cause, it would have to be either in God's very nature or outside it, that is, in another substance of another nature. For if it were of the same nature, that very supposition would concede that God exists. But a substance which was of another nature [NS: than the divine] would have nothing in common with God (by P2), and therefore could neither give him existence nor take it away. Since, then, there can be, outside the divine nature, no reason, *or,* cause which takes away the divine existence, the reason will necessarily have to be in his nature itself, if indeed he does not exist. That is, his nature would involve a contradiction [NS: as in our second example]. But it is absurd to affirm this of a Being absolutely infinite and supremely perfect. Therefore, there is no cause, *or* reason, either in God or outside God, which takes his existence away. And therefore, God necessarily exists, q.e.d.

Alternatively: To be able not to exist is to lack power, and conversely, to be able to exist is to have power (as is known through itself). So, if what now necessarily exists are only finite beings, then finite beings are more powerful than an absolutely infinite Being. But this, as is known through itself, is absurd. So, either nothing exists or an absolutely infinite Being also exists. But we exist, either in ourselves, or in something else, which necessarily exists (see A1 and P7). Therefore an absolutely infinite Being—that is (by D6), God—necessarily exists, q.e.d.

II/54   Schol.: In this last demonstration I wanted to show God's existence a posteriori, so that the demonstration would be perceived more easily—but not because God's existence does not follow a priori from the same foundation. For since being able to exist is power, it follows that the more reality belongs to the nature of a thing, the more powers it has, of itself, to exist. Therefore, an absolutely infinite Being, *or* God, has, of himself, an absolutely infinite power of existing. For that reason, he exists absolutely.

Still, there may be many who will not easily be able to see how evident this demonstration is, because they have been accustomed to contemplate only those things that flow from external causes. And of these, they see that those which quickly come to be, that is, which easily exist, also easily perish. And conversely, they judge that those things to which they conceive more things to pertain are more difficult to do, that is, that they do not exist so easily. But to free them from these prejudices, I have no need to show here in what manner this proposition—*what quickly comes to be, quickly perishes*—is true, nor whether or not all things are equally easy in respect to the whole of Nature. It is sufficient to note only this, that I am not here speaking of things that come to be from external causes, but only of substances that (by P6) can be produced by no external cause.

For things that come to be from external causes—whether they consist of many parts or of few—owe all the perfection or reality they have to the power of the external cause; and therefore their existence arises only from the perfection of their external cause, and not from their own perfection. On the other hand, whatever perfection substance has is not owed to any external cause. So its existence must follow from its nature alone; hence its existence is nothing but its essence.

Perfection, therefore, does not take away the existence of a thing, but on the contrary asserts it. But imperfection takes it away. So there is nothing of whose existence we can be more certain than we are of the existence of an absolutely infinite, *or* perfect, Being—that is, God. For since his essence excludes all imperfection, and involves absolute perfection, by that very fact it takes away every cause of doubting his existence, and gives the greatest certainty concerning it. I believe this will be clear even to those who are only moderately attentive.

P12: *No attribute of a substance can be truly conceived from which it follows* II/55
that the substance can be divided.

Dem.: For the parts into which a substance so conceived would be divided either will retain the nature of the substance or will not. If the first [NS: viz. they retain the nature of the substance], then (by P8) each part will have to be infinite, and (by P7) its own cause, and (by P5) each part will have to consist of a different attribute. And so many substances will be able to be formed from one, which is absurd (by P6). Furthermore, the parts (by P2) would have nothing in common with their whole, and the whole (by D4 and P10) could both be and be conceived without its parts, which is absurd, as no one will be able to doubt.

But if the second is asserted, namely, that the parts will not retain the nature of substance, then since the whole substance would be divided into equal parts, it would lose the nature of substance, and would cease to be, which (by P7) is absurd.

P13: *A substance which is absolutely infinite is indivisible.*

Dem.: For if it were divisible, the parts into which it would be divided will either retain the nature of an absolutely infinite substance or they will not. If the first, then there will be a number of substances of the same nature, which (by P5) is absurd. But if the second is asserted, then (as above [NS: P12]), an absolutely infinite substance will be able to cease to be, which (by P11) is also absurd.

Cor.: From these [propositions] it follows that no substance, and consequently no corporeal substance, insofar as it is a substance, is divisible.

Schol.: That substance is indivisible, is understood more simply merely from this, that the nature of substance cannot be conceived unless as infinite, and that by a part of substance nothing can be understood except a finite substance, which (by P8) implies a plain contra- II/56
diction.

P14: *Except God, no substance can be or be conceived.*

Dem.: Since God is an absolutely infinite being, of whom no attribute which expresses an essence of substance can be denied (by D6), and he necessarily exists (by P11), if there were any substance except God, it would have to be explained through some attribute of God, and so two substances of the same attribute would exist, which (by P5) is absurd. And so except God, no substance can be or, consequently, be conceived.

For if it could be conceived, it would have to be conceived as existing. But this (by the first part of this demonstration) is absurd. Therefore, except for God no substance can be or be conceived, q.e.d.

Cor. 1: From this it follows most clearly, first, that God is unique, that is (by D6), that in Nature there is only one substance, and that it is absolutely infinite (as we indicated in P10S).

Cor. 2: It follows, second, that an extended thing and a thinking thing are either attributes of God, or (by A1) affections of God's attributes.

P15: *Whatever is, is in God, and nothing can be or be conceived without God.*

Dem.: Except for God, there neither is, nor can be conceived, any substance (by P14), that is (by D3), thing that is in itself and is conceived through itself. But modes (by D5) can neither be nor be conceived without substance. So they can be in the divine nature alone, and can be conceived through it alone. But except for substances and modes there is nothing (by A1). Therefore, [NS: everything is in God and] nothing can be or be conceived without God, q.e.d.

Schol.: [I.] There are those who feign a God, like man, consisting of a body and a mind, and subject to passions. But how far they wander from the true knowledge of God, is sufficiently established by what has already been demonstrated. Them I dismiss. For everyone who has to any extent contemplated the divine nature denies that God is corporeal. They prove this best from the fact that by body we understand any quantity, with length, breadth, and depth, limited by some certain figure. Nothing more absurd than this can be said of God, namely, of a being absolutely infinite. But meanwhile, by the other arguments by which they strive to demonstrate this same conclusion they clearly show that they entirely remove corporeal, *or* extended, substance itself from the divine nature. And they maintain that it has been created by God. But by what divine power could it be created? They are completely ignorant of that. And this shows clearly that they do not understand what they themselves say. At any rate, I have demonstrated clearly enough—in my judgment, at least—that no substance can be produced or created by another thing (see P6C and P8S2). Next, we have shown (P14) that except for God, no substance can either be or be conceived, and hence [in P14C2] we have concluded that extended substance is one of God's infinite attributes. But to provide a fuller explanation, I shall refute my opponents' arguments, which all reduce to these.

[II.] *First*, they think that corporeal substance, insofar as it is substance, consists of parts. And therefore they deny that it can be infinite, and consequently, that it can pertain to God. They explain this by many examples, of which I shall mention one or two.

10

[i] If corporeal substance is infinite, they say, let us conceive it to be divided in two parts. Each part will be either finite or infinite. If the former, then an infinite is composed of two finite parts, which is absurd. If the latter [NS: i.e., if each part is infinite], then there is one infinite twice as large as another, which is also absurd. [ii] Again, if an infinite quantity is measured by parts [each] equal to a foot, it will consist of infinitely many such parts, as it will also, if it is measured by parts [each] equal to an inch. And therefore, one infinite number will be twelve times greater than another [NS: which is no less absurd]. [iii] Finally, if

we conceive that from one point of a certain infinite   II/58 quantity two lines, say AB and AC, are extended to infinity, it is certain that, although in the beginning they are a certain, determinate distance apart, the distance between B and C is continuously increased, and at last, from being determinate, it will become indeterminable. Since these absurdities follow—so they think—from the fact that an infinite quantity is supposed, they infer that corporeal substance must be finite, and consequently cannot pertain to God's essence.

[III.] Their *second* argument is also drawn from God's supreme perfection. For God, they say, since he is a supremely perfect being, cannot be acted on. But corporeal substance, since it is divisible, can be acted on. It follows, therefore, that it does not pertain to God's essence.

[IV.] These are the arguments which I find Authors using, to try to show that corporeal substance is unworthy of the divine nature, and cannot pertain to it. But anyone who is properly attentive will find that I have already replied to them, since these arguments are founded only on their supposition that corporeal substance is composed of parts, which I have already (P12 and P13C) shown to be absurd. And then anyone who wishes to consider the matter rightly will see that all those absurdities (*if indeed they are all absurd, which I am not now disputing*), from which they wish to infer that extended substance is finite, do not follow at all from the fact that an infinite quantity is supposed, but from the fact that they suppose an infinite quantity to be measurable and composed of finite parts. So from the absurdities which follow from that they can infer only that infinite quantity is not measurable, and that it is not composed of finite parts. This is the same thing we have already demonstrated above (P12, etc.). So the weapon they aim at us, they really turn against themselves. If, therefore, they still wish to infer from this absurdity of theirs that extended substance must be finite, they are indeed doing nothing more than if someone feigned that a circle has the properties of a square, and inferred from that the circle has no center,

11

from which all lines drawn to the circumference are equal. For corporeal substance, which cannot be conceived except as infinite, unique, and indivisible (see P8, 5, and 12), they conceive to be composed of finite parts, to be many, and to be divisible, in order to infer that it is finite.

II/59

So also others, after they feign that a line is composed of points, know how to invent many arguments, by which they show that a line cannot be divided to infinity. And indeed it is no less absurd to assert that corporeal substance is composed of bodies, *or* parts, than that a body is composed of surfaces, the surfaces of lines, and the lines, finally, of points. All those who know that clear reason is infallible must confess this—particularly those who deny that there is a vacuum. For if corporeal substance could be so divided that its parts were really distinct, why, then, could one part not be annihilated, the rest remaining connected with one another as before? And why must they all be so fitted together that there is no vacuum? Truly, of things which are really distinct from one another, one can be, and remain in its condition, without the other. Since, therefore, there is no vacuum in Nature (a subject I discuss elsewhere), but all its parts must so concur that there is no vacuum, it follows also that they cannot be really distinguished, that is, that corporeal substance, insofar as it is a substance, cannot be divided.

[V.] If someone should now ask why we are, by nature, so inclined to divide quantity, I shall answer that we conceive quantity in two ways: abstractly, *or* superficially, as we [NS: commonly] imagine it, or as substance, which is done by the intellect alone [NS: without the help of the imagination]. So if we attend to quantity as it is in the imagination, which we do often and more easily, it will be found to be finite, divisible, and composed of parts; but if we attend to it as it is in the intellect, and conceive it insofar as it is a substance, which happens [NS: seldom and] with great difficulty, then (as we have already sufficiently demonstrated) it will be found to be infinite, unique, and indivisible.

This will be sufficiently plain to everyone who knows how to distinguish between the intellect and the imagination—particularly if it is also noted that matter is everywhere the same, and that parts are distinguished in it only insofar as we conceive matter to be affected in different ways, so that its parts are distinguished only modally, but not really.

II/60

For example, we conceive that water is divided and its parts separated from one another—insofar as it is water, but not insofar as it is corporeal substance. For insofar as it is substance, it is neither separated nor divided. Again, water, insofar as it is water, is generated and corrupted, but insofar as it is substance, it is neither generated nor corrupted.

[VI.] And with this I think I have replied to the second argument also,

12

since it is based on the supposition that matter, insofar as it is substance, is divisible, and composed of parts. Even if this [reply] were not [sufficient], I do not know why [matter] would be unworthy of the divine nature. For (by P14) apart from God there can be no substance by which [the divine nature] would be acted on. All things, I say, are in God, and all things that happen, happen only through the laws of God's infinite nature and follow (as I shall show) from the necessity of his essence. So it cannot be said in any way that God is acted on by another, or that extended substance is unworthy of the divine nature, even if it is supposed to be divisible, so long as it is granted to be eternal and infinite. But enough of this for the present.

P16: *From the necessity of the divine nature there must follow infinitely many things in infinitely many modes, (i.e., everything which can fall under an infinite intellect).*

Dem.: This proposition must be plain to anyone, provided he attends to the fact that the intellect infers from the given definition of any thing a number of properties that really do follow necessarily from it (that is, from the very essence of the thing); and that it infers more properties the more the definition of the thing expresses reality, that is, the more reality the essence of the defined thing involves. But since the divine nature has absolutely infinite attributes (by D6), each of which also expresses an essence infinite in its own kind, from its necessity there must follow infinitely many things in infinite modes (i.e., everything which can fall under an infinite intellect), q.e.d.

Cor. 1: From this it follows that God is the efficient cause of all things which can fall under an infinite intellect.

Cor. 2: It follows, second, that God is a cause through himself and not an accidental cause. II/61

Cor. 3: It follows, third, that God is absolutely the first cause.

P17: *God acts from the laws of his nature alone, and is compelled by no one.*

Dem.: We have just shown (P16) that from the necessity of the divine nature alone, or (what is the same thing) from the laws of his nature alone, absolutely infite things follow, and in P15 we have demonstrated that nothing can be or be conceived without God, but that all things are in God. So there can be nothing outside him by which he is determined or compelled to act. Therefore, God acts from the laws of his nature alone, and is compelled by no one, q.e.d.

Cor. 1: From this it follows, first, that there is no cause, either extrinsically or intrinsically, which prompts God to action, except the perfection of his nature.

Cor. 2: It follows, second, that God alone is a free cause. For God alone exists only from the necessity of his nature (by P11 and P14C1), and acts from the necessity of his nature (by P17). Therefore (by D7) God alone is a free cause, q.e.d.

Schol.: [I.] Others think that God is a free cause because he can (so they think) bring it about that the things which we have said follow from his nature (i.e., which are in his power) do not happen or are not produced by him. But this is the same as if they were to say that God can bring it about that it would not follow from the nature of a triangle that its three angles are equal to two right angles; *or* that from a given cause the effect would not follow—which is absurd.

II/62

Further, I shall show later, without the aid of this proposition, that neither intellect nor will pertain to God's nature. Of course I know there are many who think they can demonstrate that a supreme intellect and a free will pertain to God's nature. For they say they know nothing they can ascribe to God more perfect than what is the highest perfection in us.

Moreover, though they conceive God to actually understand in the highest degree, they still do not believe that he can bring it about that all the things he actually understands exist. For they think that in that way they would destroy God's power. If he had created all the things in his intellect (they say), then he would have been able to create nothing more, which they believe to be incompatible with God's omnipotence. So they prefer to maintain that God is indifferent to all things, not creating anything except what he has decreed to create by some absolute will.

But I think I have shown clearly enough (see P16) that from God's supreme power, *or* infinite nature, infinitely many things in infinitely many modes, that is, all things, have necessarily flowed, or always follow, by the same necessity and in the same way as from the nature of a triangle it follows, from eternity and to eternity, that its three angles are equal to two right angles. So God's omnipotence has been actual from eternity and will remain in the same actuality to eternity. And in this way, at least in my opinion, God's omnipotence is maintained far more perfectly.

Indeed—to speak openly—my opponents seem to deny God's omnipotence. For they are forced to confess that God understands infinitely many creatable things, which nevertheless he will never be able to create. For otherwise, if he created everything he understood [NS: to be creatable] he would (according to them) exhaust his omnipotence and render himself imperfect. Therefore to maintain that God is perfect, they are driven to maintain at the same time that he cannot bring about everything to which his power extends. I do not see what could be

14

feigned which would be more absurd than this or more contrary to God's omnipotence.

[II.] Further—to say something here also about the intellect and will which we commonly attribute to God—if will and intellect do pertain to the eternal essence of God, we must of course understand by each of these attributes something different from what men commonly understand. For the intellect and will which would constitute God's essence would have to differ entirely from our intellect and will, and could not agree with them in anything except the name. They would not agree with one another any more than do the dog that is a heavenly constellation and the dog that is a barking animal. I shall demonstrate this.

If intellect pertains to the divine nature, it will not be able to be (like our intellect) by nature either posterior to (as most would have it), or simultaneous with, the things understood, since God is prior in causality to all things (by P16C1). On the contrary, the truth and formal essence of things is what it is because it exists objectively in that way in God's intellect. So God's intellect, insofar as it is conceived to constitute God's essence, is really the cause both of the essence and of the existence of things. This seems also to have been noticed by those who asserted that God's intellect, will, and power are one and the same.

Therefore, since God's intellect is the only cause of things (viz. as we have shown, both of their essence and of their existence), he must necessarily differ from them both as to his essence and as to his existence. For what is caused differs from its cause precisely in what it has from the cause [NS: for that reason it is called the effect of such a cause]. For example, a man is the cause of the existence of another man, but not of his essence, for the latter is an eternal truth. Hence, they can agree entirely according to their essence. But in existing they must differ. And for that reason, if the existence of one perishes, the other's existence will not thereby perish. But if the essence of one could be destroyed, and become false, the other's essence would also be destroyed [NS: and become false].

So the thing that is the cause both of the essence and of the existence of some effect, must differ from such an effect, both as to its essence and as to its existence. But God's intellect is the cause both of the essence and of the existence of our intellect. Therefore, God's intellect, insofar as it is conceived to constitute the divine essence, differs from our intellect both as to its essence and as to its existence, and cannot agree with it in anything except in name, as we supposed. The proof proceeds in the same way concerning the will, as anyone can easily see.

II/63

P18: *God is the immanent, not the transitive, cause of all things.*

II/64   Dem.: Everything that is, is in God, and must be conceived through God (by P15), and so (by P16C1) God is the cause of [NS: all] things, which are in him. That is the first [thing to be proven]. And then outside God there can be no substance (by P14), that is (by D3), thing which is in itself outside God. That was the second. God, therefore, is the immanent, not the transitive cause of all things, q.e.d.

P19: *God is eternal, or all God's attributes are eternal.*

Dem.: For God (by D6) is substance, which (by P11) necessarily exists, that is (by P7), to whose nature it pertains to exist, or (what is the same) from whose definition it follows that he exists; and therefore (by D8), he is eternal.

Next, by God's attributes are to be understood what (by D4) expresses an essence of the divine substance, that is, what pertains to substance. The attributes themselves, I say, must involve it itself. But eternity pertains to the nature of substance (as I have already demonstrated from P7). Therefore each of the attributes must involve eternity, and so, they are all eternal, q.e.d.

Schol.: This proposition is also as clear as possible from the way I have demonstrated God's existence (P11). For from that demonstration, I say, it is established that God's existence, like his essence, is an eternal truth. And then I have also demonstrated God's eternity in another way (*Descartes' Principles* IP19), and there is no need to repeat it here.

P20: *God's existence and his essence are one and the same.*

Dem.: God (by P19) and all of his attributes are eternal, that is (by D8), each of his attributes expresses existence. Therefore, the same attributes of God which (by D4) explain God's eternal essence at the same time explain his eternal existence, that is, that itself which constitutes II/65 God's essence at the same time constitutes his existence. So his existence and his essence are one and the same, q.e.d.

Cor. 1: From this it follows, first, that God's existence, like his essence, is an eternal truth.

Cor. 2: It follows, second, that God, *or* all of God's attributes, are immutable. For if they changed as to their existence, they would also (by P20) change as to their essence, that is (as is known through itself), from being true become false, which is absurd.

P21: *All the things which follow from the absolute nature of any of God's attributes have always had to exist and be infinite, or are, through the same attribute, eternal and infinite.*

Dem.: If you deny this, then conceive (if you can) that in some attribute of God there follows from its absolute nature something that is finite and has a determinate existence, *or* duration, for example, God's idea in thought. Now since thought is supposed to be an attribute of God, it is necessarily (by P11) infinite by its nature. But insofar as it has God's idea, [thought] is supposed to be finite. But (by D2) [thought] cannot be conceived to be finite unless it is determined through thought itself. But [thought can] not [be determined] through thought itself, insofar as it constitutes God's idea, for to that extent [thought] is supposed to be finite. Therefore, [thought must be determined] through thought insofar as it does not constitute God's idea, which [thought] nevertheless (by P11) must necessarily exist. Therefore, there is thought which does not constitute God's idea, and on that account God's idea does not follow necessarily from the nature [of this thought] insofar as it is absolute thought (for [thought] is conceived both as constituting God's idea and as not constituting it). [That God's idea does not follow from thought, insofar as it is absolute thought] is contrary to the hypothesis. So if God's idea in thought, or anything else in any attribute of God (for it does not matter what example is taken, since the demonstration is universal), follows from the necessity of the absolute nature of the attribute itself, it must necessarily be infinite. This was the first thing to be proven.

Next, what follows in this way from the necessity of the nature of any attribute cannot have a determinate [NS: existence, or] duration. For if you deny this, then suppose there is, in some attribute of God, a thing which follows from the necessity of the nature of that attribute—for example, God's idea in thought—and suppose that at some time [this idea] did not exist or will not exist. But since thought is supposed to be an attribute of God, it must exist necessarily and be immutable (by P11 and P20C2). So beyond the limits of the duration of God's idea (for it is supposed that at some time [this idea] did not exist or will not exist) thought will have to exist without God's idea. But this is contrary to the hypothesis, for it is supposed that God's idea follows necessarily from the given thought. Therefore, God's idea in thought, or anything else which follows necessarily from the absolute nature of some attribute of God, cannot have a determinate duration, but through the same attribute is eternal. This was the second thing [NS: to be proven]. Note that the same is to be affirmed of any thing which, in some attribute of God, follows necessarily from God's absolute nature.

P22: *Whatever follows from some attribute of God insofar as it is modified by a modification which, through the same attribute, exists necessarily and is infinite, must also exist necessarily and be infinite.*

II/66

Dem.: The demonstration of this proposition proceeds in the same way as the demonstration of the preceding one.

P23: *Every mode which exists necessarily and is infinite has necessarily had to follow either from the absolute nature of some attribute of God, or from some attribute, modified by a modification which exists necessarily and is infinite.*

Dem.: For a mode is in another, through which it must be conceived (by D5), that is (by P15), it is in God alone, and can be conceived through God alone. So if a mode is conceived to exist necessarily and be infinite, [its necessary existence and infinity] must necessarily be inferred, *or* perceived through some attribute of God, insofar as that attribute is conceived to express infinity and necessity of existence, *or* (what is the same, by D8) eternity, that is (by D6 and P19), insofar as it is considered absolutely. Therefore, the mode, which exists necessarily and is infinite, has had to follow from the absolute nature of some attribute of God—either immediately (see P21) or by some mediating modification, which follows from its absolute nature, that is (by P22), which exists necessarily and is infinite, q.e.d.

P24: *The essence of things produced by God does not involve existence.*

Dem.: This is evident from D1. For that whose nature involves existence (considered in itself), is its own cause, and exists only from the necessity of its nature.

Cor.: From this it follows that God is not only the cause of things' beginning to exist, but also of their persevering in existing, *or* (to use a Scholastic term) God is the cause of the being of things. For—whether the things [NS: produced] exist or not—so long as we attend to their essence, we shall find that it involves neither existence nor duration. So their essence can be the cause neither of their existence nor of their duration, but only God, to whose nature alone it pertains to exist [, can be the cause] (by P14C1).

P25: *God is the efficient cause, not only of the existence of things, but also of their essence.*

Dem.: If you deny this, then God is not the cause of the essence of things; and so (by A4) the essence of things can be conceived without God. But (by P15) this is absurd. Therefore God is also the cause of the essence of things, q.e.d.

Schol.: This proposition follows more clearly from P16. For from that it follows that from the given divine nature both the essence of things and their existence must necessarily be inferred; and in a word, God must be called the cause of all things in the same sense in which he is called the cause of himself. This will be established still more clearly from the following corollary.

II/67

II/68

Cor.: Particular things are nothing but affections of God's attributes, *or* modes by which God's attributes are expressed in a certain and determinate way. The demonstration is evident from P15 and D5.

P26: *A thing which has been determined to produce an effect has necessarily been determined in this way by God; and one which has not been determined by God cannot determine itself to produce an effect.*

Dem.: That through which things are said to be determined to produce an effect must be something positive (as is known through itself). And so, God, from the necessity of his nature, is the efficient cause both of its essence and of its existence (by P25 and 16); this was the first thing. And from it the second thing asserted also follows very clearly. For if a thing which has not been determined by God could determine itself, the first part of this [NS: proposition] would be false, which is absurd, as we have shown.

P27: *A thing which has been determined by God to produce an effect, cannot render itself undetermined.*

Dem.: This proposition is evident from A3.

P28: *Every singular thing,* or *any thing which is finite and has a determinate existence, can neither exist nor be determined to produce an effect unless it is determined to exist and produce an effect by another cause, which is also finite and has a determinate existence; and again, this cause also can neither exist nor be determined to produce an effect unless it is determined to exist and produce an effect by another, which is also finite and has a determinate existence, and so on, to infinity.*

II/69

Dem.: Whatever has been determined to exist and produce an effect has been so determined by God (by P26 and P24C). But what is finite and has a determinate existence could not have been produced by the absolute nature of an attribute of God; for whatever follows from the absolute nature of an attribute of God is eternal and infinite (by P21). It had, therefore, to follow either from God or from an attribute of God insofar as it is considered to be affected by some mode. For there is nothing except substance and its modes (by A1, D3, and D5) and modes (by P25C) are nothing but affections of God's attributes. But it also could not follow from God, or from an attribute of God, insofar as it is affected by a modification which is eternal and infinite (by P22). It had, therefore, to follow from, or be determined to exist and produce an effect by God or an attribute of God insofar as it is modified by a modification which is finite and has a determinate existence. This was the first thing to be proven.

And in turn, this cause, *or* this mode (by the same reasoning by which we have already demonstrated the first part of this proposition) had also to be determined by another, which is also finite and has a determinate existence; and again, this last (by the same reasoning) by another, and so always (by the same reasoning) to infinity, q.e.d.

II/70   Schol.: Since certain things had to be produced by God immediately, namely, those which follow necessarily from his absolute nature, and others (which nevertheless can neither be nor be conceived without God) had to be produced by the mediation of these first things, it follows:

I. That God is absolutely the proximate cause of the things produced immediately by him, and not [a proximate cause] in his own kind, as they say. For God's effects can neither be nor be conceived without their cause (by P15 and P24C).

II. That God cannot properly be called the remote cause of singular things, except perhaps so that we may distinguish them from those things that he has produced immediately, or rather, that follow from his absolute nature. For by a remote cause we understand one which is not conjoined in any way with its effect. But all things that are, are in God, and so depend on God that they can neither be nor be conceived without him.

P29: *In nature there is nothing contingent, but all things have been determined from the necessity of the divine nature to exist and produce an effect in a certain way.*

Dem.: Whatever is, is in God (by P15); but God cannot be called a contingent thing. For (by P11) he exists necessarily, not contingently. Next, the modes of the divine nature have also followed from it necessarily and not contingently (by P16)—either insofar as the divine nature is considered absolutely (by P21) or insofar as it is considered to be determined to act in a certain way (by P28). Further, God is the cause of these modes not only insofar as they simply exist (by P24C), but also (by P26) insofar as they are considered to be determined to produce an effect. For if they have not been determined by God, then (by P26) it is impossible, not contingent, that they should determine themselves. Conversely (by P27) if they have been determined by God, it is not

II/71   contingent, but impossible, that they should render themselves undetermined. So all things have been determined from the necessity of the divine nature, not only to exist, but to exist in a certain way, and to produce effects in a certain way. There is nothing contingent, q.e.d.

Schol.: Before I proceed further, I wish to explain here—or rather to advise [the reader]—what we must understand by *Natura naturans* and *Natura naturata*. For from the preceding I think it is already established that by *Natura naturans* we must understand what is in itself and is conceived through itself, *or* such attributes of substance as express an eternal and infinite essence, that is (by P14C1 and P17C2), God, insofar as he is considered as a free cause.

But by *Natura naturata* I understand whatever follows from the necessity of God's nature, *or* from any of God's attributes, that is, all the modes of God's attributes insofar as they are considered as things which are in God, and can neither be nor be conceived without God.

P30: *An actual intellect, whether finite or infinite, must comprehend God's attributes and God's affections, and nothing else.*

Dem.: A true idea must agree with its object (by A6), that is (as is known through itself), what is contained objectively in the intellect must necessarily be in Nature. But in Nature (by P14C1) there is only one substance, namely, God, and there are no affections other than those which are in God (by P15) and which can neither be nor be conceived without God (by P15). Therefore, an actual intellect, whether finite or infinite, must comprehend God's attributes and God's affections, and nothing else, q.e.d.

P31: *The actual intellect, whether finite or infinite, like will, desire, love, and the like, must be referred to* Natura naturata, *not to* Natura naturans.

Dem.: By intellect (as is known through itself) we understand not absolute thought, but only a certain mode of thinking, which mode differs from the others, such as desire, love, and the like, and so (by D5) must be conceived through absolute thought, that is (by P15 and D6), it must be so conceived through an attribute of God, which expresses the eternal and infinite essence of thought, that it can neither be nor be conceived without [that attribute]; and so (by P29S), like the other modes of thinking, it must be referred to *Natura naturata*, not to *Natura naturans*, q.e.d.

Schol.: The reason why I speak here of actual intellect is not because I concede that there is any potential intellect, but because, wishing to avoid all confusion, I wanted to speak only of what we perceive as clearly as possible, that is, of the intellection itself. We perceive nothing more clearly than that. For we can understand nothing that does not lead to more perfect knowledge of the intellection.

P32: *The will cannot be called a free cause, but only a necessary one.*

Dem.: The will, like the intellect, is only a certain mode of thinking. And so (by P28) each volition can neither exist nor be determined to produce an effect unless it is determined by another cause, and this cause again by another, and so on, to infinity. Even if the will be supposed to be infinite, it must still be determined to exist and produce an effect by God, not insofar as he is an absolutely infinite substance, but insofar as he has an attribute that expresses the infinite and eternal essence of thought (by P23). So in whatever way it is conceived, whether as finite or as infinite, it requires a cause by which it is determined to exist and produce an effect. And so (by D7) it cannot be called a free cause, but only a necessary or compelled one, q.e.d.

II/73   Cor. 1: From this it follows, first, that God does not produce any effect by freedom of the will.

Cor. 2: It follows, second, that will and intellect are related to God's nature as motion and rest are, and as are absolutely all natural things, which (by P29) must be determined by God to exist and produce an effect in a certain way. For the will, like all other things, requires a cause by which it is determined to exist and produce an effect in a certain way. And although from a given will, *or* intellect infinitely many things may follow, God still cannot be said, on that account, to act from freedom of the will, any more than he can be said to act from freedom of motion and rest on account of those things that follow from motion and rest (for infinitely many things also follow from motion and rest). So will does not pertain to God's nature any more than do the other natural things, but is related to him in the same way as motion and rest, and all the other things which, as we have shown, follow from the necessity of the divine nature and are determined by it to exist and produce an effect in a certain way.

P33: *Things could have been produced by God in no other way, and in no other order than they have been produced.*

Dem.: For all things have necessarily followed from God's given nature (by P16), and have been determined from the necessity of God's nature to exist and produce an effect in a certain way (by P29). Therefore, if things could have been of another nature, or could have been determined to produce an effect in another way, so that the order of Nature was different, then God's nature could also have been other than it is now, and therefore (by P11) that [other nature] would also have had to exist, and consequently, there could have been two or more Gods, which is absurd (by P14C1). So things could have been produced in no other way and no other order, and so on, q.e.d.

II/74   Schol. 1: Since by these propositions I have shown more clearly than the noon light that there is absolutely nothing in things on account of which they can be called contingent, I wish now to explain briefly what we must understand by contingent—but first, what [we must understand] by necessary and impossible.

A thing is called necessary either by reason of its essence or by reason of its cause. For a thing's existence follows necessarily either from its essence and definition or from a given efficient cause. And a thing is also

22

called impossible from these same causes—namely, either because its essence, *or* definition, involves a contradiction, or because there is no external cause which has been determined to produce such a thing.

But a thing is called contingent only because of a defect of our knowledge. For if we do not know that the thing's essence involves a contradiction, or if we do know very well that its essence does not involve a contradiction, and nevertheless can affirm nothing certainly about its existence, because the order of causes is hidden from us, it can never seem to us either necessary or impossible. So we call it contingent or possible.

Schol. 2: From the preceding it clearly follows that things have been produced by God with the highest perfection, since they have followed necessarily from a given most perfect nature. Nor does this convict God of any imperfection, for his perfection compels us to affirm this. Indeed, from the opposite, it would clearly follow (as I have just shown), that God is not supremely perfect; because if things had been produced by God in another way, we would have to attribute to God another nature, different from that which we have been compelled to attribute to him from the consideration of the most perfect being.

However, I have no doubt that many will reject this opinion as absurd, without even being willing to examine it—for no other reason than because they have been accustomed to attribute another freedom to God, far different from that we have taught (D7), namely, an absolute will. But I also have no doubt that, if they are willing to reflect on the matter, and consider properly the chain of our demonstrations, in the end they will utterly reject the freedom they now attribute to God, not only as futile, but as a great obstacle to science. Nor is it necessary for me to repeat here what I said in P17S. II/75

Nevertheless, to please them, I shall show that even if it is conceded that will pertains to God's essence, it still follows from his perfection that things could have been created by God in no other way or order. It will be easy to show this if we consider, first, what they themselves concede, namely, that it depends on God's decree and will alone that each thing is what it is. For otherwise God would not be the cause of all things. Next, that all God's decrees have been established by God himself from eternity. For otherwise he would be convicted of imperfection and inconstancy. But since, in eternity, there is neither *when*, nor *before*, nor *after*, it follows, from God's perfection alone, that he can never decree anything different, and never could have, *or* that God was not before his decrees, and cannot be without them.

But they will say that even if it were supposed that God had made another nature of things, or that from eternity he had decreed something else concerning Nature and its order, no imperfection in God would follow from that.

Still, if they say this, they will concede at the same time that God can change his decrees. For if God had decreed, concerning Nature and its order, something other than what he did decree, that is, had willed and conceived something else concerning Nature, he would necessarily have had an intellect other than he now has, and a will other than he now has. And if it is permitted to attribute to God another intellect and another will, without any change of his essence and of his perfection, why can he not now change his decrees concerning created things, and nevertheless remain equally perfect? For his intellect and will concerning created things and their order are the same in respect to his essence and his perfection, however his will and intellect may be conceived.

Further, all the philosophers I have seen concede that in God there is no potential intellect, but only an actual one. But since his intellect and his will are not distinguished from his essence, as they all also concede, it follows that if God had another actual intellect, and another will, his II/76 essence would also necessarily be other. And therefore (as I inferred at the beginning) if things had been produced by God otherwise than they now are, God's intellect and his will, that is (as is conceded), his essence, would have to be different [NS: from what it now is]. And this is absurd.

Therefore, since things could have been produced by God in no other way, and no other order, and since it follows from God's supreme perfection that this is true, no truly sound reason can persuade us to believe that God did not will to create all the things which are in his intellect, with that same perfection with which he understands them.

But they will say that there is no perfection or imperfection in things; what is in them, on account of which they are perfect or imperfect, and are called good or bad, depends only on God's will. And so, if God had willed, he could have brought it about that what is now perfection would have been the greatest imperfection, and conversely [NS: that what is now an imperfection in things would have been the most perfect]. How would this be different from saying openly that God, who necessarily understands what he wills, can bring it about by his will that he understands things in another way than he does understand them? As I have just shown, this is a great absurdity.

So I can turn the argument against them in the following way. All things depend on God's power. So in order for things to be able to be different, God's will would necessarily also have to be different. But God's will cannot be different (as we have just shown most evidently from God's perfection). So things also cannot be different.

I confess that this opinion, which subjects all things to a certain indifferent will of God, and makes all things depend on his good pleasure, is nearer the truth than that of those who maintain that God does all things for the sake of the good. For they seem to place something outside God, which does not depend on God, to which God attends, as a model, in what he does, and at which he aims, as at a certain goal. This is simply to subject God to fate. Nothing more absurd can be maintained about God, whom we have shown to be the first and only free cause, both of the essence of all things, and of their existence. So I shall waste no time in refuting this absurdity.

P34: *God's power is his essence itself.*

Dem.: For from the necessity alone of God's essence it follows that God is the cause of himself (by P11) and (by P16 and P16C) of all things. Therefore, God's power, by which he and all things are and act, is his essence itself, q.e.d. II/77

P35: *Whatever we conceive to be in God's power, necessarily exists.*

Dem.: For whatever is in God's power must (by P34) be so comprehended by his essence that it necessarily follows from it, and therefore necessarily exists, q.e.d.

P36: *Nothing exists from whose nature some effect does not follow.*

Dem: Whatever exists expresses the nature, *or* essence of God in a certain and determinate way (by P25C), that is (by P34), whatever exists expresses in a certain and determinate way the power of God, which is the cause of all things. So (by P16), from [NS: everything which exists] some effect must follow, q.e.d.

APPENDIX

With these [demonstrations] I have explained God's nature and properties: that he exists necessarily; that he is unique; that he is and acts from the necessity alone of his nature; that (and how) he is the free cause of all things; that all things are in God and so depend on him that without him they can neither be nor be conceived; and finally, that all things have been predetermined by God, not from freedom of the will *or* absolute good pleasure, but from God's absolute nature, *or* infinite power. Further, I have taken care, whenever the occasion arose, to remove prejudices that could prevent my demonstrations from being perceived. But because many prejudices remain that could, and can, be a great obstacle to men's understanding the connection of things in the way I have explained it, I considered it worthwhile to submit them here to the scrutiny of reason. All the prejudices I here undertake to expose depend on II/78 this one: that men commonly suppose that all natural things act, as men do, on account of an end; indeed, they maintain as certain that God himself directs all things to some certain end, for they say that God has made all things for man, and man that he might worship God.

So I shall begin by considering this one prejudice, asking *first* [I] why most people are satisfied that it is true, and why all are so inclined by nature to embrace it. *Then* [II] I shall show its falsity, and *finally* [III] how, from this, prejudices have arisen concerning *good* and *evil, merit* and *sin, praise* and *blame, order* and *confusion, beauty* and *ugliness*, and other things of this kind.

[I.] Of course this is not the place to deduce these things from the nature of the human mind. It will be sufficient here if I take as a foundation what everyone must acknowledge: that all men are born ignorant of the causes of things, and that they all want to seek their own advantage, and are conscious of this appetite. From these [assumptions] it follows, *first*, that men think themselves free, because they are conscious of their volitions and their appetite, and do not think, even in their dreams, of the causes by which they are disposed to wanting and willing, because they are ignorant of [those causes]. It follows, *second*, that men act always on account of an end, namely, on account of their advantage, which they want. Hence they seek to know only the final causes of what has been done, and when they have heard them, they are satisfied, because they have no reason to doubt further. But if they cannot hear them from another, nothing remains for them but to turn toward themselves, and reflect on the ends by which they are usually determined to do such things; so they necessarily judge the temperament of the other from their own temperament.

Furthermore, they find—both in themselves and outside themselves—many means that are very helpful in seeking their own advantage, for example, eyes for seeing, teeth for chewing, plants and animals for food, the sun for light, the sea for supporting fish [NS: and so with almost all other things whose natural causes they have no reason to doubt]. Hence, they consider all natural things as means to their own advantage. And knowing that they had found these means, not provided them for themselves, they had reason to believe that there was someone else who had prepared those means for their use. For after they considered things as means, they could not believe that the things had made themselves; but from the means they were accustomed to prepare for themselves, they had to infer that there was a ruler, or a number of rulers, of Nature, endowed with human freedom, who had taken care of all things for them, and made all things for their use.

And since they had never heard anything about the temperament of

II/79

26

these rulers, they had to judge it from their own. Hence, they maintained that the gods direct all things for the use of men in order to bind men to them and be held by men in the highest honor. So it has happened that each of them has thought up from his own temperament different ways of worshiping God, so that God might love him above all the rest, and direct the whole of Nature according to the needs of their blind desire and insatiable greed. Thus this prejudice was changed into superstition, and struck deep roots in their minds. This was why each of them strove with great diligence to understand and explain the final causes of all things.

But while they sought to show that Nature does nothing in vain (i.e., nothing not of use to men), they seem to have shown only that Nature and the gods are as mad as men. See, I ask you, how the matter has turned out! Among so many conveniences in Nature they had to find many inconveniences: storms, earthquakes, diseases, and the like. These, they maintain, happen because the gods [NS: (whom they judge to be of the same nature as themselves)] are angry on account of wrongs done to them by men, *or* on account of sins committed in their worship. And though their daily experience contradicted this, and though infinitely many examples showed that conveniences and inconveniences happen indiscriminately to the pious and the impious alike, they did not on that account give up their long-standing prejudice. It was easier for them to put this among the other unknown things, whose use they were ignorant of, and so remain in the state of ignorance in which they had been born, than to destroy that whole construction, and think up a new one.

So they maintained it as certain that the judgments of the gods far surpass man's grasp. This alone, of course, would have caused the truth to be hidden from the human race to eternity, if mathematics, which is concerned not with ends, but only with the essences and properties of figures, had not shown men another standard of truth. And besides mathematics, we can assign other causes also (which it is unnecessary to enumerate here), which were able to bring it about that men [NS: —but very few, in relation to the whole human race—] would notice these common prejudices and be led to the true knowledge of things.

[II.] With this I have sufficiently explained what I promised in the first place [viz. why men are so inclined to believe that all things act for an end]. Not many words will be required now to show that Nature has no end set before it, and that all final causes are nothing but human fictions. For I believe I have already sufficiently established it, both by the foundations and causes from which I have shown this prejudice to have had its origin, and also by P16, P32C1, and C2, and all those

II/80

[propositions] by which I have shown that all things proceed by a certain eternal necessity of Nature, and with the greatest perfection.

I shall, however, add this: this doctrine concerning the end turns Nature completely upside down. For what is really a cause, it considers as an effect, and conversely [NS: what is an effect it considers as a cause]. What is by nature prior, it makes posterior. And finally, what is supreme and most perfect, it makes imperfect. For—to pass over the first two, since they are manifest through themselves—as has been established in PP21–23, that effect is most perfect which is produced immediately by God, and the more something requires several intermediate causes to produce it, the more imperfect it is. But if the things which have been produced immediately by God had been made so that God would achieve his end, then the last things, for the sake of which the first would have been made, would be the most excellent of all.

Again, this doctrine takes away God's perfection. For if God acts for the sake of an end, he necessarily wants something which he lacks. And though the theologians and metaphysicians distinguish between an end of need and an end of assimilation, they nevertheless confess that God did all things for his own sake, not for the sake of the things to be created. For before creation they can assign nothing except God for whose sake God would act. And so they are necessarily compelled to confess that God lacked those things for the sake of which he willed to prepare means, and that he desired them. This is clear through itself.

Nor ought we here to pass over the fact that the followers of this doctrine, who have wanted to show off their cleverness in assigning the ends of things, have introduced—to prove this doctrine of theirs—a new way of arguing: by reducing things, not to the impossible, but to ignorance. This shows that no other way of defending their doctrine was open to them. For example, if a stone has fallen from a roof onto someone's head and killed him, they will show, in the following way, that the stone fell in order to kill the man. For if it did not fall to that end, God willing it, how could so many circumstances have concurred by chance (for often many circumstances do concur at once)? Perhaps you will answer that it happened because the wind was blowing hard and the man was walking that way. But they will persist: why was the wind blowing hard at that time? why was the man walking that way at that same time? If you answer again that the wind arose then because on the preceding day, while the weather was still calm, the sea began to toss, and that the man had been invited by a friend, they will press on—for there is no end to the questions which can be asked: but why was the sea tossing? why was the man invited at just that time? And so they will not

II/81

28

stop asking for the causes of causes until you take refuge in the will of God, that is, the sanctuary of ignorance.

Similarly, when they see the structure of the human body, they are struck by a foolish wonder, and because they do not know the causes of so great an art, they infer that it is constructed, not by mechanical, but by divine, or supernatural art, and constituted in such a way that one part does not injure another.

Hence it happens that one who seeks the true causes of miracles, and is eager, like an educated man, to understand natural things, not to wonder at them, like a fool, is generally considered an impious heretic and denounced as such by those whom the people honor as interpreters of Nature and the gods. For they know that if ignorance is taken away, then foolish wonder, the only means they have of arguing and defending their authority, is also taken away. But I leave these things, and pass on to what I have decided to treat here in the *third* place.

[III.] After men persuaded themselves that everything which happens, happens on their account, they had to judge that what is most important in each thing is what is most useful to them, and to rate as most excellent all those things by which they were most pleased. Hence, they had to form these notions, by which they explained natural things: *good, evil, order, confusion, warm, cold, beauty, ugliness*. And because they think themselves free, those notions have arisen: *praise* and *blame*, *sin* and *merit*. The latter I shall explain after I have treated human nature; but the former I shall briefly explain here.

Whatever conduces to health and the worship of God, they have called *good*; but what is contrary to these, *evil*.

And because those who do not understand the nature of things, but only imagine them, affirm nothing concerning things, and take the imagination for the intellect, they firmly believe, in their ignorance of things and of their own nature, that there is an order in things. For when things are so disposed that, when they are presented to us through the senses, we can easily imagine them, and so can easily remember them, we say that they are well-ordered; but if the opposite is true, we say that they are badly ordered, or confused.

II/82

And since those things we can easily imagine are especially pleasing to us, men prefer order to confusion, as if order were anything in Nature more than a relation to our imagination. They also say that God has created all things in order, and so, unknowingly attribute imagination to God—unless, perhaps, they mean that God, to provide for human imagination, has disposed all things so that men can very easily imagine them. Nor will it, perhaps, give them pause that infinitely many things

29

are found which far surpass our imagination, and a great many which confuse it on account of its weakness. But enough of this.

The other notions are also nothing but modes of imagining, by which the imagination is variously affected; and yet the ignorant consider them the chief attributes of things, because, as we have already said, they believe all things have been made for their sake, and call the nature of a thing good or evil, sound or rotten and corrupt, as they are affected by it. For example, if the motion the nerves receive from objects presented through the eyes is conducive to health, the objects by which it is caused are called beautiful; those which cause a contrary motion are called ugly. Those which move the sense through the nose, they call pleasant-smelling or stinking; through the tongue, sweet or bitter, tasty or tasteless; through touch, hard or soft, rough or smooth, and the like; and finally, those which move the ears are said to produce noise, sound, or harmony. Men have been so mad as to believe that God is pleased by harmony. Indeed there are philosophers who have persuaded themselves that the motions of the heavens produce a harmony.

All of these things show sufficiently that each one has judged things according to the disposition of his brain; or rather, has accepted affections of the imagination as things. So it is no wonder (to note this, too, in passing) that we find so many controversies to have arisen among men, and that they have finally given rise to skepticism. For although human bodies agree in many things, they still differ in very many. And for that reason what seems good to one, seems bad to another; what seems ordered to one, seems confused to another; what seems pleasing to one, seems displeasing to another, and so on.

II/83

I pass over the [other notions] here, both because this is not the place to treat them at length, and because everyone has experienced this [variability] sufficiently for himself. That is why we have such sayings as "So many heads, so many attitudes," "everyone finds his own judgment more than enough," and "there are as many differences of brains as of palates." These proverbs show sufficiently that men judge things according to the disposition of their brain, and imagine, rather than understand them. For if men had understood them, the things would at least convince them all, even if they did not attract them all, as the example of mathematics shows.

We see, therefore, that all the notions by which ordinary people are accustomed to explain Nature are only modes of imagining, and do not indicate the nature of anything, only the constitution of the imagination. And because they have names, as if they were [notions] of beings existing outside the imagination, I call them beings, not of reason, but of imagination. So all the arguments in which people try to use such notions against us can easily be warded off.

For many are accustomed to arguing in this way: if all things have followed from the necessity of God's most perfect nature, why are there so many imperfections in Nature? why are things corrupt to the point where they stink? so ugly that they produce nausea? why is there confusion, evil, and sin?

As I have just said, those who argue in this way are easily answered. For the perfection of things is to be judged solely from their nature and power; things are not more or less perfect because they please or offend men's senses, or because they are of use to, or are incompatible with, human nature.

But to those who ask "why God did not create all men so that they would be governed by the command of reason?" I answer only "because he did not lack material to create all things, from the highest degree of perfection to the lowest"; or, to speak more properly, "because the laws of his nature have been so ample that they sufficed for producing all things which can be conceived by an infinite intellect" (as I have demonstrated in P16).

These are the prejudices I undertook to note here. If any of this kind still remain, they can be corrected by anyone with only a little meditation. [NS: And so I find no reason to devote more time to these matters, and so on.]

SECOND PART OF THE ETHICS
OF THE NATURE AND ORIGIN OF THE MIND

II/84

I pass now to explaining those things which must necessarily follow from the essence of God, or the infinite and eternal being—not, indeed, all of them, for we have demonstrated (IP16) that infinitely many things must follow from it in infinitely many modes, but only those that can lead us, by the hand, as it were, to the knowledge of the human mind and its highest blessedness.

DEFINITIONS

D1: By body I understand a mode that in a certain and determinate way expresses God's essence insofar as he is considered as an extended thing (see IP25C).

D2: I say that to the essence of any thing belongs that which, being given, the thing is [NS: also] necessarily posited and which, being taken

31

away, the thing is necessarily [NS: also] taken away; or that without which the thing can neither be nor be conceived, and which can neither be nor be conceived without the thing.

D3: By idea I understand a concept of the mind which the mind forms because it is a thinking thing.

Exp.: *I say concept rather than perception, because the word perception seems to indicate that the mind is acted on by the object. But concept seems to express an action of the mind.*

D4: By adequate idea I understand an idea which, insofar as it is considered in itself, without relation to an object, has all the properties, *or* intrinsic denominations of a true idea.

Exp.: *I say intrinsic to exclude what is extrinsic, namely, the agreement of the idea with its object.*

D5: Duration is an indefinite continuation of existing.

Exp.: *I say indefinite because it cannot be determined at all through the very nature of the existing thing, nor even by the efficient cause, which necessarily posits the existence of the thing, and does not take it away.*

D6: By reality and perfection I understand the same thing.

D7: By singular things I understand things that are finite and have a determinate existence. And if a number of individuals so concur in one action that together they are all the cause of one effect, I consider them all, to that extent, as one singular thing.

AXIOMS

A1: The essence of man does not involve necessary existence, that is, from the order of Nature it can happen equally that this or that man does exist, or that he does not exist.

A2: Man thinks [NS: or, to put it differently, we know that we think].

A3: There are no modes of thinking, such as love, desire, or whatever is designated by the word affects of the mind, unless there is in the same individual the idea of the thing loved, desired, and the like. But there can be an idea, even though there is no other mode of thinking.

A4: We feel that a certain body [NS: our body] is affected in many ways.

A5: We neither feel nor perceive any singular things [NS: or anything of *Natura naturata*], except bodies and modes of thinking.
See the postulates after P13.

P1: *Thought is an attribute of God,* or *God is a thinking thing.*

Dem.: Singular thoughts, *or* this or that thought, are modes which express God's nature in a certain and determinate way (by IP25C). Therefore (by ID5) there belongs to God an attribute whose concept all singular thoughts involve, and through which they are also conceived. Therefore, thought is one of God's infinite attributes, which expresses an eternal and infinite essence of God (see ID6), *or* God is a thinking thing, q.e.d.

Schol.: This proposition is also evident from the fact that we can conceive an infinite thinking being. For the more things a thinking being can think, the more reality, *or* perfection, we conceive it to contain. Therefore, a being which can think infinitely many things in infinitely many ways is necessarily infinite in its power of thinking. So since we can conceive an infinite being by attending to thought alone, thought (by ID4 and D6) is necessarily one of God's infinite attributes, as we maintained.

P2: *Extension is an attribute of God,* or *God is an extended thing.*

Dem: The demonstration of this proceeds in the same way as that of the preceding proposition. II/87

P3: *In God there is necessarily an idea, both of his essence and of everything which necessarily follows from his essence.*

Dem.: For God (by P1) can think infinitely many things in infinitely many modes, *or* (what is the same, by IP16) can form the idea of his essence and of all the things which necessarily follow from it. But whatever is in God's power necessarily exists (by IP35); therefore, there is necessarily such an idea, and (by IP15) it is only in God, q.e.d.

Schol.: By God's power ordinary people understand God's free will and his right over all things which are, things which on that account are commonly considered to be contingent. For they say that God has the power of destroying all things and reducing them to nothing. Further, they very often compare God's power with the power of kings.

But we have refuted this in IP32C1 and C2, and we have shown in IP16 that God acts with the same necessity by which he understands himself, that is, just as it follows from the necessity of the divine nature (as everyone maintains unanimously) that God understands himself, with the same necessity it also follows that God does infinitely many things in infinitely many modes. And then we have shown in IP34 that God's power is nothing except God's active essence. And so it is as impossible for us to conceive that God does not act as it is to conceive that he does not exist.

Again, if it were agreeable to pursue these matters further, I could also show here that power which ordinary people fictitiously ascribe to God is not only human (which shows that ordinary people conceive God as a man, or as like a man), but also involves lack of power. But I do not wish to speak so often about the same topic. I only ask the reader to reflect repeatedly on what is said concerning this matter in Part I, from P16 to the end. For no one will be able to perceive rightly the things I maintain unless he takes great care not to confuse God's power with the human power or right of kings.

P4: *God's idea, from which infinitely many things follow in infinitely many modes, must be unique.*

Dem.: An infinite intellect comprehends nothing except God's attributes and his affections (by IP30). But God is unique (by IP14C1). Therefore God's idea, from which infinitely many things follow in infinitely many modes, must be unique, q.e.d.

P5: *The formal being of ideas admits God as a cause only insofar as he is considered as a thinking thing, and not insofar as he is explained by any other attribute. That is, ideas, both of God's attributes and of singular things, admit not the objects themselves, or the things perceived, as their efficient cause, but God himself, insofar as he is a thinking thing.*

Dem.: This is evident from P3. For there we inferred that God can form the idea of his essence, and of all the things that follow necessarily from it, solely from the fact that God is a thinking thing, and not from the fact that he is the object of his own idea. So the formal being of ideas admits God as its cause insofar as he is a thinking thing.

But another way of demonstrating this is the following. The formal being of ideas is a mode of thinking (as is known through itself), that is (by IP25C), a mode which expresses, in a certain way, God's nature insofar as he is a thinking thing. And so (by IP10) it involves the concept of no other attribute of God, and consequently (by IA4) is the effect of no other attribute than thought. And so the formal being of ideas admits God as its cause insofar as he is considered only as a thinking thing, and so on, q.e.d.

P6: *The modes of each attribute have God for their cause only insofar as he is considered under the attribute of which they are modes, and not insofar as he is considered under any other attribute.*

Dem.: For each attribute is conceived through itself without any other (by IP10). So the modes of each attribute involve the concept of their own attribute, but not of another one; and so (by IA4) they have God for their cause only insofar as he is considered under the attribute of which they are modes, and not insofar as he is considered under any other, q.e.d.

34

Cor.: From this it follows that the formal being of things which are not modes of thinking does not follow from the divine nature because [God] has first known the things; rather the objects of ideas follow and are inferred from their attributes in the same way and by the same necessity as that with which we have shown ideas to follow from the attribute of thought.

P7: *The order and connection of ideas is the same as the order and connection of things.*

Dem.: This is clear from IA4. For the idea of each thing caused depends on the knowledge of the cause of which it is the effect.

Cor.: From this it follows that God's [NS: actual] power of thinking is equal to his actual power of acting. That is, whatever follows formally from God's infinite nature follows objectively in God from his idea in the same order and with the same connection.

Schol.: Before we proceed further, we must recall here what we showed [NS: in the First Part], namely, that whatever can be perceived by an infinite intellect as constituting an essence of substance pertains to one substance only, and consequently that the thinking substance and the extended substance are one and the same substance, which is now comprehended under this attribute, now under that. So also a mode of extension and the idea of that mode are one and the same thing, but expressed in two ways. Some of the Hebrews seem to have seen this, as if through a cloud, when they maintained that God, God's intellect, and the things understood by him are one and the same. II/90

For example, a circle existing in Nature and the idea of the existing circle, which is also in God, are one and the same thing, which is explained through different attributes. Therefore, whether we conceive Nature under the attribute of extension, or under the attribute of thought, or under any other attribute, we shall find one and the same order, or one and the same connection of causes, that is, that the same things follow one another.

When I said [NS: before] that God is the cause of the idea, say of a circle, only insofar as he is a thinking thing, and [the cause] of the circle, only insofar as he is an extended thing, this was for no other reason than because the formal being of the idea of the circle can be perceived only through another mode of thinking, as its proximate cause, and that mode again through another, and so on, to infinity. Hence, so long as things are considered as modes of thinking, we must explain the order of the whole of Nature, or the connection of causes, through the attribute of thought alone. And insofar as they are considered as modes of extension, the order of the whole of Nature must be explained through the attribute of extension alone. I understand the same concerning the other attributes.

So of things as they are in themselves, God is really the cause insofar as he consists of infinite attributes. For the present, I cannot explain these matters more clearly.

P8: *The ideas of singular things, or of modes, that do not exist must be comprehended in God's infinite idea in the same way as the formal essences of the singular things, or modes, are contained in God's attributes.*

II/91   Dem.: This proposition is evident from the preceding one, but is understood more clearly from the preceding scholium.

Cor.: From this it follows that so long as singular things do not exist, except insofar as they are comprehended in God's attributes, their objective being, or ideas, do not exist except insofar as God's infinite idea exists. And when singular things are said to exist, not only insofar as they are comprehended in God's attributes, but insofar also as they are said to have duration, their ideas also involve the existence through which they are said to have duration.

Schol.: If anyone wishes me to explain this further by an example, I will, of course, not be able to give one which adequately explains what I speak of here, since it is unique. Still I shall try as far as possible to illustrate the matter: the circle is of such a nature that the rectangles formed from the segments of all the straight lines intersecting in it are equal to one another. So in a circle there are contained infinitely many rectangles which are equal to one another. Nevertheless, none of them can be said to exist except insofar as the circle exists, nor also can the idea of any of these rectangles be said

to exist except insofar as it is comprehended in the idea of the circle. Now of these infinitely many [rectangles] let two only, namely, [those formed from the segments of lines] D and E, exist. Of course their ideas also exist now, not only insofar as they are only comprehended in the idea of the circle, but also insofar as they involve the existence of those rectangles. By this they are distinguished from the other ideas of the other rectangles.

P9: *The idea of a singular thing which actually exists has God for a cause not insofar as he is infinite, but insofar as he is considered to be affected by*
II/92   *another idea of a singular thing which actually exists; and of this [idea] God is also the cause, insofar as he is affected by another third [NS: idea], and so on, to infinity.*

Dem.: The idea of a singular thing which actually exists is a singular mode of thinking, and distinct from the others (by P8C and S), and so (by P6) has God for a cause only insofar as he is a thinking thing. But not (by IP28) insofar as he is a thing thinking absolutely; rather insofar as he is considered to be affected by another [NS: determinate] mode of thinking. And God is also the cause of this mode, insofar as he is affected by another [NS: determinate mode of thinking], and so on, to infinity. But the order and connection of ideas (by P7) is the same as the order and connection of causes. Therefore, the cause of one singular idea is another idea, *or* God, insofar as he is considered to be affected by another idea; and of this also [God is the cause], insofar as he is affected by another, and so on, to infinity, q.e.d.

Cor.: Whatever happens in the singular object of any idea, there is knowledge of it in God, only insofar as he has the idea of the same object.

Dem.: Whatever happens in the object of any idea, there is an idea of it in God (by P3), not insofar as he is infinite, but insofar as he is considered to be affected by another idea of [NS: an existing] singular thing (by P9); but the order and connection of ideas (by P7) is the same as the order and connection of things; therefore, knowledge of what happens in a singular object will be in God only insofar as he has the idea of the same object, q.e.d.

P10: *The being of substance does not pertain to the essence of man, or substance does not constitute the form of man.*

Dem.: For the being of substance involves necessary existence (by IP7). Therefore, if the being of substance pertained to the essence of man, then substance being given, man would necessarily be given (by D2), and consequently man would exist necessarily, which (by A1) is absurd, q.e.d.

II/93

Schol.: This proposition is also demonstrated from IP5, namely, that there are not two substances of the same nature. Since a number of men can exist, what constitutes the form of man is not the being of substance. Further, this proposition is evident from the other properties of substance, namely, that substance is, by its nature, infinite, immutable, indivisible, and so forth, as anyone can easily see.

Cor.: From this it follows that the essence of man is constituted by certain modifications of God's attributes.

Dem.: For the being of substance does not pertain to the essence of man (by P10). Therefore, it is something (by IP15) which is in God, and which can neither be nor be conceived without God, *or* (by IP25C) an affection, *or* mode, which expresses God's nature in a certain and determinate way.

Schol.: Everyone, of course, must concede that nothing can either be

37

or be conceived without God. For all confess that God is the only cause of all things, both of their essence and of their existence. That is, God is not only the cause of the coming to be of things, as they say, but also of their being.

But in the meantime many say that anything without which a thing can neither be nor be conceived pertains to the nature of the thing. And so they believe either that the nature of God pertains to the essence of created things, or that created things can be or be conceived without God—or what is more certain, they are not sufficiently consistent.

The cause of this, I believe, was that they did not observe the [proper] order of philosophizing. For they believed that the divine nature, which they should have contemplated before all else (because it is prior both in knowledge and in nature) is last in the order of knowledge, and that the things which are called objects of the senses are prior to all. That is why, when they contemplated natural things, they thought of nothing less than they did of the divine nature; and when afterwards they directed their minds to contemplating the divine nature, they could think of nothing less than of their first fictions, on which they had built the knowledge of natural things, because these could not assist knowledge of the divine nature. So it is no wonder that they have generally contradicted themselves.

II/94

But I pass over this. For my intent here was only to give a reason why I did not say that anything without which a thing can neither be nor be conceived pertains to its essence—namely, because singular things can neither be nor be conceived without God, and nevertheless, God does not pertain to their essence. But I have said that what necessarily constitutes the essence of a thing is that which, if it is given, the thing is posited, and if it is taken away, the thing is taken away, that is, the essence is what the thing can neither be nor be conceived without, and vice versa, what can neither be nor be conceived without the thing.

P11: *The first thing which constitutes the actual being of a human Mind is nothing but the idea of a singular thing which actually exists.*

Dem.: The essence of man (by P10C) is constituted by certain modes of God's attributes, namely (by A2), by modes of thinking, of all of which (by A3) the idea is prior in nature, and when it is given, the other modes (to which the idea is prior in nature) must be in the same individual (by A3). And therefore an idea is the first thing which constitutes the being of a human mind. But not the idea of a thing which does not exist. For then (by P8C) the idea itself could not be said to exist. Therefore, it will be the idea of a thing which actually exists. But not of an infinite thing. For an infinite thing (by IP21 and 22) must always exist necessarily. But (by A1) it is absurd [that this idea should be of a necessarily existing object]. Therefore, the first thing which constitutes the actual being of a human mind is the idea of a singular thing which actually exists, q.e.d.

Cor.: From this it follows that the human mind is a part of the infinite intellect of God. Therefore, when we say that the human mind perceives this or that, we are saying nothing but that God, not insofar as he is infinite, but insofar as he is explained through the nature of the human mind, *or* insofar as he constitutes the essence of the human mind, has this or that idea; and when we say that God has this or that idea, not only insofar as he constitutes the nature of the human mind, but insofar as he also has the idea of another thing together with the human mind, then we say that the human mind perceives the thing only partially, *or* inadequately.

II/95

Schol.: Here, no doubt, my readers will come to a halt, and think of many things which will give them pause. For this reason I ask them to continue on with me slowly, step by step, and to make no judgment on these matters until they have read through them all.

P12: *Whatever happens in the object of the idea constituting the human mind must be perceived by the human mind, or there will necessarily be an idea of that thing in the mind; that is, if the object of the idea constituting a human mind is a body, nothing can happen in that body which is not perceived by the mind.*

Dem.: For whatever happens in the object of any idea, the knowledge of that thing is necessarily in God (by P9C), insofar as he is considered to be affected by the idea of the same object, that is (by P11), insofar as he constitutes the mind of some thing. Therefore, whatever happens in the object of the idea constituting the human mind, the knowledge of it is necessarily in God insofar as he constitutes the nature of the human mind, that is (by P11C), knowledge of this thing will necessarily be in the mind, *or* the mind will perceive it, q.e.d.

Schol.: This proposition is also evident, and more clearly understood from P7S, which you should consult.

P13: *The object of the idea constituting the human mind is the body*, or *a certain mode of extension which actually exists, and nothing else.*

II/96

Dem.: For if the object of the human mind were not the body, the ideas of the affections of the body would not be in God (by P9C) insofar as he constituted our mind, but insofar as he constituted the mind of another thing, that is (by P11C), the ideas of the affections of the body would not be in our mind; but (by A4) we have ideas of the affections of the body. Therefore, the object of the idea which constitutes the human mind is the body, and it (by P11) actually exists.

Next, if the object of the mind were something else also, in addition to the body, then since (by IP36) nothing exists from which there does not follow some effect, there would necessarily (by P12) be an idea in our mind of some effect of it. But (by A5) there is no idea of it. Therefore, the object of our mind is the existing body and nothing else, q.e.d.

Cor.: From this it follows that man consists of a mind and a body, and that the human body exists, as we are aware of it.

Schol.: From these [propositions] we understand not only that the human mind is united to the body, but also what should be understood by the union of mind and body. But no one will be able to understand it adequately, *or* distinctly, unless he first knows adequately the nature of our body. For the things we have shown so far are completely general and do not pertain more to man than to other individuals, all of which, though in different degrees, are nevertheless animate. For of each thing there is necessarily an idea in God, of which God is the cause in the same way as he is of the idea of the human body. And so, whatever we have said of the idea of the human body must also be said of the idea of any thing.

II/97   However, we also cannot deny that ideas differ among themselves, as the objects themselves do, and that one is more excellent than the other, and contains more reality, just as the object of the one is more excellent than the object of the other and contains more reality. And so to determine what is the difference between the human mind and the others, and how it surpasses them, it is necessary for us, as we have said, to know the nature of its object, that is, of the human body. I cannot explain this here, nor is that necessary for the things I wish to demonstrate. Nevertheless, I say this in general, that in proportion as a body is more capable than others of doing many things at once, or being acted on in many ways at once, so its mind is more capable than others of perceiving many things at once. And in proportion as the actions of a body depend more on itself alone, and as other bodies concur with it less in acting, so its mind is more capable of understanding distinctly. And from these [truths] we can know the excellence of one mind over the others, and also see the cause why we have only a completely confused knowledge of our body, and many other things which I shall deduce from them in the following [propositions]. For this reason I have thought it worthwhile to explain and demonstrate these things more accurately. To do this it is necessary to premise a few things concerning the nature of bodies.

A1': All bodies either move or are at rest.

A2': Each body moves now more slowly, now more quickly.

L1: *Bodies are distinguished from one another by reason of motion and rest, speed and slowness, and not by reason of substance.*

Dem.: I suppose that the first part of this is known through itself. But that bodies are not distinguished by reason of substance is evident both from IP5 and from IP8. But it is more clearly evident from those things which are said in IP15S.

L2: *All bodies agree in certain things.*

II/98

Dem.: For all bodies agree in that they involve the concept of one and the same attribute (by D1), and in that they can move now more slowly, now more quickly, and absolutely, that now they move, now they are at rest.

L3: *A body which moves or is at rest must be determined to motion or rest by another body, which has also been determined to motion or rest by another, and that again by another, and so on, to infinity.*

Dem.: Bodies (by D1) are singular things which (by L1) are distinguished from one another by reason of motion and rest; and so (by IP28), each must be determined necessarily to motion or rest by another singular thing, namely (by P6), by another body, which (by A1') either moves or is at rest. But this body also (by the same reasoning) could not move or be at rest if it had not been determined by another to motion or rest, and this again (by the same reasoning) by another, and so on, to infinity, q.e.d.

Cor.: From this it follows that a body in motion moves until it is determined by another body to rest; and that a body at rest also remains at rest until it is determined to motion by another.

This is also known through itself. For when I suppose that body A, say, is at rest, and do not attend to any other body in motion, I can say nothing about body A except that it is at rest. If afterwards it happens that body A moves, that of course could not have come about from the fact that it was at rest. For from that nothing else could follow but that body A would be at rest.

If, on the other hand, A is supposed to move, then as often as we II/99 attend only to A, we shall be able to affirm nothing concerning it except that it moves. If afterwards it happens that A is at rest, that of course also could not have come about from the motion it had. For from the motion nothing else could follow but that A would move. Therefore, it happens by a thing which was not in A, namely, by an external cause, by which [NS: the body in motion, A] has been determined to rest.

A1″: All modes by which a body is affected by another body follow both from the nature of the body affected and at the same time from the nature of the affecting body, so that one and the same body may be moved differently according to differences in the nature of the bodies moving it. And conversely, different bodies may be moved differently by one and the same body.

A2″: When a body in motion strikes against another which is at rest and cannot give way, then it is reflected, so that it continues to move, and the angle of the line of the reflected motion with the surface of the body at rest which it struck against will be equal to the angle which the line of the incident motion makes with the same surface.

This will be sufficient concerning the simplest bodies, which are distinguished from one another only by motion and rest, speed and slowness. Now let us move up to composite bodies.

Definition: *When a number of bodies, whether of the same or of different size, are so constrained by other bodies that they lie upon one another, or if they so move, whether with the same degree or different degrees of speed, that they communicate their motions to each other in a certain fixed manner, we shall say that those bodies are united with one another and that they all together compose one body* or *individual, which is distinguished from the others by this union of bodies.*

II/100

A3″: As the parts of an individual, or composite body, lie upon one another over a larger or smaller surface, so they can be forced to change their position with more or less difficulty; and consequently the more or less will be the difficulty of bringing it about that the individual changes its shape. And therefore the bodies whose parts lie upon one another over a large surface, I shall call *hard*; those whose parts lie upon one another over a small surface, I shall call *soft*; and finally those whose parts are in motion, I shall call *fluid*.

L4: *If, of a body, or of an individual, which is composed of a number of bodies, some are removed, and at the same time as many others of the same nature take their place, the [NS: body, or the] individual will retain its nature, as before, without any change of its form.*

Dem.: For (by L1) bodies are not distinguished in respect to substance; what constitutes the form of the individual consists [NS: only] in the union of the bodies (by the preceding definition). But this [NS: union] (by hypothesis) is retained even if a continual change of bodies occurs. Therefore, the individual will retain its nature, as before, both in respect to substance, and in respect to mode, q.e.d.

L5: *If the parts composing an individual become greater or less, but in such a proportion that they all keep the same ratio of motion and rest to each other as before, then the individual will likewise retain its nature, as before, without any change of form.*

Dem.: The demonstration of this is the same as that of the preceding lemma.

L6: *If certain bodies composing an individual are compelled to alter the motion they have from one direction to another, but so that they can continue their motions and communicate them to each other in the same ratio as before, the individual will likewise retain its nature, without any change of form.*

II/101

Dem.: This is evident through itself. For it is supposed that it retains everything which, in its definition, we said constitutes its form. [NS: See the definition before L4.]

L7: *Furthermore, the individual so composed retains its nature, whether it, as a whole, moves or is at rest, or whether it moves in this or that direction, so long as each part retains its motion, and communicates it, as before, to the others.*

Dem.: This [NS: also] is evident from the definition preceding L4.

Schol.: By this, then, we see how a composite individual can be affected in many ways, and still preserve its nature. So far we have conceived an individual which is composed only of bodies which are distinguished from one another only by motion and rest, speed and slowness, that is, which is composed of the simplest bodies. But if we should now conceive of another, composed of a number of individuals of a different nature, we shall find that it can be affected in a great many other ways, and still preserve its nature. For since each part of it is composed of a number of bodies, each part will therefore (by L7) be able, without any change of its nature, to move now more slowly, now more quickly, and consequently communicate its motion more quickly or more slowly to the others.

II/102

But if we should further conceive a third kind of individual, composed [NS: of many individuals] of this second kind, we shall find that it can be affected in many other ways, without any change of its form. And if we proceed in this way to infinity, we shall easily conceive that the whole of nature is one individual, whose parts, that is, all bodies, vary in infinite ways, without any change of the whole individual.

If it had been my intention to deal expressly with body, I ought to have explained and demonstrated these things more fully. But I have already said that I intended something else, and brought these things forward only because I can easily deduce from them the things I have decided to demonstrate.

43

POSTULATES

I. The human body is composed of a great many individuals of different natures, each of which is highly composite.

II. Some of the individuals of which the human body is composed are fluid, some soft, and others, finally, are hard.

III. The individuals composing the human body, and consequently, the human body itself, are affected by external bodies in very many ways.

IV. The human body, to be preserved, requires a great many other bodies, by which it is, as it were, continually regenerated.

II/103

V. When a fluid part of the human body is determined by an external body so that it frequently thrusts against a soft part [of the body], it changes its surface and, as it were, impresses on [the soft part] certain traces of the external body striking against [the fluid part].

VI. The human body can move and dispose external bodies in a great many ways.

P14: *The human mind is capable of perceiving a great many things, and is the more capable, the more its body can be disposed in a great many ways.*

Dem.: For the human body (by Post. 3 and 6) is affected in a great many ways by external bodies, and is disposed to affect external bodies in a great many ways. But the human mind must perceive everything which happens in the human body (by P12). Therefore, the human mind is capable of perceiving a great many things, and is the more capable [, NS: as the human body is more capable], q.e.d.

P15: *The idea that constitutes the formal being* [esse] *of the human mind is not simple, but composed of a great many ideas.*

Dem.: The idea that constitutes the formal being of the human mind is the idea of a body (by P13), which (by Post. 1) is composed of a great many highly composite individuals. But of each individual composing the body, there is necessarily (by P8C) an idea in God. Therefore (by P7), the idea of the human body is composed of these many ideas of the parts composing the body, q.e.d.

P16: *The idea of any mode in which the human body is affected by external bodies must involve the nature of the human body and at the same time the nature of the external body.*

II/104

Dem.: For all the modes in which a body is affected follow from the nature of the affected body, and at the same time from the nature of the affecting body (by A1″ [II/99]). So the idea of them (by IA4) will necessarily involve the nature of each body. And so the idea of each mode in

44

which the human body is affected by an external body involves the nature of the human body and of the external body, q.e.d.

Cor. 1: From this it follows, first, that the human mind perceives the nature of a great many bodies together with the nature of its own body.

Cor. 2: It follows, second, that the ideas which we have of external bodies indicate the condition of our own body more than the nature of the external bodies. I have explained this by many examples in the Appendix of Part I.

P17: *If the human body is affected with a mode that involves the nature of an external body, the human mind will regard the same external body as actually existing, or as present to it, until the body is affected by an affect that excludes the existence or presence of that body.*

Dem.: This is evident. For so long as the human body is so affected, the human mind (by P12) will regard this affection of the body, that is (by P16), it will have the idea of a mode that actually exists, an idea which involves the nature of the external body, that is, an idea which does not exclude, but posits, the existence or presence of the nature of the external body. And so the mind (by P16C1) will regard the external body as actually existing, or as present, until it is affected, and so on, q.e.d.

Cor.: Although the external bodies by which the human body has once been affected neither exist nor are present, the mind will still be able to regard them as if they were present.

II/105

Dem.: While external bodies so determine the fluid parts of the human body that they often thrust against the softer parts, they change (by Post. 5) their surfaces with the result (see A2″ after L3) that they are reflected from it in another way than they used to be before, and still later, when the fluid parts, by their spontaneous motion, encounter those new surfaces, they are reflected in the same way as when they were driven against those surfaces by the external bodies. Consequently, while, thus reflected, they continue to move, they will affect the human body with the same mode, concerning which the mind (by P12) will think again, that is (by P17), the mind will again regard the external body as present; this will happen as often as the fluid parts of the human body encounter the same surfaces by their spontaneous motion. So although the external bodies by which the human body has once been affected do not exist, the mind will still regard them as present, as often as this action of the body is repeated, q.e.d.

Schol.: We see, therefore, how it can happen (as it often does) that we regard as present things which do not exist. This can happen from other causes also, but it is sufficient for me here to have shown one through which I can explain it as if I had shown it through its true cause; still, I do not believe that I wander far from the true [cause] since all those postulates which I have assumed contain hardly anything which is not established by experience which we cannot doubt, after we have shown that the human body exists as we are aware of it (see P13C).

Furthermore (from P17C and P16C2), we clearly understand what is the difference between the idea of, say, Peter, which constitutes the essence of Peter's mind, and the idea of Peter which is in another man, say in Paul. For the former directly explains the essence of Peter's body, II/106 and does not involve existence, except so long as Peter exists; but the latter indicates the condition of Paul's body more than Peter's nature [NS: see P16C2], and therefore, while that condition of Paul's body lasts, Paul's mind will still regard Peter as present to itself, even though Peter does not exist.

Next, to retain the customary words, the affections of the human body whose ideas present external bodies as present to us, we shall call images of things, though they do not reproduce the [NS: external] figures of things. And when the mind regards bodies in this way, we shall say that it imagines.

And here, in order to begin to indicate what error is, I should like you to note that the imaginations of the mind, considered in themselves contain no error, *or* that the mind does not err from the fact that it imagines, but only insofar as it is considered to lack an idea which excludes the existence of those things which it imagines to be present to it. For if the mind, while it imagined nonexistent things as present to it, at the same time knew that those things did not exist, it would, of course, attribute this power of imagining to a virtue of its nature, not to a vice— especially if this faculty of imagining depended only on its own nature, that is (by ID7), if the mind's faculty of imagining were free.

P18: *If the human body has once been affected by two or more bodies at the same time, then when the mind subsequently imagines one of them, it will immediately recollect the others also.*

Dem.: The mind (by P17C) imagines a body because the human body is affected and disposed as it was affected when certain of its parts were struck by the external body itself. But (by hypothesis) the body was then so disposed that the mind imagined two [or more] bodies at once; there- fore it will now also imagine two [or more] at once, and when the mind imagines one, it will immediately recollect the other also, q.e.d.

Schol.: From this we clearly understand what memory is. For it is II/107 nothing other than a certain connection of ideas involving the nature of things which are outside the human body—a connection which is in the mind according to the order and connection of the affections of the human body.

I say, *first*, that the connection is only of those ideas which involve the nature of things outside the human body, but not of the ideas which explain the nature of the same things. For they are really (by P16) ideas of affections of the human body which involve both its nature and that of external bodies.

I say, *second*, that this connection happens according to the order and connection of the affections of the human body in order to distinguish it from the connection of ideas which happens according to the order of the intellect, by which the mind perceives things through their first causes, and which is the same in all men.

And from this we clearly understand why the mind, from the thought of one thing, immediately passes to the thought of another, which has no likeness to the first: as, for example, from the thought of the word *pomum* a Roman will immediately pass to the thought of the fruit [viz. an apple], which has no similarity to that articulate sound and nothing in common with it except that the body of the same man has often been affected by these two [NS: at the same time], that is, that the man often heard the word *pomum* while he saw the fruit.

And in this way each of us will pass from one thought to another, as each one's association has ordered the images of things in the body. For example, a soldier, having seen traces of a horse in the sand, will immediately pass from the thought of a horse to the thought of a horseman, and from that to the thought of war, and so on. But a farmer will pass from the thought of a horse to the thought of a plow, and then to that of a field, and so on. And so each one, according as he has been accustomed to join and connect the images of things in this or that way, will pass from one thought to another.

P19: *The human mind does not know the human body itself, nor does it know that it exists, except through ideas of affections by which the body is affected.*

Dem.: For the human mind is the idea itself, *or* knowledge of the human body (by P13), which (by P9) is indeed in God insofar as he is considered to be affected by another idea of a singular thing, or because (by Post. 4) the human body requires a great many bodies by which it is, as it were, continually regenerated; and [NS: because] the order and connection of ideas is (by P7) the same as the order and connection of causes, this idea will be in God insofar as he is considered to be affected by the ideas of a great many singular things. Therefore, God has the idea of the human body, *or* knows the human body, insofar as he is affected by a great many other ideas, and not insofar as he constitutes

II/108

the nature of the human mind, that is (by P11C), the human mind does not know the human body.

But the ideas of affections of the body are in God insofar as he constitutes the nature of the human mind, *or* the human mind perceives the same affections (by P12), and consequently (by P16) the human body itself, as actually existing (by P17).

Therefore to that extent only, the human mind perceives the human body itself, q.e.d.

P20: *There is also in God an idea,* or *knowledge, of the human mind, which follows in God in the same way and is related to God in the same way as the idea,* or *knowledge, of the human body.*

Dem.: Thought is an attribute of God (by P1), and so (by P3) there must necessarily be in God an idea both of [NS: thought] and of all of its affections, and consequently (by P11), of the human mind also. Next, this idea, *or* knowledge, of the mind does not follow in God insofar as he is infinite, but insofar as he is affected by another idea of a singular thing (by P9). But the order and connection of ideas is the same as the order and connection of causes (by P7). Therefore, this idea, *or* knowledge, of the mind follows in God and is related to God in the same way as the idea, *or* knowledge, of the body, q.e.d.

II/109   P21: *This idea of the mind is united to the mind in the same way as the mind is united to the body.*

Dem.: We have shown that the mind is united to the body from the fact that the body is the object of the mind (see P12 and 13); and so by the same reasoning the idea of the mind must be united with its own object, that is, with the mind itself, in the same way as the mind is united with the body, q.e.d.

Schol.: This proposition is understood far more clearly from what is said in P7S; for there we have shown that the idea of the body and the body, that is (by P13), the mind and the body, are one and the same individual, which is conceived now under the attribute of thought, now under the attribute of extension. So the idea of the mind and the mind itself are one and the same thing, which is conceived under one and the same attribute, namely, thought. The idea of the mind, I say, and the mind itself follow in God from the same power of thinking and by the same necessity. For the idea of the mind, that is, the idea of the idea, is nothing but the form of the idea insofar as this is considered as a mode of thinking without relation to the object. For as soon as someone knows something, he thereby knows that he knows it, and at the same time knows that he knows that he knows, and so on, to infinity. But more on these matters later.

48

P22: *The human mind perceives not only the affections of the body, but also the ideas of these affections.*

Dem.: The ideas of the ideas of the affections follow in God in the same way and are related to God in the same way as the ideas themselves of the affections (this is demonstrated in the same way as P20). But the ideas of the affections of the body are in the human mind (by P12), that is (by P11C), in God, insofar as he constitutes the essence of the human mind. Therefore, the ideas of these ideas will be in God insofar as he has the knowledge, *or* idea, of the human mind, that is (by P21), they will be in the human mind itself, which for that reason perceives not only the affections of the body, but also their ideas, q.e.d.

II/110

P23: *The mind does not know itself, except insofar as it perceives the ideas of the affections of the body.*

Dem.: The idea, *or* knowledge, of the mind (by P20) follows in God in the same way, and is related to God in the same way as the idea, *or* knowledge, of the body. But since (by P19) the human mind does not know the human body itself, that is (by P11C), since the knowledge of the human body is not related to God insofar as he constitutes the nature of the human mind, the knowledge of the mind is also not related to God insofar as he constitutes the essence of the human mind. And so (again by P11C) to that extent the human mind does not know itself.

Next, the ideas of the affections by which the body is affected involve the nature of the human body itself (by P16), that is (by P13), agree with the nature of the mind. So knowledge of these ideas will necessarily involve knowledge of the mind. But (by P22) knowledge of these ideas is in the human mind itself. Therefore, the human mind, to that extent only, knows itself, q.e.d.

P24: *The human mind does not involve adequate knowledge of the parts composing the human body.*

Dem.: The parts composing the human body pertain to the essence of the body itself only insofar as they communicate their motions to one another in a certain fixed manner (see the definition after L3C), and not insofar as they can be considered as individuals, without relation to the human body. For (by Post. 1) the parts of the human body are highly composite individuals, whose parts (by L4) can be separated from the human body and communicate their motions (see A1″ after L3) to other bodies in another manner, while the human body completely preserves its nature and form. And so the idea, *or* knowledge, of each part will be in God (by P3), insofar as he is considered to be affected by another idea of a singular thing (by P9), a singular thing which is prior, in the order of Nature, to the part itself (by P7). The same must also be said of each

II/111

part of the individual composing the human body. And so, the knowledge of each part composing the human body is in God insofar as he is affected with a great many ideas of things, and not insofar as he has only the idea of the human body, that is (by P13), the idea which constitutes the nature of the human mind. And so, by (P11C) the human mind does not involve adequate knowledge of the parts composing the human body, q.e.d.

P25: *The idea of any affection of the human body does not involve adequate knowledge of an external body.*

Dem.: We have shown (P16) that the idea of an affection of the human body involves the nature of an external body insofar as the external body determines the human body in a certain fixed way. But insofar as the external body is an Individual which is not related to the human body, the idea, *or* knowledge, of it is in God (by P9) insofar as God is considered to be affected with the idea of another thing which (by P7) is prior in nature to the external body itself. So adequate knowledge of the external body is not in God insofar as he has the idea of an affection of the human body, *or* the idea of an affection of the human body does not involve adequate knowledge of the external body, q.e.d.

II/112   P26: *The human mind does not perceive any external body as actually existing, except through the ideas of the affections of its own body.*

Dem.: If the human body is not affected by an external body in any way, then (by P7) the idea of the human body, that is (by P13) the human mind, is also not affected in any way by the idea of the existence of that body, *or* it does not perceive the existence of that external body in any way. But insofar as the human body is affected by an external body in some way, to that extent [the human mind] (by P16 and P16C1) perceives the external body, q.e.d.

Cor.: Insofar as the human mind imagines an external body, it does not have adequate knowledge of it.

Dem.: When the human mind regards external bodies through ideas of the affections of its own body, then we say that it imagines (see P17S); and the mind cannot in any other way (by P26) imagine external bodies as actually existing. And so (by P25), insofar as the mind imagines external bodies, it does not have adequate knowledge of them, q.e.d.

P27: *The idea of any affection of the human body does not involve adequate knowledge of the human body itself.*

Dem.: Any idea of any affection of the human body involves the nature of the human body insofar as the human body itself is considered to be affected with a certain definite mode (see P16). But insofar as the

human body is an individual, which can be affected with many other   II/113
modes, the idea of this [affection] and so on. (See P25D.)

P28: *The ideas of the affections of the human body, insofar as they are related
only to the human mind, are not clear and distinct, but confused.*

Dem.: For the ideas of the affections of the human body involve the
nature of external bodies as much as that of the human body (by P16),
and must involve the nature not only of the human body [NS: as a
whole], but also of its parts; for the affections are modes (by Post. 3)
with which the parts of the human body, and consequently the whole
body, are affected. But (by P24 and P25) adequate knowledge of external bodies and of the parts composing the human body is in God, not
insofar as he is considered to be affected with the human mind, but
insofar as he is considered to be affected with other ideas. Therefore,
these ideas of the affections, insofar as they are related only to the
human mind, are like conclusions without premises, that is (as is known
through itself), they are confused ideas, q.e.d.

Schol.: In the same way we can demonstrate that the idea which constitutes the nature of the human mind is not, considered in itself alone,
clear and distinct; we can also demonstrate the same of the idea of the
human mind and the ideas of the ideas of the human body's affections
[NS: viz. that they are confused], insofar as they are referred to the mind
alone. Anyone can easily see this.

P29: *The idea of the idea of any affection of the human body does not involve
adequate knowledge of the human mind.*

Dem.: For the idea of an affection of the human body (by P27) does
not involve adequate knowledge of the body itself, *or* does not express   II/114
its nature adequately, that is (by P13), does not agree adequately with
the nature of the mind; and so (by IA6) the idea of this idea does not
express the nature of the human mind adequately, *or* does not involve
adequate knowledge of it, q.e.d.

Cor.: From this it follows that so long as the human mind perceives
things from the common order of Nature, it does not have an adequate,
but only a confused and mutilated knowledge of itself, of its own body,
and of external bodies. For the mind does not know itself except insofar
as it perceives ideas of the affections of the body (by P23). But it does
not perceive its own body (by P19) except through the very ideas themselves of the affections [of the body], and it is also through them alone
that it perceives external bodies (by P26). And so, insofar as it has these
[ideas], then neither of itself (by P29), nor of its own body (by P27), nor
of external bodies (by P25) does it have an adequate knowledge, but
only (by P28 and P28S) a mutilated and confused knowledge, q.e.d.

Schol.: I say expressly that the mind has, not an adequate, but only a confused [NS: and mutilated] knowledge, of itself, of its own body, and of external bodies, so long as it perceives things from the common order of Nature, that is, so long as it is determined externally, from fortuitous encounters with things, to regard this or that, and not so long as it is determined internally, from the fact that it regards a number of things at once, to understand their agreements, differences, and oppositions. For so often as it is disposed internally, in this or another way, then it regards things clearly and distinctly, as I shall show below.

P30: *We can have only an entirely inadequate knowledge of the duration of our body.*

II/115

Dem.: Our body's duration depends neither on its essence (by A1), nor even on God's absolute nature (by IP21). But (by IP28) it is determined to exist and produce an effect from such [NS: other] causes as are also determined by others to exist and produce an effect in a certain and determinate manner, and these again by others, and so to infinity. Therefore, the duration of our body depends on the common order of Nature and the constitution of things. But adequate knowledge of how things are constituted is in God, insofar as he has the ideas of all of them, and not insofar as he has only the idea of the human body (by P9C). So the knowledge of the duration of our body is quite inadequate in God, insofar as he is considered to constitute only the nature of the human mind, that is (by P11C), this knowledge is quite inadequate in our mind, q.e.d.

P31: *We can have only an entirely inadequate knowledge of the duration of the singular things which are outside us.*

Dem.: For each singular thing, like the human body, must be determined by another singular thing to exist and produce effects in a certain and determinate way, and this again by another, and so to infinity (by IP28). But since (in P30) we have demonstrated from this common property of singular things that we have only a very inadequate knowledge of the duration of our body, we shall have to draw the same conclusion concerning the duration of singular things [outside us], namely, that we can have only a very inadequate knowledge of their duration, q.e.d.

Cor.: From this it follows that all particular things are contingent and corruptible. For we can have no adequate knowledge of their duration (by P31), and that is what we must understand by the contingency of things and the possibility of their corruption (see IP33S1). For (by

II/116

IP29) beyond that there is no contingency.

P32: *All ideas, insofar as they are related to God, are true.*

Dem.: For all ideas which are in God agree entirely with their objects (by P7C), and so (by IA6) they are all true, q.e.d.

P33: *There is nothing positive in ideas on account of which they are called false.*

Dem.: If you deny this, conceive (if possible) a positive mode of thinking which constitutes the form of error, *or* falsity. This mode of thinking cannot be in God (by P32). But it also can neither be nor be conceived outside God (by IP15). And so there can be nothing positive in ideas on account of which they are called false, q.e.d.

P34: *Every idea which in us is absolute,* or *adequate and perfect, is true.*

Dem.: When we say that there is in us an adequate and perfect idea, we are saying nothing but that (by P11C) there is an adequate and perfect idea in God insofar as he constitutes the essence of our mind, and consequently (by P32) we are saying nothing but that such an idea is true, q.e.d.

P35: *Falsity consists in the privation of knowledge which inadequate,* or *mutilated and confused, ideas involve.*

Dem.: There is nothing positive in ideas which constitutes the form II/117 of falsity (by P33); but falsity cannot consist in an absolute privation (for it is minds, not bodies, which are said to err, or be deceived), nor also in absolute ignorance. For to be ignorant and to err are different. So it consists in the privation of knowledge which inadequate knowledge of things, *or* inadequate and confused ideas, involve, q.e.d.

Schol.: In P17S I explained how error consists in the privation of knowledge. But to explain the matter more fully, I shall give [NS: one or two examples]: men are deceived in that they think themselves free [NS: i.e., they think that, of their own free will, they can either do a thing or forbear doing it], an opinion which consists only in this, that they are conscious of their actions and ignorant of the causes by which they are determined. This, then, is their idea of freedom—that they do not know any cause of their actions. They say, of course, that human actions depend on the will, but these are only words for which they have no idea. For all are ignorant of what the will is, and how it moves the body; those who boast of something else, who feign seats and dwelling places of the soul, usually provoke either ridicule or disgust.

Similarly, when we look at the sun, we imagine it as about two hundred feet away from us, an error which does not consist simply in this imagining, but in the fact that while we imagine it in this way, we are ignorant of its true distance and of the cause of this imagining. For even if we later come to know that it is more than six hundred diameters of the earth away from us, we nevertheless imagine it as near. For we imagine the sun so near not because we do not know its true distance, but because an affection of our body involves the essence of the sun insofar as our body is affected by the sun.

P36: *Inadequate and confused ideas follow with the same necessity as adequate, or clear and distinct ideas.*

II/118   Dem.: All ideas are in God (by IP15); and, insofar as they are related to God, are true (by P32), and (by P7C) adequate. And so there are no inadequate or confused ideas except insofar as they are related to the singular mind of someone (see P24 and P28). And so all ideas—both the adequate and the inadequate—follow with the same necessity (by P6C), q.e.d.

P37: *What is common to all things* (on this see L2, above) *and is equally in the part and in the whole, does not constitute the essence of any singular thing.*

Dem.: If you deny this, conceive (if possible) that it does constitute the essence of some singular thing, say the essence of B. Then (by D2) it can neither be nor be conceived without B. But this is contrary to the hypothesis. Therefore, it does not pertain to the essence of B, nor does it constitute the essence of any other singular thing, q.e.d.

P38: *Those things which are common to all, and which are equally in the part and in the whole, can only be conceived adequately.*

Dem.: Let A be something which is common to all bodies, and which is equally in the part of each body and in the whole. I say that A can only be conceived adequately. For its idea (by P7C) will necessarily be adequate in God, both insofar as he has the idea of the human body and insofar as he has ideas of its affections, which (by P16, P25, and P27) involve in part both the nature of the human body and that of external bodies. That is (by P12 and P13), this idea will necessarily be adequate

II/119 in God insofar as he constitutes the human mind, *or* insofar as he has ideas that are in the human mind. The mind, therefore (by P11C), necessarily perceives A adequately, and does so both insofar as it perceives itself and insofar as it perceives its own or any external body. Nor can A be conceived in another way, q.e.d.

Cor.: From this it follows that there are certain ideas, *or* notions, common to all men. For (by L2) all bodies agree in certain things, which (by P38) must be perceived adequately, *or* clearly and distinctly, by all.

P39: *If something is common to, and peculiar to, the human body and certain external bodies by which the human body is usually affected, and is equally in the part and in the whole of each of them, its idea will also be adequate in the mind.*

Dem.: Let A be that which is common to, and peculiar to, the human body and certain external bodies, which is equally in the human body and in the same external bodies, and finally, which is equally in the part of each external body and in the whole. There will be an adequate idea of A in God (by P7C), both insofar as he has the idea of the human body, and insofar as he has ideas of the posited external bodies. Let it be posited now that the human body is affected by an external body through what it has in common with it, that is, by A; the idea of this affection will involve property A (by P16), and so (by P7C) the idea of this affection, insofar as it involves property A, will be adequate in God insofar as he is affected with the idea of the human body, that is (by P13), insofar as he constitutes the nature of the human mind. And so (by P11C), this idea is also adequate in the human mind, q.e.d.

Cor.: From this it follows that the mind is the more capable of perceiving many things adequately as its body has many things in common with other bodies.

II/120

P40: *Whatever ideas follow in the mind from ideas which are adequate in the mind are also adequate.*

Dem.: This is evident. For when we say that an idea in the human mind follows from ideas which are adequate in it, we are saying nothing but that (by P11C) in the divine intellect there is an idea of which God is the cause, not insofar as he is infinite, nor insofar as he is affected with the ideas of a great many singular things, but insofar as he constitutes only the essence of the human mind [NS: and therefore, it must be adequate].

Schol. 1: With this I have explained the cause of those notions which are called *common*, and which are the foundations of our reasoning.

But some axioms, *or* notions, result from other causes which it would be helpful to explain by this method of ours. For from these [explanations] it would be established which notions are more useful than the others, and which are of hardly any use; and then, which are common, which are clear and distinct only to those who have no prejudices, and finally, which are ill-founded. Moreover, we would establish what is the origin of those notions they call *Second*, and consequently of the axioms founded on them, and other things I have thought about, from time to time, concerning these matters. But since I have set these aside for another treatise, and do not wish to give rise to disgust by too long a discussion, I have decided to pass over them here.

But not to omit anything it is necessary to know, I shall briefly add something about the causes from which the terms called *Transcendental* have had their origin—I mean terms like Being, Thing, and Something. These terms arise from the fact that the human body, being limited, is capable of forming distinctly only a certain number of images at the same time (I have explained what an image is in P17S). If that number is exceeded, the images will begin to be confused, and if the number of images the body is capable of forming distinctly in itself at once is greatly exceeded, they will all be completely confused with one another.

II/121

Since this is so, it is evident from P17C and P18, that the human mind will be able to imagine distinctly, at the same time, as many bodies as there can be images formed at the same time in its body. But when the images in the body are completely confused, the mind also will imagine all the bodies confusedly, without any distinction, and comprehend them as if under one attribute, namely, under the attribute of Being, Thing, and so forth. This can also be deduced from the fact that images are not always equally vigorous and from other causes like these, which it is not necessary to explain here. For our purpose it is sufficient to consider only one. For they all reduce to this: these terms signify ideas that are confused in the highest degree.

Those notions they call *Universal*, like Man, Horse, Dog, and the like, have arisen from similar causes, namely, because so many images (e.g., of men) are formed at one time in the human body that they surpass the power of imagining—not entirely, of course, but still to the point where the mind can imagine neither slight differences of the singular [men] (such as the color and size of each one, etc.) nor their determinate number, and imagines distinctly only what they all agree in, insofar as they affect the body. For the body has been affected most [NS: forcefully] by [what is common], since each singular has affected it [by this property]. And [NS: the mind] expresses this by the word *man*, and predicates it of infinitely many singulars. For as we have said, it cannot imagine a determinate number of singulars.

But it should be noted that these notions are not formed by all [NS: men] in the same way, but vary from one to another, in accordance with what the body has more often been affected by, and what the mind imagines or recollects more easily. For example, those who have more often regarded men's stature with wonder will understand by the word *man* an animal of erect stature. But those who have been accustomed to consider something else, will form another common image of men—for example, that man is an animal capable of laughter, or a featherless biped, or a rational animal.

And similarly concerning the others—each will form universal images of things according to the disposition of his body. Hence it is not surprising that so many controversies have arisen among the philosophers, who have wished to explain natural things by mere images of things.

Schol. 2: From what has been said above, it is clear that we perceive II/122 many things and form universal notions:

I. from singular things which have been represented to us through the senses in a way which is mutilated, confused, and without order for the intellect (see P29C); for that reason I have been accustomed to call such perceptions knowledge from random experience;

II. from signs, for example, from the fact that, having heard or read certain words, we recollect things, and form certain ideas of them, like those through which we imagine the things (P18S); these two ways of regarding things I shall henceforth call knowledge of the first kind, opinion or imagination;

III. finally, from the fact that we have common notions and adequate ideas of the properties of things (see P38C, P39, P39C, and P40). This I shall call reason and the second kind of knowledge.

[IV.] In addition to these two kinds of knowledge, there is (as I shall show in what follows) another, third kind, which we shall call intuitive knowledge. And this kind of knowing proceeds from an adequate idea of the formal essence of certain attributes of God to the adequate knowledge of the [NS: formal] essence of things.

I shall explain all these with one example. Suppose there are three numbers, and the problem is to find a fourth which is to the third as the second is to the first. Merchants do not hesitate to multiply the second by the third, and divide the product by the first, because they have not yet forgotten what they heard from their teacher without any demonstration, or because they have often found this in the simplest numbers, or from the force of the demonstration of P19 in Book VII of Euclid, namely, from the common property of proportionals. But in the simplest numbers none of this is necessary. Given the numbers 1, 2, and 3, no one fails to see that the fourth proportional number is 6—and we see this much more clearly because we infer the fourth number from the ratio which, in one glance, we see the first number to have to the second.

P41: *Knowledge of the first kind is the only cause of falsity, whereas knowledge of the second and of the third kind is necessarily true.*

Dem.: We have said in the preceding scholium that to knowledge of II/123 the first kind pertain all those ideas which are inadequate and confused; and so (by P35) this knowledge is the only cause of falsity. Next, we have said that to knowledge of the second and third kinds pertain those which are adequate; and so (by P34) this knowledge is necessarily true.

P42: *Knowledge of the second and third kinds, and not of the first kind, teaches us to distinguish the true from the false.*

Dem.: This proposition is evident through itself. For he who knows how to distinguish between the true and the false must have an adequate idea of the true and of the false, that is (P40S2), must know the true and the false by the second or third kind of knowledge.

P43: *He who has a true idea at the same time knows that he has a true idea, and cannot doubt the truth of the thing.*

Dem.: An idea true in us is that which is adequate in God insofar as he is explained through the nature of the human mind (by P11C). Let us posit, therefore, that there is in God, insofar as he is explained through the nature of the human mind, an adequate idea, A. Of this idea there must necessarily also be in God an idea which is related to God in the same way as idea A (by P20, whose demonstration is universal [NS: and can be applied to all ideas]). But idea A is supposed to be related to God insofar as he is explained through the nature of the human mind; therefore the idea of idea A must also be related to God in the same way, that is (by the same P11C), this adequate idea of idea A will be in the mind itself which has the adequate idea A. And so he who has an adequate idea, *or* (by P34) who knows a thing truly, must at the same time have an adequate idea, *or* true knowledge, of his own knowledge. That is (as is manifest through itself), he must at the same time be certain, q.e.d.

II/124

Schol.: In P21S I have explained what an idea of an idea is. But it should be noted that the preceding proposition is sufficiently manifest through itself. For no one who has a true idea is unaware that a true idea involves the highest certainty. For to have a true idea means nothing other than knowing a thing perfectly, *or* in the best way. And of course no one can doubt this unless he thinks that an idea is something mute, like a picture on a tablet, and not a mode of thinking, namely, the very [act of] understanding. And I ask, who can know that he understands some thing unless he first understands it? That is, who can know that he is certain about some thing unless he is first certain about it? What can there be which is clearer and more certain than a true idea, to serve as a standard of truth? As the light makes both itself and the darkness plain, so truth is the standard both of itself and of the false.

By this I think we have replied to these questions: if a true idea is distinguished from a false one, [NS: not insofar as it is said to be a mode of thinking, but] only insofar as it is said to agree with its object, then a true idea has no more reality or perfection than a false one (since they are distinguished only through the extrinsic denomination [NS: and not through the intrinsic denomination])—and so, does the man who has true ideas [NS: have any more reality or perfection] than he who has only false ideas? Again, why do men have false ideas? And finally, how can someone know certainly that he has ideas which agree with their objects?

To these questions, I say, I think I have already replied. For as far as the difference between a true and a false idea is concerned, it is established from P35 that the true is related to the false as being is to nonbeing. And the causes of falsity I have shown most clearly from P19 to P35S. From this it is also clear what is the difference between the man who has true ideas and the man who has only false ideas. Finally, as to the last, namely, how a man can know that he has an idea which agrees with its object? I have just shown, more than sufficiently, that this arises solely from his having an idea which does agree with its object—*or* that truth is its own standard. Add to this that our mind, insofar as it perceives things truly, is part of the infinite intellect of God (by P11C); hence, it is as necessary that the mind's clear and distinct ideas are true as that God's ideas are.

II/125

P44: *It is of the nature of reason to regard things as necessary, not as contingent.*

Dem.: It is of the nature of reason to perceive things truly (by P41), namely (by IA6), as they are in themselves, that is (by IP29), not as contingent but as necessary, q.e.d.

Cor. 1: From this it follows that it depends only on the imagination that we regard things as contingent, both in respect to the past and in respect to the future.

Schol.: I shall explain briefly how this happens. We have shown above (by P17 and P17C) that even though things do not exist, the mind still imagines them always as present to itself, unless causes occur which exclude their present existence. Next, we have shown (P18) that if the human body has once been affected by two external bodies at the same time, then afterwards, when the mind imagines one of them, it will immediately recollect the other also, that is, it will regard both as present to itself unless causes occur which exclude their present existence. Moreover, no one doubts but what we also imagine time, namely, from the fact that we imagine some bodies to move more slowly than others, or more quickly, or with the same speed.

Let us suppose, then, a child, who saw Peter for the first time yesterday, in the morning, but saw Paul at noon, and Simon in the evening, and today again saw Peter in the morning. It is clear from P18 that as soon as he sees the morning light, he will immediately imagine the sun taking the same course through the sky as he saw on the preceding day, *or* he will imagine the whole day, and Peter together with the morning, Paul with noon, and Simon with the evening. That is, he will imagine the existence of Paul and of Simon with a relation to future time. On the other hand, if he sees Simon in the evening, he will relate Paul and Peter to the time past, by imagining them together with past time. And he will do this more uniformly, the more often he has seen them in this same order.

But if it should happen at some time that on some other evening he sees James instead of Simon, then on the following morning he will imagine now Simon, now James, together with the evening time, but not both at once. For it is supposed that he has seen one or the other of them in the evening, but not both at once. His imagination, therefore, will vacillate and he will imagine now this one, now that one, with the future evening time, that is, he will regard neither of them as certainly future, but both of them as contingently future.

And this vacillation of the imagination will be the same if the imagination is of things we regard in the same way with relation to past time or to present time. Consequently we shall imagine things as contingent in relation to present time as well as to past and future time.

Cor 2: It is of the nature of reason to perceive things under a certain species of eternity.

Dem.: It is of the nature of reason to regard things as necessary and not as contingent (by P44). And it perceives this necessity of things truly (by P41), that is (by IA6), as it is in itself. But (by IP16) this necessity of things is the very necessity of God's eternal nature. Therefore, it is of the nature of reason to regard things under this species of eternity.

Add to this that the foundations of reason are notions (by P38) which explain those things which are common to all, and which (by P37) do not explain the essence of any singular thing. On that account, they must be conceived without any relation to time, but under a certain species of eternity, q.e.d.

P45: *Each idea of each body, or of each singular thing which actually exists, necessarily involves an eternal and infinite essence of God.*

Dem.: The idea of a singular thing which actually exists necessarily involves both the essence of the thing and its existence (by P8C). But singular things (by IP15) cannot be conceived without God—on the contrary, because (by P6) they have God for a cause insofar as he is considered under the attribute of which the things are modes, their ideas must involve the concept of their attribute (by IA4), that is (by ID6), must involve an eternal and infinite essence of God, q.e.d.

Schol.: By existence here I do not understand duration, that is, existence insofar as it is conceived abstractly, and as a certain species of quantity. For I am speaking of the very nature of existence, which is attributed to singular things because infinitely many things follow from the eternal necessity of God's nature in infinitely many modes (see IP16). I am speaking, I say, of the very existence of singular things insofar as they are in God. For even if each one is determined by another singular thing to exist in a certain way, still the force by which each one perseveres in existing follows from the eternal necessity of God's nature. Concerning this, see IP24C.

P46: *The knowledge of God's eternal and infinite essence which each idea involves is adequate and perfect.*

Dem.: The demonstration of the preceding proposition is universal, and whether the thing is considered as a part or as a whole, its idea, whether of the whole or of a part (by P45), will involve God's eternal and infinite essence. So what gives knowledge of an eternal and infinite essence of God is common to all, and is equally in the part and in the whole. And so (by P38) this knowledge will be adequate, q.e.d.

II/128

P47: *The human mind has an adequate knowledge of God's eternal and infinite essence.*

Dem.: The human mind has ideas (by P22) from which it perceives (by P23) itself, (by P19) its own body, and (by P16C1 and P17) external bodies as actually existing. And so (by P45 and P46) it has an adequate knowledge of God's eternal and infinite essence, q.e.d.

Schol.: From this we see that God's infinite essence and his eternity are known to all. And since all things are in God and are conceived through God, it follows that we can deduce from this knowledge a great many things which we know adequately, and so can form that third kind of knowledge of which we spoke in P40S2 and of whose excellence and utility we shall speak in Part V.

But that men do not have so clear a knowledge of God as they do of the common notions comes from the fact that they cannot imagine God, as they can bodies, and that they have joined the name *God* to the images of things which they are used to seeing. Men can hardly avoid this, because they are continually affected by external bodies.

And indeed, most errors consist only in our not rightly applying names to things. For when someone says that the lines which are drawn from the center of a circle to its circumference are unequal, he surely understands (then at least) by a circle something different from what mathematicians understand. Similarly, when men err in calculating, they have certain numbers in their mind and different ones on the paper. So if you consider what they have in mind, they really do not err, though they seem to err because we think they have in their mind the numbers which are on the paper. If this were not so, we would not believe that they were erring, just as I did not believe that he was erring whom I recently heard cry out that his courtyard had flown into his neighbor's hen [NS: although his words were absurd], because what he had in mind seemed sufficiently clear to me [viz. that his hen had flown into his neighbor's courtyard].

II/129

And most controversies have arisen from this, that men do not rightly explain their own mind, or interpret the mind of the other man badly. For really, when they contradict one another most vehemently, they either have the same thoughts, or they are thinking of different things, so that what they think are errors and absurdities in the other are not.

P48: *In the mind there is no absolute, or free, will, but the mind is determined to will this or that by a cause which is also determined by another, and this again by another, and so to infinity.*

Dem.: The mind is a certain and determinate mode of thinking (by P11), and so (by IP17C2) cannot be a free cause of its own actions, *or* cannot have an absolute faculty of willing and not willing. Rather, it must be determined to willing this or that (by IP28) by a cause which is also determined by another, and this cause again by another, and so on, q.e.d.

Schol.: In this same way it is also demonstrated that there is in the mind no absolute faculty of understanding, desiring, loving, and the like. From this it follows that these and similar faculties are either complete fictions or nothing but metaphysical beings, *or* universals, which we are used to forming from particulars. So intellect and will are to this or that idea, or to this or that volition as 'stone-ness' is to this or that stone, or man to Peter or Paul.

We have explained the cause of men's thinking themselves free in the Appendix of Part I. But before I proceed further, it should be noted here that by will I understand a faculty of affirming and denying, and not desire. I say that I understand the faculty by which the mind affirms or denies something true or something false, and not the desire by which the mind wants a thing or avoids it.

II/130

But after we have demonstrated that these faculties are universal notions which are not distinguished from the singulars from which we form them, we must now investigate whether the volitions themselves are anything beyond the very ideas of things. We must investigate, I say, whether there is any other affirmation or negation in the mind except that which the idea involves, insofar as it is an idea—on this see the following proposition and also D3—so that our thought does not fall into pictures. For by ideas I understand, not the images which are formed at the back of the eye (and, if you like, in the middle of the brain), but concepts of thought [NS: or the objective being of a thing insofar as it consists only in thought].

P49: *In the mind there is no volition, or affirmation and negation, except that which the idea involves insofar as it is an idea.*

Dem.: In the mind (by P48) there is no absolute faculty of willing and not willing, but only singular volitions, namely, this and that affirmation, and this and that negation. Let us conceive, therefore, some singular volition, say a mode of thinking by which the mind affirms that the three angles of a triangle are equal to two right angles.

This affirmation involves the concept, *or* idea, of the triangle, that is, it cannot be conceived without the idea of the triangle. For to say that A must involve the concept of B is the same as to say that A cannot be conceived without B. Further, this affirmation (by A3) also cannot be without the idea of the triangle. Therefore, this affirmation can neither be nor be conceived without the idea of the triangle.

Next, this idea of the triangle must involve this same affirmation, namely, that its three angles equal two right angles. So conversely, this idea of the triangle also can neither be nor be conceived without this affirmation.

So (by D2) this affirmation pertains to the essence of the idea of the triangle and is nothing beyond it. And what we have said concerning this volition (since we have selected it at random), must also be said concerning any volition, namely, that it is nothing apart from the idea, q.e.d.

Cor.: The will and the intellect are one and the same.

II/131

Dem.: The will and the intellect are nothing apart from the singular volitions and ideas themselves (by P48 and P48S). But the singular volitions and ideas are one and the same (by P49). Therefore the will and the intellect are one and the same, q.e.d.

Schol.: [I.] By this we have removed what is commonly maintained to be the cause of error. Moreover, we have shown above that falsity consists only in the privation which mutilated and confused ideas involve. So a false idea, insofar as it is false, does not involve certainty. When we say that a man rests in false ideas, and does not doubt them, we do not, on that account, say that he is certain, but only that he does not doubt, or that he rests in false ideas because there are no causes to bring it about that his imagination wavers [NS: or to cause him to doubt them]. On this, see P44S.

Therefore, however stubbornly a man may cling to something false [NS: so that we cannot in any way make him doubt it], we shall still never say that he is certain of it. For by certainty we understand something positive (see P43 and P43S), not the privation of doubt. But by the privation of certainty, we understand falsity.

However, to explain the preceding proposition more fully, there remain certain things I must warn you of. And then I must reply to the objections which can be made against this doctrine of ours. And finally, to remove every uneasiness, I thought it worthwhile to indicate some of the advantages of this doctrine. Some, I say—for the most important ones will be better understood from what we shall say in Part V.

[II.] I begin, therefore, by warning my readers, first, to distinguish accurately between an idea, *or* concept, of the mind, and the images of things which we imagine. And then it is necessary to distinguish between ideas and the words by which we signify things. For because many people either completely confuse these three—ideas, images, and words—or do not distinguish them accurately enough, or carefully enough, they have been completely ignorant of this doctrine concerning the will. But it is quite necessary to know it, both for the sake of speculation and in order to arrange one's life wisely.

II/132

Indeed, those who think that ideas consist in images which are formed in us from encounters with [NS: external] bodies, are convinced that those ideas of things [NS: which can make no trace in our brains, or] of which we can form no similar image [NS: in our brain] are not ideas, but only fictions which we feign from a free choice of the will. They look on ideas, therefore, as mute pictures on a panel, and preoccupied with this prejudice, do not see that an idea, insofar as it is an idea, involves an affirmation or negation.

And then, those who confuse words with the idea, or with the very affirmation which the idea involves, think that they can will something contrary to what they are aware of, when they only affirm or deny with words something contrary to what they are aware of. But these prejudices can easily be put aside by anyone who attends to the nature of thought, which does not at all involve the concept of extension. He will then understand clearly that an idea (since it is a mode of thinking) consists neither in the image of anything, nor in words. For the essence of words and of images is constituted only by corporeal motions, which do not at all involve the concept of thought.

It should suffice to have issued these few words of warning on this matter, so I pass to the objections mentioned above.

[III.A.(i)] The first of these is that they think it clear that the will extends more widely than the intellect, and so is different from the intellect. The reason why they think the will extends more widely than the intellect is that they say they know by experience that they do not require a greater faculty of assenting, *or* affirming, and denying, than we already have, in order to assent to infinitely many other things which we do not perceive—but they do require a greater faculty of understanding. The will, therefore, is distinguished from the intellect because the intellect is finite and the will is infinite.

[III.A.(ii)] Second, it can be objected to us that experience seems to teach nothing more clearly than that we can suspend our judgment so as not to assent to things we perceive. This also seems to be confirmed from the fact that no one is said to be deceived insofar as he perceives something, but only insofar as he assents or dissents. For example, someone who feigns a winged horse does not on that account grant that there is a winged horse, that is, he is not on that account deceived unless at the same time he grants that there is a winged horse. Therefore, experience seems to teach nothing more clearly than that the will, *or* faculty of assenting, is free, and different from the faculty of understanding.

II/133

[III.A.(iii)] Third, it can be objected that one affirmation does not seem to contain more reality than another, that is, we do not seem to require a greater power to affirm that what is true, is true, than to affirm that something false is true. But [NS: with ideas it is different, for] we perceive that one idea has more reality, *or* perfection, than another. As some objects are more excellent than others, so also some ideas of objects are more perfect than others. This also seems to establish a difference between the will and the intellect.

[III.A.(iv)] Fourth, it can be objected that if man does not act from freedom of the will, what will happen if he is in a state of equilibrium, like Buridan's ass? Will he perish of hunger and of thirst? If I concede that he will, I would seem to conceive an ass, or a statue of a man, not a man. But if I deny that he will, then he will determine himself, and consequently have the faculty of going where he wills and doing what he wills.

Perhaps other things in addition to these can be objected. But because I am not bound to force on you what anyone can dream, I shall only take the trouble to reply to these objections—and that as briefly as I can.

[III.B.(i)] To the first I say that I grant that the will extends more widely than the intellect, if by intellect they understand only clear and distinct ideas. But I deny that the will extends more widely than perceptions, *or* the faculty of conceiving. And indeed, I do not see why the faculty of willing should be called infinite, when the faculty of sensing

65

is not. For just as we can affirm infinitely many things by the same faculty of willing (but one after another, for we cannot affirm infinitely many things at once), so also we can sense, *or* perceive, infinitely many bodies by the same faculty of sensing (viz. one after another [NS: and not at once]).

If they say that there are infinitely many things which we cannot perceive, I reply that we cannot reach them by any thought, and consequently, not by any faculty of willing. But, they say, if God willed to bring it about that we should perceive them also, he would have to give us a greater faculty of perceiving, but not a greater faculty of willing than he has given us. This is the same as if they said that, if God should will to bring it about that we understood infinitely many other beings, it would indeed be necessary for him to give us a greater intellect, but not a more universal idea of being, in order for us to embrace the same infinity of beings. For we have shown that the will is a universal being, *or* idea, by which we explain all the singular volitions, that is, it is what is common to them all.

Therefore, since they believe that this common *or* universal idea of all volitions is a faculty, it is not at all surprising if they say that this faculty extends beyond the limits of the intellect to infinity. For the universal is said equally of one, a great many, or infinitely many individuals.

[III.B(ii)] To the second objection I reply by denying that we have a free power of suspending judgment. For when we say that someone suspends judgment, we are saying nothing but that he sees that he does not perceive the thing adequately. Suspension of judgment, therefore, is really a perception, not [an act of] free will.

To understand this clearly, let us conceive a child imagining a winged horse, and not perceiving anything else. Since this imagination involves the existence of the horse (by P17C), and the child does not perceive anything else which excludes the existence of the horse, he will necessarily regard the horse as present. Nor will he be able to doubt its existence, though he will not be certain of it.

We find this daily in our dreams, and I do not believe there is anyone who thinks that while he is dreaming he has a free power of suspending judgment concerning the things he dreams, and of bringing it about that he does not dream the things he dreams he sees. Nevertheless, it happens that even in dreams we suspend judgment, namely, when we dream that we dream.

Next, I grant that no one is deceived insofar as he perceives, that is, I grant that the imaginations of the mind, considered in themselves, involve no error. But I deny that a man affirms nothing insofar as he perceives. For what is perceiving a winged horse other than affirming

II/134

wings of the horse? For if the mind perceived nothing else except the winged horse, it would regard it as present to itself, and would not have any cause of doubting its existence, or any faculty of dissenting, unless either the imagination of the winged horse were joined to an idea which excluded the existence of the same horse, or the mind perceived that its idea of a winged horse was inadequate. And then either it will necessarily deny the horse's existence, or it will necessarily doubt it.

[III.B.(iii)] As for the third objection, I think what has been said will II/135 be an answer to it too: namely, that the will is something universal, which is predicated of all ideas, and which signifies only what is common to all ideas, namely, the affirmation, whose adequate essence, therefore, insofar as it is thus conceived abstractly, must be in each idea and in this way only must be the same in all, but not insofar as it is considered to constitute the idea's essence; for in that regard the singular affirmations differ from one another as much as the ideas themselves do. For example, the affirmation which the idea of a circle involves differs from that which the idea of a triangle involves as much as the idea of the circle differs from the idea of the triangle.

Next, I deny absolutely that we require an equal power of thinking, to affirm that what is true is true, as to affirm that what is false is true. For if you consider the mind, they are related to one another as being to not-being. For there is nothing positive in ideas which constitutes the form of falsity (see P35, P35S, and P47S). So the thing to note here, above all, is how easily we are deceived when we confuse universals with singulars, and beings of reason and abstractions with real beings.

[III.B. (iv)] Finally, as far as the fourth objection is concerned, I say that I grant entirely that a man placed in such an equilibrium (viz. who perceives nothing but thirst and hunger, and such food and drink as are equally distant from him) will perish of hunger and thirst. If they ask me whether such a man should not be thought an ass, rather than a man, I say that I do not know—just as I also do not know how highly we should esteem one who hangs himself, or children, fools, and madmen, and so on.

[IV.] It remains now to indicate how much knowledge of this doctrine is to our advantage in life. We shall see this easily from the following considerations:

[A.] Insofar as it teaches that we act only from God's command, that we share in the divine nature, and that we do this the more, the more perfect our actions are, and the more and more we understand God. This doctrine, then, in addition to giving us complete peace of mind, also teaches us wherein our greatest happiness, *or* blessedness, consists: namely, in the knowledge of God alone, by which we are led to do only II/136 those things which love and morality advise. From this we clearly understand how far they stray from the true valuation of virtue, who expect to be honored by God with the greatest rewards for their virtue and best actions, as for the greatest bondage—as if virtue itself, and the service of God, were not happiness itself, and the greatest freedom.

[B.] Insofar as it teaches us how we must bear ourselves concerning matters of fortune, *or* things which are not in our power, that is, concerning things which do not follow from our nature—that we must expect and bear calmly both good fortune and bad. For all things follow from God's eternal decree with the same necessity as from the essence of a triangle it follows that its three angles are equal to two right angles.

[C.] This doctrine contributes to social life, insofar as it teaches us to hate no one, to disesteem no one, to mock no one, to be angry at no one, to envy no one; and also insofar as it teaches that each of us should be content with his own things, and should be helpful to his neighbor, not from unmanly compassion, partiality, or superstition, but from the guidance of reason, as the time and occasion demand. I shall show this in the Fourth Part.

[D.] Finally, this doctrine also contributes, to no small extent, to the common society insofar as it teaches how citizens are to be governed and led, not so that they may be slaves, but that they may do freely the things which are best.

And with this I have finished what I had decided to treat in this scholium, and put an end to this our Second Part. In it I think that I have explained the nature and properties of the human mind in sufficient detail, and as clearly as the difficulty of the subject allows, and that I have set out doctrines from which we can infer many excellent things, which are highly useful and necessary to know, as will be established partly in what follows.

II/137

THIRD PART OF THE ETHICS
OF THE ORIGIN AND NATURE OF THE AFFECTS

PREFACE

Most of those who have written about the affects, and men's way of living, seem to treat, not of natural things, which follow the common laws of Nature, but of things which are outside Nature. Indeed they seem to conceive man in Nature as a dominion within a dominion. For they believe that man disturbs, rather than follows, the order of Nature, that he has absolute power over his actions, and that he is determined only by himself. And they attribute the cause of human impotence and inconstancy, not to the common power of Nature, but to I know not what vice of human nature, which they therefore bewail, or laugh at, or disdain, or (as usually happens) curse. And he who knows how to censure more eloquently and cunningly the weakness of the human mind is held to be godly.

It is true that there have been some very distinguished men (to whose work and diligence we confess that we owe much), who have written many admirable things about the right way of living, and given men advice full of prudence. But no one, to my knowledge, has determined the nature and powers of the affects, nor what, on the other hand, the mind can do to moderate them. I know, of course, that the celebrated Descartes, although he too believed that the mind has absolute power over its own actions, nevertheless sought to explain II/138 *human affects through their first causes, and at the same time to show the way by which the mind can have absolute dominion over its affects. But in my opinion, he showed nothing but the cleverness of his understanding, as I shall show in the proper place.*

For now I wish to return to those who prefer to curse or laugh at the affects and actions of men, rather than understand them. To them it will doubtless seem strange that I should undertake to treat men's vices and absurdities in the geometric style, and that I should wish to demonstrate by certain reasoning things which are contrary to reason, and which they proclaim to be empty, absurd, and horrible.

But my reason is this: nothing happens in Nature which can be attributed to any defect in it, for Nature is always the same, and its virtue and power of acting are everywhere one and the same, that is, the laws and rules of Nature, according to which all things happen, and change from one form to another, are always and everywhere the same. So the way of understanding the nature of anything, of whatever kind, must also be the same, namely, through the universal laws and rules of Nature.

The affects, therefore, of hate, anger, envy, and the like, considered in themselves, follow with the same necessity and force of Nature as the other singular things. And therefore they acknowledge certain causes, through which they are understood, and have certain properties, as worthy of our knowledge as the properties of any other thing, by the mere contemplation of which we are pleased. Therefore, I shall treat the nature and powers of the affects, and the power of the mind over them, by the same method by which, in the preceding parts, I treated God and the mind, and I shall consider human actions and appetites just as if it were a question of lines, planes, and bodies.

DEFINITIONS II/139

D1: I call that cause adequate whose effect can be clearly and distinctly perceived through it. But I call it partial, *or* inadequate, if its effect cannot be understood through it alone.

D2: I say that we act when something happens, in us or outside us, of which we are the adequate cause, that is (by D1), when something in us or outside us follows from our nature, which can be clearly and distinctly understood through it alone. On the other hand, I say that we are acted on when something happens in us, or something follows from our nature, of which we are only a partial cause.

D3: By affect I understand affections of the body by which the body's power of acting is increased or diminished, aided or restrained, and at the same time, the ideas of these affections.

Therefore, if we can be the adequate cause of any of these affections, I understand by the affect an action; otherwise, a passion.

POSTULATES

Post. 1: The human body can be affected in many ways in which its power of acting is increased or diminished, and also in others which render its power of acting neither greater nor less.

This postulate, or axiom, rests on Post. 1, L5, and L7 (after IIP13).

II/140 Post. 2: The human body can undergo many changes, and nevertheless retain impressions, *or* traces, of the objects (on this see IIPost. 5), and consequently, the same images of things. (For the definition of images, see IIP17S.)

P1: *Our mind does certain things [acts] and undergoes other things, namely, insofar as it has adequate ideas, it necessarily does certain things, and insofar as it has inadequate ideas, it necessarily undergoes other things.*

Dem.: In each human mind some ideas are adequate, but others are mutilated and confused (by IIP40S). But ideas which are adequate in someone's mind are adequate in God insofar as he constitutes the essence of that mind [only] (by IIP11C). And those which are inadequate in the mind are also adequate in God (by the same Cor.), not insofar as he contains only the essence of that mind, but insofar as he also contains in himself, at the same time, the minds of other things. Next, from any given idea some effect must necessarily follow (IP36), of which effect God is the adequate cause (see D1), not insofar as he is infinite, but insofar as he is considered to be affected by that given idea (see IIP9). But if God, insofar as he is affected by an idea which is adequate in someone's mind, is the cause of an effect, that same mind is the effect's adequate cause (by IIP11C). Therefore, our mind (by D2), insofar as it has adequate ideas, necessarily does certain things [acts]. This was the first thing to be proven.

Next, if something necessarily follows from an idea which is adequate in God, not insofar as he has in himself the mind of one man only, but insofar as he has in himself the minds of other things together with the mind of that man, that man's mind (by the same IIP11C) is not its adequate cause, but its partial cause. Hence (by D2), insofar as the mind has inadequate ideas, it necessarily undergoes certain things. This was the second point. Therefore, our mind, and so on, q.e.d.

Cor.: From this it follows that the mind is more liable to passions the more it has inadequate ideas, and conversely, is more active the more it has adequate ideas.

II/141

P2: *The body cannot determine the mind to thinking, and the mind cannot determine the body to motion, to rest, or to anything else (if there is anything else).*

Dem.: All modes of thinking have God for a cause, insofar as he is a thinking thing, and not insofar as he is explained by another attribute (by IIP6). So what determines the mind to thinking is a mode of thinking and not of extension, that is (by IID1), it is not the body. This was the first point.

Next, the motion and rest of the body must arise from another body, which has also been determined to motion or rest by another; and absolutely, whatever arises in the body must have arisen from God insofar as he is considered to be affected by some mode of extension, and not insofar as he is considered to be affected by some mode of thinking (also by IIP6), that is, it cannot arise from the mind, which (by IIP11) is a mode of thinking. This was the second point. Therefore, the body cannot determine the mind, and so on, q.e.d.

Schol.: These things are more clearly understood from what is said in IIP7S, namely, that the mind and the body are one and the same thing, which is conceived now under the attribute of thought, now under the attribute of extension. The result is that the order, *or* connection, of things is one, whether Nature is conceived under this attribute or that; hence the order of actions and passions of our body is, by nature, at one with the order of actions and passions of the mind. This is also evident from the way in which we have demonstrated IIP12.

But although these things are such that no reason for doubt remains, still, I hardly believe that men can be induced to consider them fairly unless I confirm them by experience. They are so firmly persuaded that the body now moves, now is at rest, solely from the mind's command, and that it does a great many things which depend only on the mind's will and its art of thinking.

II/142

For indeed, no one has yet determined what the body can do, that is, experience has not yet taught anyone what the body can do from the laws of Nature alone, insofar as Nature is only considered to be corporeal, and what the body can do only if it is determined by the mind. For no one has yet come to know the structure of the body so accurately that he could explain all its functions—not to mention that many things are observed in the lower animals which far surpass human ingenuity, and that sleepwalkers do a great many things in their sleep which they would not dare to awake. This shows well enough that the body itself, simply from the laws of its own nature, can do many things which its mind wonders at.

Again, no one knows how, or by what means, the mind moves the body, nor how many degrees of motion it can give the body, nor with what speed it can move it. So it follows that when men say that this or that action of the body arises from the mind, which has dominion over the body, they do not know what they are saying, and they do nothing but confess, in fine-sounding words, that they are ignorant of the true cause of that action, and that they do not wonder at it.

But they will say [i] that—whether or not they know by what means the mind moves the body—they still know by experience that unless the human mind were capable of thinking, the body would be inactive. And then [ii], they know by experience, that it is in the mind's power alone both to speak and to be silent, and to do many other things which they therefore believe depend on the mind's decision.

[i] As far as the first [objection] is concerned, I ask them, does not experience also teach that if, on the other hand, the body is inactive, the mind is at the same time incapable of thinking? For when the body is at rest in sleep, the mind at the same time remains senseless with it, nor does it have the power of thinking, as it does when awake. And then I believe everyone has found by experience that the mind is not always equally capable of thinking of the same object, but that as the body is more susceptible to having the image of this or that object aroused in it, so the mind is more capable of regarding this or that object.

II/143 They will say, of course, that it cannot happen that the causes of buildings, of paintings, and of things of this kind, which are made only by human skill, should be able to be deduced from the laws of Nature alone, insofar as it is considered to be only corporeal; nor would the human body be able to build a temple, if it were not determined and guided by the mind.

But I have already shown that they do not know what the body can do, or what can be deduced from the consideration of its nature alone, and that they know from experience that a great many things happen from the laws of Nature alone which they never would have believed could happen without the direction of the mind—such as the things sleepwalkers do in their sleep, which they wonder at while they are awake.

I add here the very structure of the human body, which, in the ingenuity of its construction, far surpasses anything made by human skill—not to mention that I have shown above that infinitely many things follow from Nature, under whatever attribute it may be considered.

[ii] As for the second [objection], human affairs, of course, would be conducted far more happily if it were equally in man's power to be silent and to speak. But experience teaches all too plainly that men have nothing less in their power than their tongue, and can do nothing less than moderate their appetites.

That is why most men believe that we do freely only those things we have a weak inclination toward (because the appetite for these things can easily be reduced by the memory of another thing which we frequently recollect), but that we do not at all do freely those things we seek by a strong affect, which cannot be calmed by the memory of another thing. But if they had not found by experience that we do many things we afterwards repent, and that often we see the better and follow the worse (viz. when we are torn by contrary affects), nothing would prevent them from believing that we do all things freely.

So the infant believes he freely wants the milk; the angry child that he wants vengeance; and the timid, flight. So the drunk believes it is from a free decision of the mind that he speaks the things he later, when sober, wishes he had not said. So the madman, the chatterbox, the child, and a great many people of this kind believe they speak from a free decision of the mind, when really they cannot contain their impulse to speak.

So experience itself, no less clearly than reason, teaches that men believe themselves free because they are conscious of their own actions, and ignorant of the causes by which they are determined, that the decisions of the mind are nothing but the appetites themselves, which therefore vary as the disposition of the body varies. For each one governs everything from his affect; those who are torn by contrary affects do not know what they want, and those who are not moved by any affect are very easily driven here and there. II/144

All these things, indeed, show clearly that both the decision of the mind and the appetite and the determination of the body by nature exist together—or rather are one and the same thing, which we call a decision when it is considered under, and explained through, the attribute of thought, and which we call a determination when it is considered under the attribute of extension and deduced from the laws of motion and rest. This will be still more clearly evident from what must presently be said.

For there is something else I wish particularly to note here, that we can do nothing from a decision of the mind unless we recollect it. For example, we cannot speak a word unless we recollect it. And it is not in the free power of the mind to either recollect a thing or forget it. So this only is believed to be in the power of the mind—that from the mind's decision alone we can either be silent about or speak about a thing we recollect.

But when we dream that we speak, we believe that we speak from a free decision of the mind—and yet we do not speak, or, if we do, it is from a spontaneous motion of the body. And we dream that we conceal certain things from men, and this by the same decision of the mind by which, while we wake, we are silent about the things we know. We dream, finally, that, from a decision of the mind, we do certain things we do not dare to do while we are awake.

So I should very much like to know whether there are in the mind two kinds of decisions—those belonging to our fantasies and those that are free? And if we do not want to go that far in our madness, it must be granted that this decision of the mind which is believed to be free is not distinguished from the imagination itself, *or* the memory, nor is it anything beyond that affirmation which the idea, insofar as it is an idea, necessarily involves (see IIP49). And so these decisions of the mind arise by the same necessity as the ideas of things which actually exist. Those, therefore, who believe that they either speak or are silent, or do anything from a free decision of the mind, dream with open eyes.

P3: *The actions of the mind arise from adequate ideas alone; the passions depend on inadequate ideas alone.*

Dem.: The first thing which constitutes the essence of the mind is nothing but the idea of an actually existing body (by IIP11 and P13); this idea (by IIP15) is composed of many others, of which some are adequate (IIP38C), and others inadequate (by IIP29C). Therefore, whatever follows from the nature of the mind and has the mind as its proximate cause, through which it must be understood, must necessarily follow from an adequate idea or an inadequate one. But insofar as the mind has inadequate ideas (by P1), it necessarily is acted on. Therefore, the actions of the mind follow from adequate ideas alone; hence, the mind is acted on only because it has inadequate ideas, q.e.d.

Schol.: We see, then, that the passions are not related to the mind except insofar as it has something which involves a negation, *or* insofar as it is considered as a part of Nature which cannot be perceived clearly and distinctly through itself, without the others. In this way I could show that the passions are related to singular things in the same way as to the mind, and cannot be perceived in any other way. But my purpose is only to treat of the human mind.

P4: *No thing can be destroyed except through an external cause.*

Dem.: This proposition is evident through itself. For the definition of any thing affirms, and does not deny, the thing's essence, *or* it posits the thing's essence, and does not take it away. So while we attend only to the thing itself, and not to external causes, we shall not be able to find anything in it which can destroy it, q.e.d.

P5: *Things are of a contrary nature, that is, cannot be in the same subject, insofar as one can destroy the other.*

Dem.: For if they could agree with one another, or be in the same subject at once, then there could be something in the same subject which could destroy it, which (by P4) is absurd. Therefore, things and so on, q.e.d.

II/146

P6: *Each thing, as far as it can by its own power, strives to persevere in its being.*

Dem.: For singular things are modes by which God's attributes are expressed in a certain and determinate way (by IP25C), that is (by IP34), things that express, in a certain and determinate way, God's power, by which God is and acts. And no thing has anything in itself by which it can be destroyed, *or* which takes its existence away (by P4). On the contrary, it is opposed to everything which can take its existence away (by P5). Therefore, as far as it can, and it lies in itself, it strives to persevere in its being, q.e.d.

P7: *The striving by which each thing strives to persevere in its being is nothing but the actual essence of the thing.*

Dem.: From the given essence of each thing some things necessarily follow (by IP36), and things are able [to produce] nothing but what follows necessarily from their determinate nature (by IP29). So the power of each thing, *or* the striving by which it (either alone or with others) does anything, or strives to do anything—that is (by P6), the power, *or* striving, by which it strives to persevere in its being, is nothing but the given, *or* actual, essence of the thing itself, q.e.d.

P8: *The striving by which each thing strives to persevere in its being involves no finite time, but an indefinite time.*

II/147

Dem.: For if [the striving by which a thing strives to persevere in its being] involved a limited time, which determined the thing's duration, then it would follow just from that very power by which the thing exists that it could not exist after that limited time, but that it would have to be destroyed. But (by P4) this is absurd. Therefore, the striving by which a thing exists involves no definite time. On the contrary, since (by P4) it will always continue to exist by the same power by which it now

75

exists, unless it is destroyed by an external cause, this striving involves indefinite time, q.e.d.

P9: *Both insofar as the mind has clear and distinct ideas, and insofar as it has confused ideas, it strives, for an indefinite duration, to persevere in its being and it is conscious of this striving it has.*

Dem.: The essence of the mind is constituted by adequate and by inadequate ideas (as we have shown in P3). So (by P7) it strives to persevere in its being both insofar as it has inadequate ideas and insofar as it has adequate ideas; and it does this (by P8) for an indefinite duration. But since the mind (by IIP23) is necessarily conscious of itself through ideas of the body's affections, the mind (by P7) is conscious of its striving, q.e.d.

Schol.: When this striving is related only to the mind, it is called will; but when it is related to the mind and body together, it is called appetite. This appetite, therefore, is nothing but the very essence of man, from whose nature there necessarily follow those things that promote his preservation. And so man is determined to do those things.

II/148 Between appetite and desire there is no difference, except that desire is generally related to men insofar as they are conscious of their appetite. So *desire* can be defined as *Appetite together with consciousness of the appetite.*

From all this, then, it is clear that we neither strive for, nor will, neither want, nor desire anything because we judge it to be good; on the contrary, we judge something to be good because we strive for it, will it, want it, and desire it.

P10: *An idea that excludes the existence of our body cannot be in our mind, but is contrary to it.*

Dem.: Whatever can destroy our body cannot be in it (by P5), and so the idea of this thing cannot be in God insofar as he has the idea of our body (by IIP9C), that is (by IIP11 and P13), the idea of this thing cannot be in our mind. On the contrary, since (by IIP11 and P13) the first thing that constitutes the essence of the mind is the idea of an actually existing body, the first and principal [tendency] of the striving of our mind (by P7) is to affirm the existence of our body. And so an idea that denies the existence of our body is contrary to our mind, and so on, q.e.d.

P11: *The idea of any thing that increases or diminishes, aids or restrains, our body's power of acting, increases or diminishes, aids or restrains, our mind's power of thinking.*

Dem.: This proposition is evident from IIP7, or also from IIP14.

Schol.: We see, then, that the mind can undergo great changes, and pass now to a greater, now to a lesser perfection. These passions, indeed, explain to us the affects of joy and sadness. By *joy*, therefore, I shall understand in what follows that *passion by which the mind passes to a greater perfection*. And by *sadness*, that *passion by which it passes to a lesser perfection*. The *affect of joy which is related to the mind and body at once* I call *pleasure* or *cheerfulness*, and that of *sadness*, *pain* or *melancholy*.

But it should be noted [NS: here] that pleasure and pain are ascribed to a man when one part of him is affected more than the rest, whereas cheerfulness and melancholy are ascribed to him when all are equally affected.

Next, I have explained in P9S what desire is, and apart from these three I do not acknowledge any other primary affect. For I shall show in what follows that the rest arise from these three. But before I proceed further, I should like to explain P10 more fully here, so that it may be more clearly understood how one idea is contrary to another.

In IIP17S we have shown that the idea which constitutes the essence of the mind involves the existence of the body so long as the body itself exists. Next from what we have shown in IIP8C and its scholium, it follows that the present existence of our mind depends only on this, that the mind involves the actual existence of the body. Finally, we have shown that the power of the mind by which it imagines things and recollects them also depends on this (see IIP17, P18, P18S), that it involves the actual existence of the body.

From these things it follows that the present existence of the mind and its power of imagining are taken away as soon as the mind ceases to affirm the present existence of the body. But the cause of the mind's ceasing to affirm this existence of the body cannot be the mind itself (by P4), nor also that the body ceases to exist. For (by IIP6) the cause of the mind's affirming the body's existence is not that the body has begun to exist. So by the same reasoning, it does not cease to affirm the body's existence because the body ceases to exist, but (by IIP8) this [sc. ceasing to affirm the body's existence] arises from another idea which excludes the present existence of our body, and consequently of our mind, and which is thus contrary to the idea that constitutes our mind's essence.

P12: *The mind as far as it can, strives to imagine those things that increase or aid the body's power of acting.* II/150

Dem.: So long as the human body is affected with a mode that involves the nature of an external body, the human mind will regard the same body as present (by IIP17) and consequently (by IIP7) so long as the human mind regards some external body as present, that is (by IIP17S), imagines it, the human body is affected with a mode that involves the nature of that external body. Hence, so long as the mind imagines those things that increase or aid our body's power of acting, the body is affected with modes that increase or aid its power of acting (see Post. 1), and consequently (by P11) the mind's power of thinking is increased or aided. Therefore (by P6 or P9), the mind, as far as it can, strives to imagine those things, q.e.d.

P13: *When the mind imagines those things that diminish or restrain the body's power of acting, it strives, as far as it can, to recollect things which exclude their existence.*

Dem.: So long as the mind imagines anything of this kind, the power both of mind and of body is diminished or restrained (as we have demonstrated in P12); nevertheless, the mind will continue to imagine this thing until it imagines something else that excludes the thing's present existence (by IIP17), that is (as we have just shown), the power both of mind and of body is diminished or restrained until the mind imagines something else that excludes the existence of this thing; so the mind (by P9), as far as it can, will strive to imagine or recollect that other thing, q.e.d.

II/151 Cor.: From this it follows that the mind avoids imagining those things that diminish or restrain its or the body's power.

Schol.: From this we understand clearly what love and hate are. *Love is nothing but joy with the accompanying idea of an external cause*, and *hate is nothing but sadness with the accompanying idea of an external cause*. We see, then, that one who loves necessarily strives to have present and preserve the thing he loves; and on the other hand, one who hates strives to remove and destroy the thing he hates. But all of these things will be discussed more fully in what follows.

P14: *If the mind has once been affected by two affects at once, then afterwards, when it is affected by one of them, it will also be affected by the other.*

Dem.: If the human body has once been affected by two bodies at once, then afterwards, when the mind imagines one of them, it will immediately recollect the other also (by IIP18). But the imaginations of the mind indicate the affects of our body more than the nature of external bodies (by IIP16C2). Therefore, if the body, and consequently the mind (see D3), has once been affected by two affects [NS: at once], then afterwards, when it is affected by one of them, it will also be affected by the other, q.e.d.

P15: *Any thing can be the accidental cause of joy, sadness, or desire.*

Dem.: Suppose the mind is affected by two affects at once, one of which neither increases nor diminishes its power of acting, while the other either increases it or diminishes it (see Post. 1). From P14 it is clear that when the mind is afterwards affected with the former affect as by its true cause, which (by hypothesis) through itself neither increases nor diminishes its power of thinking, it will immediately be affected with the latter also, which increases or diminishes its power of thinking, that is (by P11S), with joy, or sadness. And so the former thing will be the cause of joy or sadness—not through itself, but accidentally. And in the same way it can easily be shown that that thing can be the accidental cause of desire, q.e.d.

II/152

Cor.: From this alone—that we have regarded a thing with an affect of joy or sadness, of which it is not itself the efficient cause, we can love it or hate it.

Dem.: For from this alone it comes about (by P14) that when the mind afterwards imagines this thing, it is affected with an affect of joy or sadness, that is (by P11S), that the power both of the mind and of the body is increased or diminished. And consequently (by P12), the mind desires to imagine the thing or (by P13C) avoids it, that is (by P13S), it loves it or hates it, q.e.d.

Schol.: From this we understand how it can happen that we love or hate some things without any cause known to us, but only (as they say) from sympathy or antipathy. And to this must be related also those objects that affect us with joy or sadness only because they have some likeness to objects that usually affect us with these affects, as I shall show in P16. I know, of course, that the authors who first introduced the words sympathy and antipathy intended to signify by them certain occult qualities of things. Nevertheless, I believe we may be permitted to understand by them also qualities that are known or manifest.

P16: *From the mere fact that we imagine a thing to have some likeness to an object which usually affects the mind with joy or sadness, we love it or hate it, even though that in which the thing is like the object is not the efficient cause of these affects.*

II/153

Dem.: What is like the object, we have (by hypothesis) regarded in the object itself with an affect of joy or sadness. And so (by P14), when the mind is affected by its image, it will immediately be affected also with this or that affect. Consequently the thing we perceive to have this same [quality] will (by P15) be the accidental cause of joy or sadness; and so (by P15C) although that in which it is like the object is not the efficient cause of these affects, we shall still love it or hate it, q.e.d.

P17: *If we imagine that a thing which usually affects us with an affect of sadness is like another which usually affects us with an equally great affect of joy, we shall hate it and at the same time love it.*

Dem.: For (by hypothesis) this thing is through itself the cause of sadness, and (by P13S) insofar as we imagine it with this affect, we hate it. And moreover, insofar as it has some likeness to the other thing, which usually affects us with an equally great affect of joy, we shall love it with an equally great striving of joy (by P16). And so we shall both hate it and at the same time love it, q.e.d.

Schol.: This *constitution of the mind which arises from two contrary affects* is called *vacillation of mind*, which is therefore related to the affect as doubt is to the imagination (see IIP44S); nor do vacillation of mind and doubt differ from one another except in degree.

But it should be noted that in the preceding proposition I have deduced these vacillations of mind from causes which are the cause through themselves of one affect and the accidental cause of the other. I have done this because in this way they could more easily be deduced from what has gone before, not because I deny that vacillations of mind for the most part arise from an object which is the efficient cause of each affect. For the human body (by IIPost. 1) is composed of a great many individuals of different natures, and so (by IIA1″ [at II/99]), it can be affected in a great many different ways by one and the same body. And on the other hand, because one and the same thing can be affected in many ways, it will also be able to affect one and the same part of the body in many different ways. From this we can easily conceive that one and the same object can be the cause of many and contrary affects.

P18: *Man is affected with the same affect of joy or sadness from the image of a past or future thing as from the image of a present thing.*

Dem.: So long as a man is affected by the image of a thing, he will regard the thing as present, even if it does not exist (by IIP17 and P17C); he imagines it as past or future only insofar as its image is joined to the image of a past or future time (see IIP44S). So the image of a thing, considered only in itself, is the same, whether it is related to time past or future, or to the present, that is (by IIP16C2), the constitution of the body, *or* affect, is the same, whether the image is of a thing past or future, or of a present thing. And so, the affect of joy or sadness is the same, whether the image is of a thing past or future, or of a present thing, q.e.d.

Schol. 1: I call a thing past or future here, insofar as we have been affected by it, or will be affected by it. For example, insofar as we have seen it or will see it, insofar as it has refreshed us or will refresh us, has injured us or will injure us. For insofar as we imagine it in this way, we affirm its existence, that is, the body is not affected by any affect that excludes the thing's existence. And so (by IIP17) the body is affected with the image of the thing in the same way as if the thing itself were present. However, because it generally happens that those who have experienced many things vacillate so long as they regard a thing as future or past, and most often doubt the thing's outcome (see IIP44S), the affects which arise from similar images of things are not so constant, but are generally disturbed by the images of other things, until men become more certain of the thing's outcome.

II/155

Schol. 2: From what has just been said, we understand what hope and fear, confidence and despair, gladness and remorse are. For *hope* is nothing but *an inconstant joy which has arisen from the image of a future or past thing whose outcome we doubt; fear*, on the other hand, is *an inconstant sadness, which has also arisen from the image of a doubtful thing.* Next, if the doubt involved in these affects is removed, hope becomes *confidence*, and fear, *despair—*namely, *a joy or sadness which has arisen from the image of a thing we feared or hoped for.* Finally, *gladness is a joy which has arisen from the image of a past thing whose outcome we doubted*, while *remorse is a sadness which is opposite to gladness.*

P19: *He who imagines that what he loves is destroyed will be saddened; but he who imagines it to be preserved, will rejoice.*

Dem.: Insofar as it can, the mind strives to imagine those things which increase or aid the body's power of acting (by P12), that is (by P13S), those it loves. But the imagination is aided by what posits the existence of a thing, and on the other hand, is restrained by what excludes the existence of a thing (by IIP17). Therefore, the images of things that posit the existence of a thing loved aid the mind's striving to imagine the thing loved, that is (by P11S), affect the mind with joy. On the other hand, those which exclude the existence of a thing loved, restrain the same striving of the mind, that is (by P11S), affect the mind with sadness. Therefore, he who imagines that what he loves is destroyed will be saddened, and so on, q.e.d.

P20: *He who imagines that what he hates is destroyed will rejoice.*

II/156

Dem.: The mind (by P13) strives to imagine those things that exclude the existence of things by which the body's power of acting is diminished or restrained, that is (by P13S), strives to imagine those things which exclude the existence of things it hates. So the image of a thing which excludes the existence of what the mind hates aids this striving of the mind, that is (by P11S), affects the mind with joy. Therefore, he who imagines that what he hates is destroyed will rejoice, q.e.d.

P21: *He who imagines what he loves to be affected with joy or sadness will also be affected with joy or sadness; and each of those affects will be greater or lesser in the lover as they are greater or lesser in the thing loved.*

Dem.: The images of things (as we have demonstrated in P19) which

81

posit the existence of a thing loved aid the striving by which the mind strives to imagine the thing loved. But joy posits the existence of the joyous thing, and posits more existence, the greater the affect of joy is. For (by P11S) it is a transition to a greater perfection. Therefore, the image in the lover of the loved thing's joy aids his mind's striving, that is (by P11S), affects the lover with joy, and the more so, the greater this affect was in the thing loved. This was the first thing to be proved.

Next, insofar as a thing is affected with sadness, it is destroyed, and the more so, the greater the sadness with which it is affected (by P11S). So (by P19) he who imagines what he loves to be affected with sadness, will also be affected with sadness, and the more so, the greater this affect was in the thing loved, q.e.d.

II/157 P22: *If we imagine someone to affect with joy a thing we love, we shall be affected with love toward him. If, on the other hand, we imagine him to affect the same thing with sadness, we shall also be affected with hate toward him.*

Dem.: He who affects a thing we love with joy or sadness affects us also with joy or sadness, if we imagine that the thing loved is affected by that joy or sadness (by P21). But this joy or sadness is supposed to be accompanied in us by the idea of an external cause. Therefore (by P13S), if we imagine that someone affects with joy or sadness a thing we love, we shall be affected with love or hate toward him, q.e.d.

Schol.: P21 explains to us what *pity* is, which we can define as *sadness which has arisen from injury to another*. By what name we should call the joy which arises from another's good I do not know. *Next, love toward him who has done good to another* we shall call *favor*, and *hatred toward him who has done evil to another* we shall call *indignation*.

Finally, it should be noted that we do not pity only a thing we have loved (as we have shown in P21), but also one toward which we have previously had no affect, provided that we judge it to be like us (as I shall show below). And so also we favor him who has benefited someone like us, and are indignant at him who has injured one like us.

P23: *He who imagines what he hates to be affected with sadness will rejoice; if, on the other hand, he should imagine it to be affected with joy, he will be saddened. And both these affects will be the greater or lesser, as its contrary is greater or lesser in what he hates.*

II/158 Dem.: Insofar as a hateful thing is affected with sadness, it is destroyed, and the more so, the greater the sadness by which it is affected (by P11S). Therefore (by P20), he who imagines a thing he hates to be affected with sadness will on the contrary be affected with joy, and the more so, the greater the sadness with which he imagines the hateful thing to have been affected. This was the first point.

Next, joy posits the existence of the joyous thing (by P11S), and the more so, the greater the joy is conceived to be. [Therefore] if someone imagines him whom he hates to be affected with joy, this imagination (by P13) will restrain his striving, that is (by P11S), he who hates will be affected with sadness, and so on, q.e.d.

Schol.: This joy can hardly be enduring and without any conflict of mind. For (as I shall show immediately in P27) insofar as one imagines a thing like oneself to be affected with an affect of sadness, one must be saddened. And the opposite, if one imagines the same thing to be affected with joy. But here we attend only to hate.

P24: *If we imagine someone to affect with joy a thing we hate, we shall be affected with hate toward him also. On the other hand, if we imagine him to affect the same thing with sadness, we shall be affected with love toward him.*

Dem.: This proposition is demonstrated in the same way as P22.

Schol.: These and similar affects of hate are related to *envy* which, therefore, is nothing but *hate, insofar as it is considered so to dispose a man that he is glad at another's ill fortune and saddened by his good fortune.*

P25: *We strive to affirm, concerning ourselves and what we love, whatever we imagine to affect with joy ourselves or what we love. On the other hand, we strive to deny whatever we imagine affects with sadness ourselves or what we love.*

II/159

Dem.: Whatever we imagine to affect what we love with joy or sadness, affects us with joy or sadness (by P21). But the mind (by P12) strives as far as it can to imagine those things which affect us with joy, that is (by IIP17 and P17C), to regard them as present; and on the other hand (by P13) it strives to exclude the existence of those things which affect us with sadness. Therefore, we strive to affirm, concerning ourselves and what we love, whatever we imagine to affect with joy ourselves or what we love, and conversely, q.e.d.

P26: *We strive to affirm, concerning what we hate, whatever we imagine to affect it with sadness, and on the other hand, to deny whatever we imagine to affect it with joy.*

Dem.: This proposition follows from P23, as P25 follows from P21.

Schol.: From these propositions we see that it easily happens that a man thinks more highly of himself and what he loves than is just, and on the other hand, thinks less highly than is just of what he hates. When this imagination concerns the man himself who thinks more highly of himself than is just, it is called pride, and is a species of madness, because the man dreams, with open eyes, that he can do all those things which he achieves only in his imagination, and which he therefore regards as real and triumphs in, so long as he cannot imagine those things which exclude the existence [of these achievements] and determine his power of acting.

II/160   *Pride, therefore, is joy born of the fact that a man thinks more highly of himself than is just.* And the *joy born of the fact that a man thinks more highly of another than is just* is called *overestimation*, while *that which stems from thinking less highly of another than is just* is called *scorn*.

P27: *If we imagine a thing like us, toward which we have had no affect, to be affected with some affect, we are thereby affected with a like affect.*

Dem.: The images of things are affections of the human body whose ideas represent external bodies as present to us (by IIP17S), that is (by IIP16), whose ideas involve the nature of our body and at the same time the present nature of the external body. So if the nature of the external body is like the nature of our body, then the idea of the external body we imagine will involve an affection of our body like the affection of the external body. Consequently, if we imagine someone like us to be affected with some affect, this imagination will express an affection of our body like this affect. And so, from the fact that we imagine a thing like us to be affected with an affect, we are affected with a like affect. But if we hate a thing like us, then (by P23) we shall be affected with an affect contrary to its affect, not like it, q.e.d.

Schol.: This imitation of the affects, when it is related to sadness is called *pity* (on which, see P22S); but related to desire it is called *emulation*, which, therefore, *is* nothing but *the desire for a thing which is generated in us from the fact that we imagine others like us to have the same desire.*

Cor. 1: If we imagine that someone toward whom we have had no affect affects a thing like us with joy, we shall be affected with love toward him. On the other hand, if we imagine him to affect it with sadness, we shall be affected with hate toward him.

II/161   Dem.: This is demonstrated from P27 in the same way P22 is demonstrated from P21.

Cor. 2: We cannot hate a thing we pity from the fact that its suffering affects us with sadness.

Dem.: For if we could hate it because of that, then (by P23) we would rejoice in its sadness, which is contrary to the hypothesis.

Cor. 3: As far as we can, we strive to free a thing we pity from its suffering.

Dem.: Whatever affects with sadness what we pity, affects us also with a like sadness (by P27). And so (by P13) we shall strive to think of whatever can take away the thing's existence, *or* destroy the thing, that

84

is (by P9S), we shall want to destroy it, *or* shall be determined to destroy it. And so we strive to free the thing we pity from its suffering, q.e.d.

Schol.: This will, *or* appetite to do good, born of our pity for the thing on which we wish to confer a benefit, is called *benevolence*, which *is* therefore nothing but a *desire born of pity*. As for love and hate toward him who has done well or ill to a thing we imagine to be like us, see P22S.

P28: *We strive to further the occurrence of whatever we imagine will lead to joy, and to avert or destroy what we imagine is contrary to it, or will lead to sadness.*

Dem.: We strive to imagine, as far as we can, what we imagine will lead to joy (by P12), that is (by IIP17), we strive, as far as we can, to regard it as present, *or* as actually existing. But the mind's striving, *or* power of thinking, is equal to and at one in nature with the body's striving, *or* power of acting (as clearly follows from IIP7C and P11C). Therefore, we strive absolutely, *or* (what, by P9S, is the same) want and intend that it should exist. This was the first point. II/162

Next, if we imagine that what we believe to be the cause of sadness, that is (by P13S), what we hate, is destroyed, we shall rejoice (by P20), and so (by the first part of this [NS: proposition]) we shall strive to destroy it, *or* (by P13) to avert it from ourselves, so that we shall not regard it as present. This was the second point. Therefore, [we strive to further the occurrence of] whatever we imagine will lead to joy, and so on, q.e.d.

P29: *We shall strive to do also whatever we imagine men to look on with joy, and on the other hand, we shall be averse to doing what we imagine men are averse to.*

Dem.: From the fact that we imagine men to love or hate something, we shall love or hate it (by P27), that is (by P13S), we shall thereby rejoice in or be saddened by the thing's presence. And so (by P28) we shall strive to do whatever we imagine men to love, or to look on with joy, and so on, q.e.d.

Schol.: *This striving to do something (and also to omit doing something) solely to please men* is called *ambition*, especially when we strive so eagerly to please the people that we do or omit certain things to our own injury, or another's. In other cases, it is usually called *human kindness*. Next, *the* II/163 *joy with which we imagine the action of another by which he has striven to please us* I call *praise*. On the other hand, *the sadness with which we are averse to his action* I call *blame*.

P30: *If someone has done something which he imagines affects others with joy, he will be affected with joy accompanied by the idea of himself as cause,* or *he will regard himself with joy. If, on the other hand, he has done something which he imagines affects others with sadness, he will regard himself with sadness.*

Dem.: He who imagines that he affects others with joy or sadness will thereby (by P27) be affected with joy or sadness. But since man (by IIP19 and P23) is conscious of himself through the affections by which he is determined to act, then he who has done something which he imagines affects others with joy will be affected with joy, together with a consciousness of himself as the cause, *or,* he will regard himself with joy, and the converse, q.e.d.

Schol.: Since love (by P13S) is joy, accompanied by the idea of an external cause, and hate is sadness, accompanied also by the idea of an external cause, this joy and sadness are species of love and hate. But because love and hate are related to external objects, we shall signify these affects by other names. *Joy accompanied by the idea of an internal cause,* we shall call *love of esteem,* and *the sadness contrary to it, shame*—I mean *when the joy or sadness arises from the fact that the man believes that he is praised or blamed.* Otherwise, I shall call *joy accompanied by the idea of an internal cause, self-esteem,* and *the sadness contrary to it, repentance.*

Next, because (by IIP17C) it can happen that the joy with which someone imagines that he affects others is only imaginary, and (by P25) everyone strives to imagine concerning himself whatever he imagines affects himself with joy, it can easily happen that one who exults at being esteemed is proud and imagines himself to be pleasing to all, when he is burdensome to all.

P31: *If we imagine that someone loves, desires, or hates something we ourselves love, desire, or hate, we shall thereby love, desire, or hate it with greater constancy. But if we imagine that he is averse to what we love, or the opposite [NS: that he loves what we hate], then we shall undergo vacillation of mind.*

Dem.: Simply because we imagine that someone loves something, we thereby love the same thing (by P27). But we suppose that we already love it without this [cause of love]; so there is added to the love a new cause, by which it is further encouraged. As a result, we shall love what we love with greater constancy.

Next, from the fact that we imagine someone to be averse to something, we shall be averse to it (by P27). But if we suppose that at the same time we love it, then at the same time we shall both love and be averse to the same thing, *or* (see P17S) we shall undergo vacillation of mind, q.e.d.

Cor.: From this and from P28 it follows that each of us strives, so far as he can, that everyone should love what he loves, and hate what he hates. Hence that passage of the poet:

> Speremus pariter, pariter metuamus amantes;
> Ferreus est, si quis, quod sinit alter, amat.[1]

Schol.: This striving to bring it about that everyone should approve his love and hate is really ambition (see P29S). And so we see that each of us, by his nature, wants the others to live according to his temperament; when all alike want this, they are alike an obstacle to one another, and when all wish to be praised, *or* loved, by all, they hate one another.

P32: *If we imagine that someone enjoys some thing that only one can possess, we shall strive to bring it about that he does not possess it.*

II/165

Dem.: From the mere fact that we imagine someone to enjoy something (by P27 and P27C1), we shall love that thing and desire to enjoy it. But (by hypothesis) we imagine his enjoyment of this thing as an obstacle to our joy. Therefore (by P28), we shall strive that he not possess it, q.e.d.

Schol.: We see, therefore, that for the most part human nature is so constituted that men pity the unfortunate and envy the fortunate, and (by P32) [envy them] with greater hate the more they love the thing they imagine the other to possess. We see, then, that from the same property of human nature from which it follows that men are compassionate, it also follows that the same men are envious and ambitious.

Finally, if we wish to consult experience, we shall find that it teaches all these things, especially if we attend to the first years of our lives. For we find from experience that children, because their bodies are continually, as it were, in a state of equilibrium, laugh or cry simply because they see others laugh or cry. Moreover, whatever they see others do, they immediately desire to imitate it. And finally, they desire for themselves all those things by which they imagine others are pleased—because, as we have said, the images of things are the very affections of the human body, *or* modes by which the human body is affected by external causes, and disposed to do this or that.

P33: *When we love a thing like ourselves, we strive, as far as we can, to bring it about that it loves us in return.*

---

[1] The lines are from Ovid's *Amores* II, xix, 4–5. It appears from the context that Spinoza understands them as follows: "As lovers, let us hope together and fear together; he has a heart of steel, who loves what another man leaves alone." It is not clear, however, that that would be a correct translation in the Ovidian context. Cf. Guy Lee's translation of the *Amores* (London: John Murray, 1968).

Dem.: As far as we can, we strive to imagine, above all others, the thing we love (by P12). Therefore, if a thing is like us, we shall strive to affect it with joy above all others (by P29), *or* we shall strive, as far as we can, to bring it about that the thing we love is affected with joy, accompanied by the idea of ourselves [as cause], that is (by P13S), that it loves us in return, q.e.d.

II/166

P34: *The greater the affect with which we imagine a thing we love to be affected toward us, the more we shall exult at being esteemed.*

Dem.: We strive (by P33), as far as we can, that a thing we love should love us in return, that is (by P13S), that a thing we love should be affected with joy, accompanied by the idea of ourselves [as cause]. So the greater the joy with which we imagine a thing we love to be affected on our account, the more this striving is aided, that is (by P11 and P11S), the greater the joy with which we are affected. But since we rejoice because we have affected another, like us, with joy, then we regard ourselves with joy (by P30). Therefore, the greater the affect with which we imagine a thing we love to be affected toward us, the greater the joy with which we shall regard ourselves, *or* (by P30S) the more we shall exult at being esteemed, q.e.d.

P35: *If someone imagines that a thing he loves is united with another by as close, or by a closer, bond of friendship than that with which he himself, alone, possessed the thing, he will be affected with hate toward the thing he loves, and will envy the other.*

Dem.: The greater the love with which someone imagines a thing he loves to be affected toward him, the more he will exult at being esteemed (by P34), that is (by P30S), the more he will rejoice. And so (by P28) he will strive, as far as he can, to imagine the thing he loves to be bound to him as closely as possible. This striving, *or* appetite, is encouraged if he imagines another to desire the same thing he does (by P31).

II/167

But this striving, *or* appetite, is supposed to be restrained by the image of the thing he loves, accompanied by the image of him with whom the thing he loves is united. So (by P11S) he will thereby be affected with sadness, accompanied by the idea of the thing he loves as a cause, together with the image of the other; that is (by P13S), he will be affected with hate toward the thing he loves, and, at the same time, toward the other (by P15C), whom he will envy because of the pleasure the other takes in the thing he loves (by P23), q.e.d.

Schol.: This hatred toward a thing we love, combined with envy, is called *jealousy,* which is therefore nothing but *a vacillation of mind born of love and hatred together, accompanied by the idea of another who is envied.* Moreover, this hatred toward the thing he loves will be greater in proportion to the joy with which the jealous man was usually affected from the love returned to him by the thing he loves, and also in proportion to the affect with which he was affected toward him with whom he imagines the thing he loves to unite itself. For if he hated him, he will thereby hate the thing he loves (by P24), because he imagines that what he loves affects with joy what he hates, and also (by P15C) because he is forced to join the image of the thing he loves to the image of him he hates.

This latter reason is found, for the most part, in love toward a woman. For he who imagines that a woman he loves prostitutes herself to another not only will be saddened, because his own appetite is restrained, but also will be repelled by her, because he is forced to join the image of the thing he loves to the shameful parts and excretions of the other. To this, finally, is added the fact that she no longer receives the jealous man with the same countenance as she used to offer him. From this cause, too, the lover is saddened, as I shall show.

P36: *He who recollects a thing by which he was once pleased desires to possess it in the same circumstances as when he first was pleased by it.*

Dem.: Whatever a man sees together with a thing that pleased him (by P15) will be the accidental cause of joy. And so (by P28) he will desire to possess it all, together with the thing that pleased him, *or* he will desire to possess the thing with all the same circumstances as when he first was pleased by it, q.e.d. II/168

Cor.: Therefore, if the lover has found that one of those circumstances is lacking, he will be saddened.

Dem.: For insofar as he finds that a circumstance is lacking, he imagines something which excludes the existence of this thing. But since, from love, he desires this thing, *or* circumstance (by P36), then insofar as he imagines it to be lacking, he will be saddened, q.e.d.

Schol.: This sadness, insofar as it concerns the absence of what we love, is called longing.

P37: *The desire which arises from sadness or joy, and from hatred or love, is greater, the greater the affect is.*

Dem.: Sadness diminishes or restrains a man's power of acting (by P11S), that is (by P7), diminishes or restrains the striving by which a man strives to persevere in his being; so it is contrary to this striving (by P5), and all a man affected by sadness strives for is to remove sadness. But (by the definition of sadness) the greater the sadness, the greater is the part of the man's power of acting to which it is necessarily opposed. Therefore, the greater the sadness, the greater the power of acting with which the man will strive to remove the sadness, that is (by P9S), the greater the desire, *or* appetite, with which he will strive to remove the sadness.

Next, since joy (by the same P11S) increases or aids man's power of acting, it is easily demonstrated in the same way that the man affected with joy desires nothing but to preserve it, and does so with the greater desire, as the joy is greater.

II/169

Finally, since hate and love are themselves affects of sadness or of joy, it follows in the same way that the striving, appetite, or desire which arises from hate or love will be greater as the hate and love are greater, q.e.d.

P38: *If someone begins to hate a thing he has loved, so that the love is completely destroyed, then (from an equal cause) he will have a greater hate for it than if he had never loved it, and this hate will be the greater as the love before was greater.*

Dem.: For if someone begins to hate a thing he loves, more of his appetites will be restrained than if he had not loved it. For love is a joy (by P13S), which the man, as far as he can (by P28), strives to preserve; and (by the same scholium) he does this by regarding the thing he loves as present, and by affecting it, as far as he can, with joy (by P21). This striving (by P37) is greater as the love is greater, as is the striving to bring it about that the thing he loves loves him in return (see P33). But these strivings are restrained by hatred toward the thing he loves (by P13C and P23); therefore, the lover (by P11S) will be affected with sadness from this cause also, and the more so as his love was greater. That is, apart from the sadness which was the cause of the hate, another arises from the fact that he loved the thing. And consequently he will regard the thing he loved with a greater affect of sadness, that is (by P13S), he will have a greater hatred for it than if he had not loved it. And this hate will be the greater as the love was greater, q.e.d.

P39: *He who hates someone will strive to do evil to him, unless he fears that a greater evil to himself will arise from this; and on the other hand, he who loves someone will strive to benefit him by the same law.*

II/170

Dem.: To hate someone (by P13S) is to imagine him as the cause of [NS: one's] sadness; and so (by P28), he who hates someone will strive to remove or destroy him. But if from that he fears something sadder, *or* (what is the same) a greater evil to himself, and believes that he can avoid this sadness by not doing to the one he hates the evil he was contemplating, he will desire to abstain from doing evil (by the same P28)—and that (by P37) with a greater striving than that by which he was bound to do evil. So this greater striving will prevail, as we maintained.

The second part of this demonstration proceeds in the same way. Therefore, he who hates someone, and so on, q.e.d.

Schol.: By good here I understand every kind of joy, and whatever leads to it, and especially what satisfies any kind of longing, whatever that may be. And by evil [l understand here] every kind of sadness, and especially what frustrates longing. For we have shown above (in P9S) that we desire nothing because we judge it to be good, but on the contrary, we call it good because we desire it. Consequently, what we are averse to we call evil.

So each one, from his own affect, judges, *or* evaluates, what is good and what is bad, what is better and what is worse, and finally, what is best and what is worst. So the greedy man judges an abundance of money best, and poverty worst. The ambitious man desires nothing so much as esteem and dreads nothing so much as shame. To the envious nothing is more agreeable than another's unhappiness, and nothing more burdensome than another's happiness. And so, each one, from his own affect, judges a thing good or bad, useful or useless.

Further, this affect, by which a man is so disposed that he does not will what he wills, and wills what he does not will, is called *timidity*, which is therefore nothing but *fear insofar as a man is disposed by it to avoid an evil he judges to be future by encountering a lesser evil* (see P28). But if *the evil he is timid toward is shame*, then the timidity is called *a sense of shame*. Finally, if *the desire to avoid a future evil is restrained by timidity regarding another evil, so that he does not know what he would rather do*, then the fear is called *consternation*, particularly if each evil he fears is of the greatest.

II/171

P40: *He who imagines he is hated by someone, and believes he has given the other no cause for hate, will hate the other in return.*

Dem.: He who imagines someone to be affected with hate will thereby also be affected with hate (by P27), that is (by P13S), with sadness accompanied by the idea of an external cause. But (by hypothesis) he imagines no cause of this sadness except the one who hates him. So from imagining himself to be hated by someone, he will be affected with sadness, accompanied by the idea of the one who hates him [as a cause of the sadness] *or* (by the same scholium) he will hate the other, q.e.d.

Schol. If he imagines he has given just cause for this hatred, he will be affected with shame (by P30 and P30S). But this rarely happens (by P25). Moreover, this reciprocity of hatred can also arise from the fact that hatred is followed by a striving to do evil to him who is hated (by P39). He, therefore, who imagines that someone hates him will imagine the other to be the cause of an evil, *or* sadness. And so, he will be affected with sadness, *or* fear, accompanied by the idea of the one who hates him, as a cause. That is, he will be affected with hate in return, as above.

Cor. 1: He who imagines one he loves to be affected with hate toward him will be tormented by love and hate together. For insofar as he imagines that [the one he loves] hates him, he is determined to hate [that person] in return (by P40). But (by hypothesis) he nevertheless loves him. So he will be tormented by love and hate together.

II/172 Cor. 2: If someone imagines that someone else, toward whom he has previously had no affect, has, out of hatred, done him some evil, he will immediately strive to return the same evil.

Dem.: He who imagines someone to be affected with hate toward him, will hate him in return (by P40), and (by P26) will strive to think of everything which can affect [that person] with sadness, and be eager to bring it to him (by P39). But (by hypothesis) the first thing he imagines of this kind is the evil done him. So he will immediately strive to do the same to [that person], q.e.d.

Schol.: *The striving to do evil to him we hate* is called *anger*; and *the striving to return an evil done us* is called *vengeance*.

P41: *If someone imagines that someone loves him, and does not believe he has given any cause for this, he will love [that person] in return.*

Dem.: This proposition is demonstrated in the same way as the preceding one. See also its scholium.

Schol.: But if he believes that he has given just cause for this love, he will exult at being esteemed (by P30 and P30S). This, indeed, happens rather frequently (by P25) and is the opposite of what we said happens when someone imagines that someone hates him (see P40S).

Next, this *reciprocal love, and consequent* (by P39) *striving to benefit one who loves us, and strives* (by the same P39) *to benefit us*, is called *thankfulness, or gratitude*. And so it is evident that men are far more ready for vengeance than for returning benefits.

II/173 Cor.: He who imagines he is loved by one he hates will be torn by hate and love together. This is demonstrated in the same way as P40C1.

Schol.: But if the hate has prevailed, he will strive to do evil to the one who loves him. This affect is called *cruelty*, especially if it is believed that the one who loves has given no ordinary cause for hatred.

P42: *He who has benefited someone—whether moved to do so by love or by the hope of esteem—will be saddened if he sees his benefit accepted in an ungrateful spirit.*

Dem.: He who loves a thing like himself strives, as far as he can, to be loved by it in return (by P33). So he who has benefited someone from love does this from a longing by which he is bound that he may be loved in return—that is (by P34), from the hope of Esteem *or* (by P30S) Joy;

so (by P12) he will strive, as far as he can, to imagine this cause of Esteem, *or* to regard it as actually existing. But (by hypothesis) he imagines something else that excludes the existence of this cause. So (by P19) he will be saddened by this.

P43: *Hate is increased by being returned, but can be destroyed by love.*

Dem.: He who imagines one he hates to be affected with hate toward him will feel a new hate (by P40), while the first (by hypothesis) continues. If, on the other hand, he imagines that the one he hates is affected with love toward him, then insofar as he imagines this, he regards himself with joy (by P30) and will strive to please the one he hates (by P29), that is (by P41), he strives not to hate him and not to affect him with sadness. This striving (by P37) will be greater or lesser in proportion to the affect from which it arises. So if it is greater than that which arises from hate, and by which he strives to affect the thing he hates with sadness (by P26), then it will prevail over it and efface the hate from his mind, q.e.d.

II/174

P44: *Hate completely conquered by love passes into love, and the love is therefore greater than if hate had not preceded it.*

Dem.: The proof of this proceeds in the same way as that of P38. For he who begins to love a thing he has hated, *or* used to regard with sadness, rejoices because he loves, and to this joy which love involves (see its definition in P13S) there is also added a joy arising from this—the striving to remove the sadness hate involves (as we have shown in P37) is strengthened in every respect, and accompanied by the idea of the one he hated, [who is regarded] as a cause [of joy].

Schol.: Although this is so, still, no one will strive to hate a thing, or to be affected with sadness, in order to have this greater joy, that is, no one will desire to suffer injury in the hope of recovering, or long to be sick in the hope of getting better. For each one will strive always to preserve his being, and to put aside sadness as far as he can. But if, on the contrary, one could conceive that a man could desire to hate someone, in order afterwards to have the greater love for him, then he would always desire to hate him. For as the hate was greater, so the love would be greater, and so he would always desire his hate to become greater and greater. And by the same cause, a man would strive to become more and more ill, so that afterwards he might have the greater joy from restoring his health; and so he would always strive to become ill, which (by P6) is absurd.

P45: *If someone imagines that someone like himself is affected with hate toward a thing like himself which he loves, he will hate that [person].*

II/175

Dem.: For the thing he loves hates in return the one who hates it (by

93

P40), and so the lover, who imagines that someone hates the thing he loves, thereby imagines the thing he loves to be affected with hate, that is (by P13S), with sadness. And consequently (by P21), he is saddened, and his sadness is accompanied by the idea of the one who hates the thing he loves—[this other being regarded] as the cause [of the sadness]. That is (by P13S), he will hate him, q.e.d.

P46: *If someone has been affected with joy or sadness by someone of a class, or nation, different from his own, and this joy or sadness is accompanied by the idea of that person as its cause, under the universal name of the class or nation, he will love or hate, not only that person, but everyone of the same class or nation.*

Dem.: The demonstration of this matter is evident from P16.

P47: *The joy which arises from our imagining that a thing we hate is destroyed, or affected with some other evil, does not occur without some sadness of mind.*

Dem.: This is evident from P27. For insofar as we imagine a thing like us to be affected with sadness, we are saddened.

Schol.: This proposition can also be demonstrated from IIP17C. For as often as we recollect a thing—even though it does not actually exist—we still regard it as present, and the body is affected in the same way [NS: as if it were present]. So insofar as the memory of the thing is strong, the man is determined to regard it with sadness. While the image of the thing still remains, this determination is, indeed, restrained by the memory of those things that exclude its existence; but it is not taken away. And so the man rejoices only insofar as this determination is restrained.

So it happens that this joy, which arises from the misfortune occurring to the thing we hate, is repeated as often as we recollect the thing. For as we have said, when the image of this thing is aroused, because it involves the existence of the thing, it determines the man to regard the thing with the same sadness as he used to before, when it existed. But because he has joined to the image of this thing other images which exclude its existence, this determination to sadness is immediately restrained, and the man rejoices anew. This happens as often as the repetition occurs.

This is also the cause of men's rejoicing when they recall some evil now past, and why they enjoy telling of dangers from which they have been freed. For when they imagine a danger, they regard it as future, and are determined to fear it. This determination is restrained anew by the idea of freedom, which they have joined to the idea of the danger, when they have been freed from it. This renders them safe again, and so they rejoice again.

II/176

P48: *Love or hate—say, of Peter—is destroyed if the sadness the hate in-*
volves, or the joy the love involves, is attached to the idea of another cause, and
each is diminished to the extent that we imagine that Peter was not its only
cause.

Dem.: This is evident simply from the definitions of love and hate—
see P13S. For this joy is called love of Peter, or this sadness, hatred of
Peter, only because Peter is considered to be the cause of the one affect
or the other. If this is taken away—either wholly or in part—the affect
toward Peter is also diminished, either wholly or in part, q.e.d.   II/177

P49: *Given an equal cause of love, love toward a thing will be greater if we*
imagine the thing to be free than if we imagine it to be necessary. And similarly
for hate.

Dem.: A thing we imagine to be free must be perceived through itself,
without others (by ID7). So if we imagine it to be the cause of joy or
sadness, we shall thereby love or hate it (by P13S), and shall do so with
the greatest love or hate that can arise from the given affect (by P48).
But if we should imagine as necessary the thing which is the cause of this
affect, then (by the same ID7) we shall imagine it to be the cause of the
affect, not alone, but with others. And so (by P48) our love or hate
toward it will be less, q.e.d.

Schol.: From this it follows that because men consider themselves to
be free, they have a greater love or hate toward one another than toward
other things. To this is added the imitation of the affects, on which see
PP27, 34, 40, and 43.

P50: *Anything whatever can be the accidental cause of hope or fear.*

Dem.: This proposition is demonstrated in the same way as P15.
Consult it together with P18S2.

Schol.: Things which are accidental causes of hope or fear are called
good or bad omens. And insofar as these same omens are causes of hope
or fear, they are causes of joy or sadness (by the definitions of hope and   II/178
fear; see P18S2); consequently (by P15C), we love them or hate them,
and strive (by P28) either to use them as means to the things we hope
for, or to remove them as obstacles or causes of fear.

Furthermore, as follows from P25, we are so constituted by nature
that we easily believe the things we hope for, but believe only with difficulty those we fear, and that we regard them more or less highly than is
just. This is the source of the superstitions by which men are everywhere troubled.

For the rest, I do not think it worth the trouble to show here the
vacillations of mind which stem from hope and fear since it follows
simply from the definition of these affects that there is no hope without
fear, and no fear without hope (as we shall explain more fully in its

place). Moreover, insofar as we hope for or fear something, we love it or hate it; so whatever we have said of love and hate, anyone can easily apply to hope and fear.

P51: *Different men can be affected differently by one and the same object; and one and the same man can be affected differently at different times by one and the same object.*

Dem.: The human body (by IIPost. 3) is affected in a great many ways by external bodies. Therefore, two men can be differently affected at the same time, and so (by IIA1″ [II/99]) they can be affected differently by one and the same object.

Next (by the same Post.) the human body can be affected now in this way, now in another. Consequently (by the same axiom) it can be affected differently at different times by one and the same object, q.e.d.

Schol.: We see, then, that it can happen that what the one loves, the other hates, what the one fears, the other does not, and that one and the same man may now love what before he hated, and now dare what before he was too timid for.

II/179 Next, because each one judges from his own affect what is good and what is bad, what is better and what worse (see P39S) it follows that men can vary as much in judgment as in affect. The result is that when we compare one with another, we distinguish them only by a difference of affects, and call some intrepid, others timid, and others, finally, by another name.

For example, I shall call him *intrepid* who disdains an evil I usually fear. Moreover, if I attend to the fact that his desire to do evil to one he hates, and good to one he loves, is not restrained by timidity regarding an evil by which I am usually restrained, I shall call him *daring*. Someone will seem *timid* to me if he is afraid of an evil I usually disdain. If, moreover, I attend to the fact that his desire [to do evil to those he hates and good to those he loves] is restrained by timidity regarding an evil which cannot restrain me, I shall call him *cowardly*. In this way will everyone judge.

Finally, because of this inconstancy of man's nature and judgment, and also because he often judges things only from an affect, because the things which he believes will make for joy or sadness, and which he therefore strives to promote or prevent (by P28), are often only imaginary not to mention the other conclusions we have reached in Part II about the uncertainty of things we easily conceive that a man can often be the cause both of his own sadness and his own joy, *or* that he is affected both with joy and with sadness, accompanied by the idea of himself as their cause. So we easily understand what repentance and self-esteem are: *repentance is sadness accompanied by the idea of oneself as cause*, and *self-esteem is joy accompanied by the idea of oneself as cause*. Because men believe themselves free, these affects are very violent (see P49).

P52: *If we have previously seen an object together with others, or we imagine it has nothing but what is common to many things, we shall not consider it so long as one which we imagine to have something singular.*

Dem.: As soon as we imagine an object we have seen with others, we shall immediately recollect the others (by IIP18 and P18S), and so from considering one we immediately pass to considering another. And the reasoning is the same concerning the object we imagine to have nothing but what is common to many things. For imagining that is supposing that we consider nothing in it but what we have seen before with others.

But when we suppose that we imagine in an object something singular, which we have never seen before, we are only saying that when the mind considers that object, it has nothing in itself which it is led to consider from considering that. And so it is determined to consider only that. Therefore, if we have seen, and so on, q.e.d.

Schol.: This affection of the mind, *or* this *imagination of a singular thing, insofar as it is alone in the mind*, is called *wonder*. But *if it is aroused by an object we fear*, it is called *consternation*, because wonder at an evil keeps a man so suspended in considering it that he cannot think of other things by which he could avoid that evil. But *if what we wonder at is a man's prudence, diligence, or something else of that kind, because we consider him as far surpassing us in this*, then the wonder is called *veneration*. Otherwise, *if what we wonder at is the man's anger, envy, and the like*, the wonder is called *dread*.

Next, if we wonder at the prudence, diligence, and the like, of a man we love, the love will thereby (by P12) be greater and this *love joined to wonder*, or *veneration*, we call *devotion*. In this way we can also conceive hate, hope, confidence, and other affects to be joined to wonder, and so we can deduce more affects than those which are usually indicated by the accepted words. So it is clear that the names of the affects are found more from the ordinary usage [of words] than from an accurate knowledge [of the affects].

To wonder is opposed *disdain*, the cause of which, however, is generally this: because we see that someone wonders at, loves, or fears something, or something appears at first glance like things we admire, love, fear, and so on (by P15, P15C, and P27), we are determined to wonder at, love, fear, and so on, the same thing; but if, from the thing's presence, or from considering it more accurately, we are forced to deny it whatever can be the cause of wonder, love, fear, and the like, then the mind remains determined by the thing's presence to think more of the

II/180

II/181

things which are not in the object than of those which are (though the object's presence usually determines [the mind] to think chiefly of what is in the object).

Next, as devotion stems from wonder at a thing we love, so *mockery* stems from *disdain for a thing we hate or fear*, and *contempt* from *disdain for folly*, as veneration stems from wonder at prudence. Finally, we can conceive love, hope, love of esteem, and other affects joined to disdain, and from that we can deduce in addition other affects, which we also do not usually distinguish from the others by any single term.

P53: *When the mind considers itself and its power of acting, it rejoices, and does so the more, the more distinctly it imagines itself and its power of acting.*

Dem.: A man does not know himself except through affections of his body and their ideas (by IIP19 and P23). So when it happens that the mind can consider itself, it is thereby supposed to pass to a greater perfection, that is (by P11S), to be affected with joy, and with greater joy the more distinctly it can imagine its power of acting, q.e.d.

Cor.: This joy is more and more encouraged the more the man imagines himself to be praised by others. For the more he imagines himself to be praised by others, the greater the joy with which he imagines himself to affect others, a joy accompanied by the idea of himself (by P29S). And so (by P27) he himself is affected with a greater joy, accompanied by the idea of himself, q.e.d.

II/182

P54: *The mind strives to imagine only those things which posit its power of acting.*

Dem.: The mind's striving, *or* power, is its very essence (by P7); but the mind's essence (as is known through itself) affirms only what the mind is and can do, not what it is not and cannot do. So it strives to imagine only what affirms, *or* posits, its power of acting, q.e.d.

P55: *When the mind imagines its own lack of power, it is saddened by it.*

Dem.: The mind's essence affirms only what the mind is and can do, *or* it is of the nature of the mind to imagine only those things which posit its power of acting (by P54). So when we say that the mind, in considering itself, imagines its lack of power, we are saying nothing but that the mind's striving to imagine something which posits its power of acting is restrained, *or* (by P11S) that it is saddened, q.e.d.

Cor.: This sadness is more and more encouraged if we imagine ourselves to be blamed by others. This is demonstrated in the same way as P53C.

Schol.: This *sadness, accompanied by the idea of our own weakness* is called *humility*. But *joy arising from considering ourselves*, is called *self-love* or

II/183

self-esteem. And since this is renewed as often as a man considers his virtues, *or* his power of acting, it also happens that everyone is anxious to tell his own deeds, and show off his powers, both of body and of mind and that men, for this reason, are troublesome to one another.

From this it follows, again, that men are by nature envious (see P24S and P32S), *or* are glad of their equals' weakness and saddened by their equals' virtue. For whenever anyone imagines his own actions, he is affected with joy (by P53), and with a greater joy, the more his actions express perfection, and the more distinctly he imagines them, that is (by IIP40S1), the more he can distinguish them from others, and consider them as singular things. So everyone will have the greatest gladness from considering himself, when he considers something in himself which he denies concerning others.

But if he relates what he affirms of himself to the universal idea of man or animal, he will not be so greatly gladdened. And on the other hand, if he imagines that his own actions are weaker, compared to others' actions, he will be saddened (by P28), and will strive to put aside this sadness, either by wrongly interpreting his equals' actions or by magnifying his own as much as he can. It is clear, therefore, that men are naturally inclined to hate and envy.

Education itself adds to natural inclination. For parents generally spur their children on to virtue only by the incentive of honor and envy.

But perhaps this doubt remains: that not infrequently we admire and venerate men's virtues. To remove this scruple, I shall add the following corollary.

Cor.: No one envies another's virtue unless he is an equal.

Dem.: Envy is hatred itself (see P24S), *or* (by P13S) a sadness, that is (by P11S), an affection by which a man's power of acting, *or* striving, is restrained. But a man (by P9S) neither strives to do, nor desires, anything unless it can follow from his given nature. So no man desires that there be predicated of him any power of acting, *or* (what is the same) virtue, which is peculiar to another's nature and alien to his own. Hence, his desire cannot be restrained, that is (by P11S), he cannot be saddened because he considers a virtue in someone unlike himself. Consequently he also cannot envy him. But he can, indeed, envy his equal, who is supposed to be of the same nature as he, q.e.d.

Schol.: So when we said above (in P52S) that we venerate a man because we wonder at his prudence, strength of character, and so on, that happens (as is evident from the proposition itself) because we imagine these virtues to be peculiarly in him, and not as common to our nature. Therefore, we shall not envy him these virtues any more than we envy trees their height, or lions their strength.

II/184

P56: *There are as many species of joy, sadness, and desire, and consequently of each affect composed of these (like vacillation of mind) or derived from them (like love, hate, hope, fear, etc.), as there are species of objects by which we are affected.*

Dem.: Joy and sadness, and consequently the affects composed of them or derived from them, are passions (by P11S). But we are necessarily acted on (by P1) insofar as we have inadequate ideas, and only insofar as we have them (by P3) are we acted on, that is (see IIP40S), necessarily we are acted on only insofar as we imagine, *or* (see IIP17 and P17S) insofar as we are affected with an affect which involves both the nature of our body and the nature of an external body. Therefore, the nature of each passion must necessarily be so explained that the nature of the object by which we are affected is expressed.

II/185   For example, the joy arising from A involves the nature of object A, that arising from object B involves the nature of object B, and so these two affects of joy are by nature different, because they arise from causes of a different nature. So also the affect of sadness arising from one object is different in nature from the sadness stemming from another cause. The same must also be understood of love, hate, hope, fear, vacillation of mind, and so on.

Therefore, there are as many species of joy, sadness, love, hate, and the like, as there are species of objects by which we are affected.

But desire is the very essence, *or* nature, of each [man] insofar as it is conceived to be determined, by whatever constitution he has, to do something (see P9S). Therefore, as each [man] is affected by external causes with this or that species of joy, sadness, love, hate, and so on, that is, as his nature is constituted in one way or the other, so his desires vary and the nature of one desire must differ from the nature of the other as much as the affects from which each arises differ from one another.

Therefore, there are as many species of desire as there are species of joy, sadness, love, and the like, and consequently (through what has already been shown) as there are species of objects by which we are affected, q.e.d.

Schol.: Noteworthy among these species of affects, which (by P56) must be very many, are gluttony, drunkenness, lust, greed, and ambition, which are only notions of love or desire which explain the nature of each of these affects through the objects to which they are related. For by gluttony, drunkenness, lust, greed, and ambition we understand nothing but an immoderate love or desire for eating, drinking, sexual union, wealth, and esteem.

Moreover, these affects, insofar as we distinguish them from the others only through the object to which they are related, do not have opposites. For moderation, which we usually oppose to gluttony, sobriety which we usually oppose to drunkenness, and chastity, which we usually oppose to lust, are not affects *or* passions, but indicate the power of the mind, a power which moderates these affects.

I cannot explain the other species of affects here, for there are as many as there are species of objects. But even if I could, it is not necessary. For our purpose, which is to determine the powers of the affects and the power of the mind over the affects, it is enough to have a general definition of each affect. It is enough, I say, for us to understand the common properties of the affects and of the mind, so that we can determine what sort of power, and how great a power, the mind has to moderate and restrain the affects. So though there is a great difference between this or that affect of love, hate or desire for example, between the love of one's children and the love of one's wife, it is still not necessary for us to know these differences, nor to investigate the nature and origin of the affects further. II/186

P57: *Each affect of each individual differs from the affect of another as much as the essence of the one from the essence of the other.*

Dem.: This proposition is evident from IIA1" [II/99]. But nevertheless we shall demonstrate it from the definitions of the three primitive affects.

All the affects are related to desire, joy, or sadness, as the definitions we have given of them show. But desire is the very nature, *or* essence, of each [individual] (see the definition of desire in P9S). Therefore, the desire of each individual differs from the desire of another as much as the nature, *or* essence, of the one differs from the essence of the other.

Next, joy and sadness are passions by which each one's power, *or* striving to persevere in his being, is increased or diminished, aided or restrained (by P11 and P11S). But by the striving to persevere in one's being, insofar as it is related to the mind and body together, we understand appetite and desire (see P9S). So joy and sadness are the desire, *or* appetite, itself insofar as it is increased or diminished, aided or restrained, by external causes. That is (by the same scholium), it is the very nature of each [individual]. And so, the joy or sadness of each [individual] also differs from the joy or sadness of another as much as the nature, *or* essence, of the one differs from the essence of the other. Consequently, each affect of each individual differs from the affect of another as much, and so on, q.e.d. II/187

Schol.: From this it follows that the affects of the animals which are called irrational (for after we know the origin of the mind, we cannot in any way doubt that the lower animals feel things) differ from men's affects as much as their nature differs from human nature. Both the horse and the man are driven by a lust to procreate; but the one is driven by an equine lust, the other by a human lust. So also the lusts and appetites of insects, fish, and birds must vary. Therefore, though each individual lives content with his own nature, by which he is constituted, and is glad of it, nevertheless that life with which each one is content, and that gladness, are nothing but the idea, *or* soul, of the individual. And so the gladness of the one differs in nature from the gladness of the other as much as the essence of the one differs from the essence of the other.

Finally, from P57 it follows that there is no small difference between the gladness by which a drunk is led and the gladness a philosopher possesses. I wished to mention this in passing.

This will be enough concerning the affects which are related to man insofar as he is acted on. It remains to add a few words about those which are related to him insofar as he acts.

P58: *Apart from the joy and desire which are passions, there are other affects of joy and desire which are related to us insofar as we act.*

Dem.: When the mind conceives itself and its power of acting, it rejoices (by P53). But the mind necessarily considers itself when it conceives a true, *or* adequate, idea (by IIP43). But the mind conceives some adequate ideas (by IIP40S2). Therefore, it also rejoices insofar as it conceives adequate ideas, that is (by P1), insofar as it acts.

II/188

Next, the mind strives to persevere in its being, both insofar as it has clear and distinct ideas and insofar as it has confused ideas (by P9). But by striving we understand [NS: here] desire (by P9S). Therefore, desire also is related to us insofar as we understand, *or* (by P1) insofar as we act, q.e.d.

P59: *Among all the affects which are related to the mind insofar as it acts, there are none which are not related to joy or desire.*

Dem.: All the affects are related to desire, joy, or sadness, as the definitions we have given of them show. But by sadness we understand the fact that the mind's power of acting is diminished or restrained (by P11 and P11S). And so insofar as the mind is saddened, its power of understanding, that is (by P1), of acting, is diminished or restrained. Hence no affects of sadness can be related to the mind insofar as it acts, but only affects of joy and desire, which (by P58) are also so far related to the mind, q.e.d.

Schol.: *All actions that follow from affects related to the mind insofar as it understands* I relate to *strength of character*, which I divide into tenacity and nobility. For by *tenacity* I understand *the desire by which each one strives, solely from the dictate of reason, to preserve his being.* By *nobility* I understand *the desire by which each one strives, solely from the dictate of reason, to aid other men and join them to him in friendship.*

Those actions, therefore, which aim only at the agent's advantage, I relate to tenacity, and those which aim at another's advantage, I relate to nobility. So moderation, sobriety, presence of mind in danger, and so forth, are species of tenacity, whereas courtesy, mercy, and so forth, are species of nobility.

And with this I think I have explained and shown through their first causes the main affects and vacillations of mind which arise from the composition of the three primitive affects, namely, desire, joy, and sadness. From what has been said it is clear that we are driven about in many ways by external causes, and that, like waves on the sea, driven by contrary winds, we toss about, not knowing our outcome and fate.

II/189

But I said that I have shown only the main [NS: affects], not all the conflicts of mind there can be. For by proceeding in the same way as above, we can easily show that love is joined to repentance, contempt, shame, and so on. Indeed, from what has already been said I believe it is clear to anyone that the various affects can be compounded with one another in so many ways, and that so many variations can arise from this composition that they cannot be defined by any number. But it is sufficient for my purpose to enumerate only the main affects. [To consider] those I have omitted would be more curious than useful.

Nevertheless, this remains to be noted about love: very often it happens that while we are enjoying a thing we wanted, the body acquires from this enjoyment a new constitution, by which it is differently determined, and other images of things are aroused in it; and at the same time the mind begins to imagine other things and desire other things.

For example, when we imagine something which usually pleases us by its taste, we desire to enjoy it—that is, to consume it. But while we thus enjoy it, the stomach is filled, and the body constituted differently. So if (while the body is now differently disposed) the presence of the food or drink encourages the image of it, and consequently also the striving, *or* desire to consume it, then that new constitution will be opposed to this desire, *or* striving. Hence, the presence of the food or drink we used to want will be hateful. This is what we call *disgust* and *weariness*.

As for the external affections of the body, which are observed in the affects—such as trembling, paleness, sobbing, laughter, and the like—I have neglected them, because they are related to the body only, without any relation to the mind. Finally, there are certain things to be noted about the definitions of the affects. I shall therefore repeat them here in order, interposing the observations required on each one.

DEFINITIONS OF THE AFFECTS

I. Desire is man's very essence, insofar as it is conceived to be determined, from any given affection of it, to do something.

Exp.: We said above, in P9S, that desire is appetite together with the consciousness of it. And appetite is the very essence of man, insofar as it is determined to do what promotes his preservation.

But in the same scholium I also warned that I really recognize no difference between human appetite and desire. For whether a man is conscious of his appetite or not, the appetite still remains one and the same. And so—not to seem to commit a tautology—I did not wish to explain desire by appetite, but was anxious to so define it that I would comprehend together all the strivings of human nature that we signify by the name of appetite, will, desire, or impulse. For I could have said that desire is man's very essence, insofar as it is conceived to be determined to do something. But from this definition (by IIP23) it would not follow that the mind could be conscious of its desire, *or* appetite. Therefore, in order to involve the cause of this consciousness, it was necessary (by the same proposition) to add: *insofar as it is conceived, from some given affection of it, to be determined*, and so on. For by an affection of the human essence we understand any constitution of that essence, whether it is innate [NS: or has come from outside], whether it is conceived through the attribute of thought alone, or through the attribute of extension alone, or is referred to both at once.

Here, therefore, by the word *desire* I understand any of a man's strivings, impulses, appetites, and volitions, which vary as the man's constitution varies, and which are not infrequently so opposed to one another that the man is pulled in different directions and knows not where to turn.

II. Joy is a man's passage from a lesser to a greater perfection.

III. Sadness is a man's passage from a greater to a lesser perfection.

Exp.: I say a passage. For joy is not perfection itself. If a man were born with the perfection to which he passes, he would possess it without an affect of joy.

This is clearer from the affect of sadness, which is the opposite of joy. For no one can deny that sadness consists in a passage to a lesser perfection, not in the lesser perfection itself, since a man cannot be saddened insofar as he participates in some perfection. Nor can we say that sadness consists in the privation of a greater perfection. For a privation is nothing, whereas the affect of sadness is an act, which can therefore be no other act than that of passing to a lesser perfection, that is, an act by which man's power of acting is diminished or restrained (see P11S).

As for the definitions of cheerfulness, pleasure, melancholy, and pain, I omit them, because they are chiefly related to the body, and are only species of joy or sadness.

IV. Wonder is an imagination of a thing in which the mind remains fixed because this singular imagination has no connection with the others. (See P52 and P52S.)

Exp.: In IIP18S we showed the cause why the mind, from considering one thing, immediately passes to the thought of another—because the images of these things are connected with one another, and so ordered that one follows the other. This, of course, cannot be conceived when the image of the thing is new. Rather the mind will be detained in regarding the same thing until it is determined by other causes to think of other things.

So the imagination of a new thing, considered in itself, is of the same nature as the other [imaginations], and for this reason I do not number wonder among the affects. Nor do I see why I should, since this distraction of the mind does not arise from any positive cause which distracts the mind from other things, but only from the fact that there is no cause determining the mind to pass from regarding one thing to thinking of others. II/192

So as I pointed out in P11S, I recognize only three primitive, *or* primary, affects: joy, sadness, and desire. I have spoken of wonder only because it has become customary for some to indicate the affects derived from these three by other names when they are related to objects we wonder at. For the same reason I shall also add the definition of disdain to these.

V. Disdain is an imagination of a thing which touches the mind so little that the thing's presence moves the mind to imagining more what is not in it than what is. (See P52S).

I omit, here, the definitions of veneration and contempt because no affects that I know of derive their names from them.

VI. Love is a joy, accompanied by the idea of an external cause.

Exp.: This definition explains the essence of love clearly enough. But the definition of those authors who define *love* as *a will of the lover to join himself to the thing loved* expresses a property of love, not its essence. And because these authors did not see clearly enough the essence of love, they could not have any clear concept of this property. Hence everyone has judged their definition quite obscure.

But it should be noted that when I say it is a property in the lover, that he wills to join himself to the thing loved, I do not understand by will a consent, or a deliberation of the mind, *or* free decision (for we have demonstrated that this is a fiction in IIP48). Nor do I understand a desire of joining oneself to the thing loved when it is absent or continu- II/193 ing in its presence when it is present. For love can be conceived without either of these desires. Rather, by will I understand a satisfaction in the lover on account of the presence of the thing loved, by which the lover's joy is strengthened or at least encouraged.

VII. Hate is a sadness, accompanied by the idea of an external cause.

Exp.: The things to be noted here will be perceived easily from what has been said in the explanation of the preceding definition. (See also P13S.)

VIII. Inclination is a joy accompanied by the idea of a thing which is the accidental cause of joy.

IX. Aversion is a sadness accompanied by the idea of something which is the accidental cause of sadness. (On this see P15S.)

X. Devotion is a love of one whom we wonder at.

Exp.: That wonder arises from the newness of the thing we have shown in P52. So if it happens that we often imagine what we wonder at, we shall cease to wonder at it. And so we see that the affect of devotion easily changes into simple love.

XI. Mockery is a joy born of the fact that we imagine something we disdain in a thing we hate.

Exp.: Insofar as we disdain a thing we hate, we deny existence to it (see P52S), and so far we rejoice (by P20). But since we suppose that man nevertheless hates what he mocks, it follows that this joy is not enduring. (See P47S.)

II/194 XII. Hope is an inconstant joy, born of the idea of a future or past thing whose outcome we to some extent doubt.

XIII. Fear is an inconstant sadness, born of the idea of a future or past thing whose outcome we to some extent doubt. (See P18S2.)

Exp.: From these definitions it follows that there is neither hope without fear, nor fear without hope. For he who is suspended in hope and doubts a thing's outcome is supposed to imagine something which excludes the existence of the future thing. And so to that extent he is saddened (by P19), and consequently, while he is suspended in hope, he fears that the thing [he imagines] will happen.

Conversely, he who is in fear, that is, who doubts the outcome of a thing he hates, also imagines something which excludes the existence of that thing. And so (by P20) he rejoices, and hence, to that extent has hope that the thing will not take place.

XIV. Confidence is a joy born of the idea of a future or past thing, concerning which the cause of doubting has been removed.

XV. Despair is a sadness born of the idea of a future or past thing concerning which the cause of doubting has been removed.

Exp.: Confidence, therefore, is born of hope and despair of fear, when the cause of doubt concerning the thing's outcome is removed. This happens because man imagines that the past or future thing is there, and regards it as present, or because he imagines other things, excluding the existence of the things which put him in doubt. For though we can never be certain of the outcome of singular things (by IIP31C), it can still happen that we do not doubt their outcome. As we have shown (see IIP49S), it is one thing not to doubt a thing, and another to be certain of it. And so it can happen that we are affected, from the image of a past or future thing, with the same affect of joy or sadness as from the image of a present thing (as we have demonstrated in P18; see also its [first] scholium).

XVI. Gladness is a joy, accompanied by the idea of a past thing which has turned out better than we had hoped.

XVII. Remorse is a sadness, accompanied by the idea of a past thing which has turned out worse than we had hoped.

XVIII. Pity is a sadness, accompanied by the idea of an evil which has happened to another whom we imagine to be like us. (See P22S and P27S.)

Exp.: There seems to be no difference between pity and compassion, except perhaps that pity concerns the singular affect, whereas compassion concerns the habitual disposition of this affect.

XIX. Favor is a love toward someone who has benefited another.

XX. Indignation is a hate toward someone who has done evil to another.

Exp.: I know that in their common usage these words mean something else. But my purpose is to explain the nature of things, not the meaning of words. I intend to indicate these things by words whose usual meaning is not entirely opposed to the meaning with which I wish to use them. One warning of this should suffice. As for the cause of these affects, see P27C1 and P22S.

XXI. Overestimation is thinking more highly of someone than is just, out of love.

XXII. Scorn is thinking less highly of someone than is just, out of hate.

Exp.: Overestimation, therefore, is an effect, *or* property, of love, and scorn an effect of hate. And so *overestimation* can also be defined as *love insofar as it so affects a man that he thinks more highly than is just of the thing loved*. On the other hand, scorn can be defined as *hate insofar as it so affects a man that he thinks less highly than is just of the one he hates.* (See P26S.)

XXIII. Envy is hate insofar as it so affects a man that he is saddened by another's happiness and, conversely, glad at his ill fortune.

II/195

II/196

Exp.: To envy one commonly opposes compassion, which can therefore (in spite of the meaning of the word) be defined as follows.

XXIV. Compassion is love, insofar as it so affects a man that he is glad at another's good fortune, and saddened by his ill fortune.

Exp.: As far as envy is concerned, see P24S and P32S. These are the affects of joy and sadness which are accompanied by the idea of an external thing as cause, either through itself or accidentally. I pass now to the others, which are accompanied by the idea of an internal thing as cause.

XXV. Self-esteem is a joy born of the fact that a man considers himself and his own power of acting.

XXVI. Humility is a sadness born of the fact that a man considers his own lack of power, or weakness.

II/197 Exp.: Self-esteem is opposed to humility, insofar as we understand by it a joy born of the fact that we consider our power of acting. But insofar as we also understand by it a joy, accompanied by the idea of some deed which we believe we have done from a free decision of the mind, it is opposed to repentance, which we define as follows.

XXVII. Repentance is a sadness accompanied by the idea of some deed we believe ourselves to have done from a free decision of the mind.

Exp.: We have shown the causes of these affects in P51S, P53, P54, P55, and P55S. On the free decision of the mind, see IIP35S.

But we ought also to note here that it is no wonder sadness follows absolutely all those acts which from custom are called *wrong*, and joy, those which are called *right*. For from what has been said above we easily understand that this depends chiefly on education. Parents—by blaming the former acts, and often scolding their children on account of them, and on the other hand, by recommending and praising the latter acts—have brought it about that emotions of sadness were joined to the one kind of act, and those of joy to the other.

Experience itself also confirms this. For not everyone has the same custom and religion. On the contrary, what among some is holy, among others is unholy; and what among some is honorable, among others is dishonorable. Hence, according as each one has been educated, so he either repents of a deed or exults at being esteemed for it.

XXVIII. Pride is thinking more highly of oneself than is just, out of love of oneself.

Exp.: The difference, therefore, between pride and overestimation is that the latter is related to an external object, whereas pride is related to the man himself, who thinks more highly of himself than is just. Further, as overestimation is an effect or property of love, so *pride* is an effect or property of self-love. Therefore, it can also be defined as *love of oneself*, or *self-esteem, insofar as it so affects a man that he thinks more highly of himself than is just*. (See P26S.)

There is no opposite of this affect. For no one, out of hate, thinks less highly of himself than is just. Indeed, no one thinks less highly of himself than is just, insofar as he imagines that he cannot do this or that. For whatever man imagines he cannot do, he necessarily imagines; and he is so disposed by this imagination that he really cannot do what he imagines he cannot do. For so long as he imagines that he cannot do this or that, he is not determined to do it, and consequently it is impossible for him to do it.

But if we attend to those things which depend only on opinion, we shall be able to conceive it possible that a man thinks less highly of himself than is just. For it can happen that, while someone sad considers his weakness, he imagines himself to be disdained by everyone—even while the others think of nothing less than to disdain him. Moreover, it can happen that a man thinks less highly of himself than is just, if in the present he denies something of himself in relation to a future time of which he is uncertain—for example, if he denies that he can conceive of anything certain, or that he can desire or do anything but what is wrong or dishonorable. Again, we can say that someone thinks less highly of himself than is just, when we see that, from too great a fear of shame, he does not dare things which others equal to him dare.

So we can oppose this affect—which I shall call despondency—to pride. For as pride is born of self-esteem, so despondency is born of humility. We can therefore define it as follows.

XXIX. Despondency is thinking less highly of oneself than is just, out of sadness.

Exp.: We are, nevertheless, often accustomed to oppose humility to pride. But then we attend more to the effects than to the nature of the two. For we usually call him proud who exults too much at being esteemed (see P30S), who tells of nothing but his own virtues and the vices of others, who wishes to be given precedence over all others, and finally who proceeds with the gravity and attire usually adopted by others who are placed far above him.

On the other hand, we call him humble who quite often blushes, who confesses his own vices and tells the virtues of others, who yields to all, and finally, who walks with head bowed, and neglects to adorn himself.

These affects—humility and despondency—are very rare. For human nature, considered in itself, strains against them, as far as it can (see P13 and P54). So those who are believed to be most despondent and humble are usually most ambitious and envious.

XXX. Love of esteem is a joy accompanied by the idea of some action of ours which we imagine that others praise.

XXXI. Shame is a sadness, accompanied by the idea of some action [NS: of ours] which we imagine that others blame.

Exp.: On these, see P30S. But the difference between shame and a sense of shame should be noted here. For shame is a sadness which follows a deed one is ashamed of; whereas a sense of shame is a fear of, *or* timidity regarding, shame, by which man is restrained from doing something dishonorable. To a sense of shame is usually opposed shamelessness, but the latter is really not an affect, as I shall show in the proper place. But as I have already pointed out, the names of the affects are guided more by usage than by nature.

And with this I have finished what I had set out to explain concerning the affects of joy and sadness. So I proceed to those I relate to desire.

XXXII. Longing is a desire, *or* appetite, to possess something which is encouraged by the memory of that thing, and at the same time restrained by the memory of other things which exclude the existence of the thing wanted.

Exp.: When we recollect a thing (as we have often said before), we are thereby disposed to regard it with the same affect as if it were present. But while we are awake, this disposition, *or* striving, is generally restrained by images of things which exclude the existence of what we recollect. So when we remember a thing which affects us with some kind of joy, we thereby strive to regard it as present with the same affect of joy—a striving which, of course, is immediately restrained by the memory of things which exclude its existence.

II/200

Longing, therefore, is really a sadness which is opposed to that joy which arises from the absence of a thing we hate (see P47S). But because the word *longing* seems to concern desire, I relate this affect to the affects of desire.

XXXIII. Emulation is a desire for a thing which is generated in us because we imagine that others have the same desire.

Exp.: If someone flees because he sees others flee, or is timid because he sees others timid, or, because he sees that someone else has burned his hand, withdraws his own hand and moves his body as if his hand were burned, we shall say that he imitates the other's affect, but not that he emulates it—not because we know that emulation has one cause and imitation another, but because it has come about by usage that we call emulous only one who imitates what we judge to be honorable, useful, or pleasant.

As for the cause of emulation, see P27 and P27S. And on why envy is generally joined to this affect, see P32 and P32S.

XXXIV. Thankfulness, *or* gratitude, is a desire, *or* eagerness of love, by which we strive to benefit one who has benefited us from a like affect of love. (See P39 and P41S.)

XXXV. Benevolence is a desire to benefit one whom we pity. (See P27S.)

XXXVI. Anger is a desire by which we are spurred, from hate, to do evil to one we hate. (See P39.)

XXXVII. Vengeance is a desire by which, from reciprocal hate, we are roused to do evil to one who, from a like affect, has injured us. (See P40C2 and P40C2S.)

II/201

XXXVIII. Cruelty, *or* severity, is a desire by which someone is roused to do evil to one whom we love or pity.

Exp.: To cruelty is opposed mercy, which is not a passion, but a power of the mind, by which a man governs anger and vengeance.

XXXIX. Timidity is a desire to avoid a greater evil, which we fear, by a lesser one. (See P39S.)

XL. Daring is a desire by which someone is spurred to do something dangerous which his equals fear to take on themselves.

XLI. Cowardice is ascribed to one whose desire is restrained by timidity regarding a danger which his equals dare to take on themselves.

Exp.: Cowardice, therefore, is nothing but fear of some evil, which most people do not usually fear. So I do not relate it to affects of desire. Nevertheless I wished to explain it here, because insofar as we attend to the desire, it is really opposed to daring.

XLII. Consternation is attributed to one whose desire to avoid an evil is restrained by wonder at the evil he fears.

Exp.: Consternation, therefore, is a species of cowardice. But because consternation arises from a double timidity, it can be more conveniently defined as *a fear which keeps a man senseless or vacillating so that he cannot avert the evil.* I say *senseless* insofar as we understand that his desire to avert the evil is restrained by wonder, and *vacillating* insofar as we conceive that that desire is restrained by timidity regarding another evil, which torments him equally, so that he does not know which of the two to avert. On these see P39S and P52S. As for cowardice and daring, see P51S.

II/202

XLIII. Human kindness, *or* courtesy, is a desire to do what pleases men and not do what displeases them.

XLIV. Ambition is an excessive desire for esteem.

Exp.: Ambition is a desire by which all the affects are encouraged and strengthened (by P27 and P31); so this affect can hardly be overcome. For as long as a man is bound by any desire, he must at the same time be bound by this one. As Cicero says, *Every man is led by love of esteem, and the more so, the better he is. Even the philosophers who write books on how esteem is to be disdained put their names to these works.*

XLV. Gluttony is an immoderate desire for and love of eating.

XLVI. Drunkenness is an immoderate desire for and love of drinking.

XLVII. Greed is an immoderate desire for and love of wealth.

XLVIII. Lust is also a desire for and love of joining one body to another.

Exp.: Whether this desire for sexual union is moderate or not, it is usually called lust.

Moreover, these five affects (as I pointed out in P56S) have no opposites. For courtesy is a species of ambition (see P29S), and I have already pointed out also that moderation, sobriety, and chastity indicate the power of the mind, and not a passion. And even if it can happen that a greedy, ambitious, or timid man abstains from too much food, drink, and sexual union, still, greed, ambition, and timidity are not opposites of gluttony, drunkenness, or lust.

For the greedy man generally longs to gorge himself on another's food and drink. And the ambitious will not be moderate in anything, provided he can hope he will not be discovered; if he lives among the drunken and the lustful, then because he is ambitious, he will be the more inclined to these vices. Finally, the timid man does what he does not wish to do. For though he may hurl his wealth into the sea to avoid death, he still remains greedy. And if the lustful man is sad because he cannot indulge his inclinations, he does not on that account cease to be lustful.

Absolutely, these affects do not so much concern the acts of eating, drinking, and so forth, as the appetite itself and the love. Therefore, nothing can be opposed to these affects except nobility and tenacity, which will be discussed later on.

I pass over in silence the definitions of jealousy and the other vacillations of mind, both because they arise from the composition of affects we have already defined, and because most of them do not have names. This shows that it is sufficient for practical purposes to know them only in general. Furthermore, from the definitions of the affects which we have explained it is clear that they all arise from desire, joy, or sadness—*or* rather, that they are nothing but these three, each one generally being called by a different name on account of its varying relations and extrinsic denominations. If we wish now to attend to these primitive affects, and to what was said above about the nature of the mind, we shall be able to define the affects, insofar as they are related only to the mind, as follows.

GENERAL DEFINITION OF THE AFFECTS

An affect which is called a passion of the mind is a confused idea, by which the mind affirms of its body, or of some part of it, a greater or lesser force of existing than before, which, when it is given, determines the mind to think of this rather than that.

Exp.: I say, first, that an affect, *or* passion of the mind, is a *confused idea.*   II/204
For we have shown (P3) that the mind is acted on only insofar as it has
inadequate, *or* confused, ideas.

Next, I say *by which the mind affirms of its body or of some part of it a
greater or lesser force of existing than before.* For all the ideas we have of
bodies indicate the actual constitution of our own body (by IIP16C2)
more than the nature of the external body. But this [idea], which constitutes the form of the affect, must indicate or express a constitution of
the body (or of some part of it), which the body (or some part of it) has
because its power of acting, *or* force of existing, is increased or diminished, aided or restrained.

But it should be noted that, when I say *a greater or lesser force of existing
than before,* I do not understand that the mind compares its body's present constitution with a past constitution, but that the idea which constitutes the form of the affect affirms of the body something which really
involves more or less of reality than before.

And because the essence of the mind consists in this (by IIP11 and
P13), that it affirms the actual existence of its body, and we understand
by perfection the very essence of the thing, it follows that the mind
passes to a greater or lesser perfection when it happens that it affirms of
its body (or of some part of the body) something which involves more
or less reality than before. So when I said above that the mind's power
of thinking is increased or diminished, I meant nothing but that the
mind has formed of its body (or of some part of it) an idea which expresses more or less reality than it had affirmed of the body. For the
excellence of ideas and the [mind's] actual power of thinking are measured by the excellence of the object.

Finally, I added *which determines the mind to think of this rather than
that* in order to express also, in addition to the nature of joy and sadness
(which the first part of the definition explains), the nature of desire.

FOURTH PART OF THE ETHICS   II/205
Of Human Bondage, *or* the Powers
of the Affects

PREFACE

Man's lack of power to moderate and restrain the affects I call bondage.
For the man who is subject to affects is under the control, not of himself, but of fortune, in whose power he so greatly is that often, though
he sees the better for himself, he is still forced to follow the worse. In
this part, I have undertaken to demonstrate the cause of this, and what

there is of good and evil in the affects. But before I begin, I choose to say a few words first on perfection and imperfection, good and evil.

If someone has decided to make something, and has finished it, then he will call his thing perfect—and so will anyone who rightly knows, or thinks he knows, the mind and purpose of the author of the work. For example, if someone sees a work (which I suppose to be not yet completed), and knows that the purpose of the author of that work is to build a house, he will say that it is imperfect. On the other hand, he will call it perfect as soon as he sees that the work has been carried through to the end which its author had decided to give it. But if someone sees a work whose like he has never seen, and does not know the mind of its maker, he will, of course, not be able to know whether that work is perfect or imperfect. And this seems to have been the first meaning of these words.

II/206

But after men began to form universal ideas, and devise models of houses, buildings, towers, and the like, and to prefer some models of things to others, it came about that each one called perfect what he saw agreed with the universal idea he had formed of this kind of thing, and imperfect, what he saw agreed less with the model he had conceived, even though its maker thought he had entirely finished it.

Nor does there seem to be any other reason why men also commonly call perfect or imperfect natural things, which have not been made by human hand. For they are accustomed to form universal ideas of natural things as much as they do of artificial ones. They regard these universal ideas as models of things, and believe that Nature (which they think does nothing except for the sake of some end) looks to them, and sets them before itself as models. So when they see something happen in Nature which does not agree with the model they have conceived of this kind of thing, they believe that Nature itself has failed or sinned, and left the thing imperfect.

We see, therefore, that men are accustomed to call natural things perfect or imperfect more from prejudice than from true knowledge of those things. For we have shown in the Appendix of Part I, that Nature does nothing on account of an end. That eternal and infinite being we call God, *or* Nature, acts from the same necessity from which he exists. For we have shown (IP16) that the necessity of nature from which he acts is the same as that from which he exists. The reason, therefore, *or* cause, why God, *or* Nature, acts, and the reason why he exists, are one and the same. As he exists for the sake of no end, he also acts for the sake of no end. Rather, as he has no principle or end of existing, so he also has none of acting. What is called a final cause is nothing but a human appetite insofar as it is considered as a principle, *or* primary cause, of some thing.

II/207

For example, when we say that habitation was the final cause of this or that house, surely we understand nothing but that a man, because he imagined the conveniences of domestic life, had an appetite to build a house. So habitation, insofar as it is considered as a final cause, is nothing more than this singular appetite. It is really an efficient cause, which is considered as a first cause, because men are commonly ignorant of the causes of their appetites. For as I have often said before, they are conscious of their actions and appetites, but not aware of the causes by which they are determined to want something.

As for what they commonly say—that Nature sometimes fails or sins, and produces imperfect things—I number this among the fictions I treated in the Appendix of Part I.

Perfection and imperfection, therefore, are only modes of thinking, that is, notions we are accustomed to feign because we compare individuals of the same species or genus to one another. This is why I said above (IID6) that by reality and perfection I understand the same thing. For we are accustomed to refer all individuals in Nature to one genus, which is called the most general, that is, to the notion of being, which pertains absolutely to all individuals in Nature. So insofar as we refer all individuals in Nature to this genus, compare them to one another, and find that some have more being, or reality, than others, we say that some are more perfect than others. And insofar as we attribute something to them which involves negation, like a limit, an end, lack of power, and so on, we call them imperfect, because they do not affect our mind as much as those we call perfect, and not because something is lacking in them which is theirs, or because Nature has sinned. For nothing belongs to the nature of anything except what follows from the necessity of the nature of the efficient cause. And whatever follows from the necessity of the nature of the efficient cause happens necessarily.

II/208

As far as good and evil are concerned, they also indicate nothing positive in things, considered in themselves, nor are they anything other than modes of thinking, or notions we form because we compare things to one another. For one and the same thing can, at the same time, be good, and bad, and also indifferent. For example, music is good for one who is melancholy, bad for one who is mourning, and neither good nor bad to one who is deaf.

But though this is so, still we must retain these words. For because we desire to form an idea of man, as a model of human nature which we may look to, it will be useful to us to retain these same words with the meaning I have indicated. In what follows, therefore, I shall understand by good what we know certainly is a means by which we may approach nearer and nearer to the model of human nature we set before ourselves. By evil, what we certainly know prevents us from becoming like that model. Next, we shall say that men are more perfect or imperfect, insofar as they approach more or less near to this model.

For the main thing to note is that when I say that someone passes from a lesser to a greater perfection, and the opposite, I do not understand that he is changed from one essence, or form, to another. For example, a horse is destroyed as much if it is changed into a man as if it is changed into an insect. Rather, we conceive that his power of acting, insofar as it is understood through his nature, is increased or diminished.

II/209 Finally, by perfection in general I shall, as I have said, understand reality, that is, the essence of each thing insofar as it exists and produces an effect, having no regard to its duration. For no singular thing can be called more perfect for having persevered in existing for a longer time. Indeed, the duration of things cannot be determined from their essence, since the essence of things involves no certain and determinate time of existing. But any thing whatever, whether it is more perfect or less, will always be able to persevere in existing by the same force by which it begins to exist; so they are all equal in this regard.

DEFINITIONS

D1: By good I shall understand what we certainly know to be useful to us.

D2: By evil, however, I shall understand what we certainly know prevents us from being masters of some good.

Exp.: On these definitions, see the preceding preface [208/18–22].

D3: I call singular things contingent insofar as we find nothing, while we attend only to their essence, which necessarily posits their existence or which necessarily excludes it.

D4: I call the same singular things possible, insofar as, while we attend to the causes from which they must be produced, we do not know whether those causes are determined to produce them.

In IP33S1 I drew no distinction between the possible and the contingent, because there was no need there to distinguish them accurately.

D5: By opposite affects I shall understand, in what follows, those which II/210 pull a man differently, although they are of the same genus—such as gluttony and greed, which are species of love, and are opposite, not by nature, but accidentally.

D6: I have explained in IIIP18S1 and S2 what I shall understand by an affect toward a future thing, a present one, and a past.

116

But here it should be noted in addition that just as we can distinctly imagine distance of place only up to a certain limit, so also we can distinctly imagine distance of time only up to a certain limit. That is, we usually imagine all those objects which are more than two hundred feet away from us, or whose distance from the place where we are surpasses what we can distinctly imagine, to be equally far from us; we therefore usually imagine them as if they were in the same plane; in the same way, we imagine to be equally far from the present all those objects whose time of existing we imagine to be separated from the present by an interval longer than that we are used to imagining distinctly; so we relate them, as it were, to one moment of time.

D7: By the end for the sake of which we do something I understand appetite.

D8: By virtue and power I understand the same thing, that is (by IIIP7), virtue, insofar as it is related to man, is the very essence, or nature, of man, insofar as he has the power of bringing about certain things, which can be understood through the laws of his nature alone.

AXIOM

[A1:] There is no singular thing in Nature than which there is not another more powerful and stronger. Whatever one is given, there is another more powerful by which the first can be destroyed.

P1: *Nothing positive which a false idea has is removed by the presence of the true insofar as it is true.* II/211

Dem.: Falsity consists only in the privation of knowledge which inadequate ideas involve (by IIP35), and they do not have anything positive on account of which they are called false (by IIP33). On the contrary, insofar as they are related to God, they are true (by IIP32). So if what a false idea has which is positive were removed by the presence of the true insofar as it is true, then a true idea would be removed by itself, which (by IIIP4) is absurd. Therefore, nothing positive which a false idea has, and so on, q.e.d.

Schol.: This proposition is understood more clearly from IIP16C2. For an imagination is an idea which indicates the present constitution of the human body more than the nature of an external body—not distinctly, of course, but confusedly. This is how it happens that the mind is said to err.

For example, when we look at the sun, we imagine it to be about two hundred feet away from us. In this we are deceived so long as we are ignorant of its true distance; but when its distance is known, the error is removed, not the imagination, that is, the idea of the sun, which explains its nature only so far as the body is affected by it. And so, although we come to know the true distance, we shall nevertheless imagine it as near us. For as we said in IIP35S, we do not imagine the sun to be so near because we are ignorant of its true distance, but because the mind conceives the sun's size insofar as the body is affected by the sun. Thus, when the rays of the sun, falling on the surface of the water, are reflected to our eyes, we imagine it as if it were in the water, even if we know its true place.

And so it is with the other imaginations by which the mind is deceived, whether they indicate the natural constitution of the body, or II/212 that its power of acting is increased or diminished: they are not contrary to the true, and do not disappear on its presence. It happens, of course, when we wrongly fear some evil, that the fear disappears on our hearing news of the truth. But on the other hand, it also happens, when we fear an evil which is certain to come, that the fear vanishes on our hearing false news. So imaginations do not disappear through the presence of the true insofar as it is true, but because there occur others, stronger than them, which exclude the present existence of the things we imagine, as we showed in IIP17.

P2: *We are acted on, insofar as we are a part of Nature, which cannot be conceived through itself, without the others.*

Dem.: We say that we are acted on when something arises in us of which we are only the partial cause (by IIID2), that is (by IIID1), something which cannot be deduced from the laws of our nature alone. Therefore, we are acted on insofar as we are a part of Nature, which cannot be conceived through itself without the others, q.e.d.

P3: *The force by which a man perseveres in existing is limited, and infinitely surpassed by the power of external causes.*

Dem.: This is evident from A1. For given a man, there is something else, say A, more powerful. And given A, there is something else again, say B, more powerful than A, and so on, to infinity. Therefore, the power of man is limited by the power of another thing and infinitely surpassed by the power of external causes, q.e.d.

P4: *It is impossible that a man should not be a part of Nature, and that he should be able to undergo no changes except those which can be understood through his own nature alone, and of which he is the adequate cause.*

II/213 Dem.: [i] The power by which singular things (and consequently, [any] man) preserve their being is the power itself of God, *or* Nature (by IP24C), not insofar as it is infinite, but insofar as it can be explained

118

through the man's actual essence (by IIIP7). The man's power, therefore, insofar as it is explained through his actual essence, is part of God *or* Nature's infinite power, that is (by IP34), of its essence. This was the first point.

[ii] Next, if it were possible that a man could undergo no changes except those which can be understood through the man's nature alone, it would follow (by IIIP4 and P6) that he could not perish, but that necessarily he would always exist. And this would have to follow from a cause whose power would be either finite or infinite, namely, either from the power of the man alone, who would be able to avert from himself other changes which could arise from external causes, or from the infinite power of Nature, by which all singular things would be directed so that the man could undergo no other changes except those which assist his preservation. But the first is absurd (by P3, whose demonstration is universal and can be applied to all singular things).

Therefore, if it were possible for a man to undergo no changes except those which could be understood through the man's nature alone, so that (as we have already shown) he would necessarily always exist, this would have to follow from God's infinite power; and consequently (by IP16) the order of the whole of Nature, insofar as it is conceived under the attributes of extension and thought, would have to be deduced from the necessity of the divine nature, insofar as it is considered to be affected with the idea of some man. And so (by IP21) it would follow that the man would be infinite. But this (by part [i] of this demonstration) is absurd.

Therefore, it is impossible that a man should undergo no other changes except those of which he himself is the adequate cause, q.e.d.

Cor.: From this it follows that man is necessarily always subject to passions, that he follows and obeys the common order of Nature, and accommodates himself to it as much as the nature of things requires.

P5: *The force and growth of any passion, and its perseverance in existing, are not defined by the power by which we strive to persevere in existing, but by the power of an external cause compared with our own.*

II/214

Dem.: The essence of a passion cannot be explained through our essence alone (by IIID1 and D2), that is (by IIIP7), the power of a passion cannot be defined by the power by which we strive to persevere in our being; but (as has been shown in IIP16) it must necessarily be defined by the power of an external cause compared with our own, q.e.d.

P6: *The force of any passion, or affect, can surpass the other actions, or power, of a man, so that the affect stubbornly clings to the man.*

Dem.: The force and growth of any passion, and its perseverance in

119

existing, are defined by the power of an external cause compared with our own (by P5). And so (by P3) it can surpass the power of a man, and so on, q.e.d.

P7: *An affect cannot be restrained or taken away except by an affect opposite to, and stronger than, the affect to be restrained.*

Dem.: An affect, insofar as it is related to the mind, is an idea by which the mind affirms of its body a greater or lesser force of existing than before (by the general Definition of the Affects [II/203/29–33]). When, therefore, the mind is troubled by some affect, the body is at the same time affected with an affection by which its power of acting is increased or diminished.

II/215   Next, this affection of the body (by P5) receives from its cause its force for persevering in its being, which, therefore, can neither be restrained nor removed, except by a corporeal cause (by IIP6) which affects the body with an affection opposite to it (by IIIP5), and stronger than it (by A1).

And so (by IIP12), the mind will be affected with the idea of an affection stronger than, and opposite to, the first affection, that is (by the general definition of the affects), the mind will be affected with an affect stronger than, and opposite to, the first affect, which will exclude or take away the existence of the first affect.

Therefore, an affect can neither be taken away nor restrained except through an opposite and stronger affect, q.e.d.

Cor.: An affect, insofar as it is related to the mind, can neither be restrained nor taken away except by the idea of an opposite affection of the body stronger than the affection by which we are acted on. For an affect by which we are acted on can neither be restrained nor taken away except by an affect stronger than it and contrary to it (by P7), that is (by the general definition of the affects), except by an idea of an affection of the body stronger than and contrary to the affection by which we are acted on.

P8: *The knowledge of good and evil is nothing but an affect of joy or sadness, insofar as we are conscious of it.*

Dem.: We call good, or evil, what is useful to, or harmful to, preserving our being (by D1 and D2), that is (by IIIP7), what increases or diminishes, aids or restrains, our power of acting. Therefore (by the definitions of joy and sadness in IIIP11S), insofar as we perceive that a thing affects us with joy or sadness, we call it good or evil. And so knowledge of good and evil is nothing but an idea of joy or sadness which follows necessarily from the affect of joy or sadness itself (by IIP22).

But this idea is united to the affect in the same way as the mind is united to the body (by IIP21), that is (as I have shown in IIP21S), this idea is not really distinguished from the affect itself, *or* (by the general definition of the affects) from the idea of the body's affection; it is only conceptually distinguished from it. Therefore, this knowledge of good and evil is nothing but the affect itself, insofar as we are conscious of it, q.e.d.

II/216

P9: *An affect whose cause we imagine to be with us in the present is stronger than if we did not imagine it to be with us.*

Dem.: An imagination is an idea by which the mind considers a thing as present (see its definition in IIP17S), which nevertheless indicates the constitution of the human body more than the nature of the external thing (by IIP16C2). An affect, therefore (by the general definition of the affects), is an imagination, insofar as [the affect] indicates the constitution of the body. But an imagination (by IIP17) is more intense so long as we imagine nothing which excludes the present existence of the external thing. Hence, an affect whose cause we imagine to be with us in the present is more intense, *or* stronger, than if we did not imagine it to be with us, q.e.d.

Schol.: I said above (in IIIP18) that when we imagine a future or past thing, we are affected with the same affect as if we were imagining something present; but I expressly warned then that this is true insofar as we attend to the thing's image only. For it is of the same nature whether we have imagined the thing as present or not. But I did not deny that it is made weaker when we consider as present to us other things, which exclude the present existence of the future thing. I neglected to point this out then, because I had decided to treat the powers of the affects in this Part.

Cor.: Other things equal, the image of a future or past thing (i.e., of a thing we consider in relation to a future or past time, the present being excluded) is weaker than the image of a present thing; and consequently, an affect toward a future or past thing is milder, other things equal, than an affect toward a present thing.

II/217

P10: *We are affected more intensely toward a future thing which we imagine will quickly be present, than if we imagined the time when it will exist to be further from the present. We are also affected more intensely by the memory of a thing we imagine to be not long past, than if we imagined it to be long past.*

Dem.: Insofar as we imagine that a thing will quickly be present, or is not long past, we thereby imagine something which excludes the presence of the thing less than if we imagined that the time when it will exist were further from the present, or that it were far in the past (as is known through itself). And so (by P9), to that extent we will be affected more intensely toward it, q.e.d.

Schol.: From what we noted at D6, it follows that we are still affected equally mildly toward objects separated from the present by an interval of time longer than that we can determine by imagining, even though we may understand that they are separated from one another by a long interval of time.

P11: *An affect toward a thing we imagine as necessary is more intense, other things equal, than one toward a thing we imagine as possible or contingent, or not necessary.*

Dem.: Insofar as we imagine a thing to be necessary, we affirm its existence. On the other hand, we deny its existence insofar as we imagine it not to be necessary (by IP33S1), and therefore (by P9), an affect toward a necessary thing is more intense, other things equal, than toward one not necessary, q.e.d.

II/218

P12: *An affect toward a thing which we know does not exist in the present, and which we imagine as possible, is more intense, other things equal, than one toward a contingent thing.*

Dem.: Insofar as we imagine a thing as contingent, we are not affected by any image of another thing which posits the thing's existence (by D3); but on the other hand (according to the hypothesis), we imagine certain things which exclude its present existence. But insofar as we imagine a thing in the future to be possible, we imagine certain things which posit its existence (by D4), that is (by IIIP18), which encourage hope or fear. And so an affect toward a possible thing is more violent [, other things equal, than one toward a contingent thing], q.e.d.

Cor.: An affect toward a thing which we know does not exist in the present, and which we imagine as contingent, is much milder than if we imagined the thing as with us in the present.

Dem.: An affect toward a thing which we imagine to exist in the present is more intense than if we imagined it as future (by P9C), and [an affect toward a thing we imagine to exist in the future is] much more violent if we imagine the future time to be not far from the present (by P10). Therefore, an affect toward a thing which we imagine will exist at a time far from the present is much milder than if we imagined it as present. And nevertheless (by P12), it is more intense than if we imagined that thing as contingent. And so an affect toward a contingent thing will be much milder than if we imagined the thing to be with us in the present, q.e.d.

II/219

P13: *An affect toward a contingent thing which we know does not exist in the present is milder, other things equal, than an affect toward a past thing.*

Dem.: Insofar as we imagine a thing as contingent, we are not affected by any image of another thing which posits the thing's existence (by D3). But on the other hand (according to the hypothesis), we imagine certain things which exclude its present existence. Now insofar as we imagine a thing in relation to past time, we are supposed to imagine something which brings it back to our memory, *or* that arouses the image of the thing (see IIP18 and P18S), and therefore brings it about that we consider it as if it were present (by IIP17C). And so (by P9) an affect toward a contingent thing which we know does not exist in the present will be milder, other things equal, than an affect toward a past thing, q.e.d.

P14: *No affect can be restrained by the true knowledge of good and evil insofar as it is true, but only insofar as it is considered as an affect.*

Dem.: An affect is an idea by which the mind affirms of its body a greater or lesser force of existing than before (by the general Definition of the Affects). So (by P1), it has nothing positive which could be removed by the presence of the true. Consequently the true knowledge of good and evil, insofar as it is true, cannot restrain any affect.

But insofar as it is an affect (see P8), if it is stronger than the affect to be restrained, to that extent only (by P7) can it restrain the affect, q.e.d.

P15: *A desire which arises from a true knowledge of good and evil can be extinguished or restrained by many other desires which arise from affects by which we are tormented.*

II/220

Dem.: From a true knowledge of good and evil, insofar as this is an affect (by P8), there necessarily arises a desire (by Def. Aff. I), which is the greater as the affect from which it arises is greater (by IIIP37). But because this desire arises (by hypothesis) from the fact that we understand something truly, it follows in us insofar as we act (by IIIP3). And so it must be understood through our essence alone (by IIID2), and consequently (by IIIP7), its force and growth can be defined only by human power alone.

Next, desires which arise from affects by which we are torn are also greater as these affects are more violent. And so their force and growth (by P5) must be defined by the power of external causes, which, if it were compared with ours, would indefinitely surpass our power (by P3). Hence, desires which arise from such affects can be more violent than the desire which arises from a true knowledge of good and evil, and can therefore (by P7) restrain or extinguish it, q.e.d.

P16: *A desire which arises from a true knowledge of good and evil, insofar as this knowledge concerns the future, can be quite easily restrained or extinguished by a desire for the pleasures of the moment.*

Dem.: An affect toward a thing we imagine as future is milder than one toward a present thing (by P9C). But a desire which arises from a true knowledge of good and evil, even if this knowledge concerns things which are good now, can be restrained or extinguished by some rash desire (by P15, whose demonstration is universal). Therefore, a desire which arises from the same knowledge, insofar as this concerns a future thing, can be quite easily restrained or extinguished, and so on, q.e.d.

II/221

P17: *A desire which arises from a true knowledge of good and evil, insofar as this concerns contingent things, can be restrained much more easily still by a desire for things which are present.*

Dem.: This proposition is demonstrated in the same way as the preceding one, from P12C.

Schol.: With this I believe I have shown the cause why men are moved more by opinion than by true reason, and why the true knowledge of good and evil arouses disturbances of the mind, and often yields to lust of every kind. Hence that verse of the Poet:

> . . . video meliora, proboque,
> deteriora sequor. . . .[2]

Ecclesiastes also seems to have had the same thing in mind when he said: "He who increases knowledge increases sorrow."[3]

I do not say these things in order to infer that it is better to be ignorant than to know, or that there is no difference between the fool and the man who understands when it comes to moderating the affects. My reason, rather, is that it is necessary to come to know both our nature's power and its lack of power, so that we can determine what reason can do in moderating the affects, and what it cannot do. I said that in this part I would treat only of man's lack of power. For I have decided to treat reason's power over the affects separately.

P18: *A desire which arises from joy is stronger, other things equal, than one which arises from sadness.*

Dem.: Desire is the very essence of man (by Def. Aff. I), that is (by IIIP7), a striving by which a man strives to persevere in his being. So a desire which arises from joy is aided or increased by the affect of joy itself (by the Def. of joy in IIIP11S), whereas one which arises from

II/222

[2] Ovid, *Metamorphoses* VII, 20–21: "I see and approve the better, but follow the worse." Medea is torn between reason's demand that she obey her father and her passion for Jason.
[3] *Ecclesiastes* 1:18.

sadness is diminished or restrained by the affect of sadness (by the same Schol.). And so the force of a desire which arises from joy must be defined both by human power and the power of the external cause, whereas the force of a desire which arises from sadness must be defined by human power alone. The former, therefore, is stronger than the latter, q.e.d.

Schol.: With these few words I have explained the causes of man's lack of power and inconstancy, and why men do not observe the precepts of reason. Now it remains for me to show what reason prescribes to us, which affects agree with the rules of human reason, and which, on the other hand, are contrary to those rules. But before I begin to demonstrate these things in our cumbersome geometric order, I should like first to show briefly here the dictates of reason themselves, so that everyone may more easily perceive what I think.

Since reason demands nothing contrary to Nature, it demands that everyone love himself, seek his own advantage, what is really useful to him, want what will really lead a man to greater perfection, and absolutely, that everyone should strive to preserve his own being as far as he can. This, indeed, is as necessarily true as that the whole is greater than its part (see IIIP4).

Further, since virtue (by D8) is nothing but acting from the laws of one's own nature, and no one strives to preserve his being (by IIIP7) except from the laws of his own nature, it follows:

(i) that the foundation of virtue is this very striving to preserve one's own being, and that happiness consists in a man's being able to preserve his being;

(ii) that we ought to want virtue for its own sake, and that there is not anything preferable to it, or more useful to us, for the sake of which we ought to want it; and finally (iii) that those who kill themselves are weak-minded and completely conquered by external causes contrary to their nature.

Again, from IIPost. 4 [II/102/29–31] it follows that we can never bring it about that we require nothing outside ourselves to preserve our being, nor that we live without having dealings with things outside us. Moreover, if we consider our mind, our intellect would of course be more imperfect if the mind were alone and did not understand anything except itself. There are, therefore, many things outside us which are useful to us, and on that account to be sought.

Of these, we can think of none more excellent than those which agree entirely with our nature. For if, for example, two individuals of entirely the same nature are joined to one another, they compose an individual twice as powerful as each one. To man, then, there is nothing more

II/223

useful than man. Man, I say, can wish for nothing more helpful to the preservation of his being than that all should so agree in all things that the minds and bodies of all would compose, as it were, one mind and one body; that all should strive together, as far as they can, to preserve their being; and that all, together, should seek for themselves the common advantage of all.

From this it follows that men who are governed by reason—that is, men who, from the guidance of reason, seek their own advantage—want nothing for themselves which they do not desire for other men. Hence, they are just, honest, and honorable.

These are those dictates of reason which I promised to present briefly here before I began to demonstrate them in a more cumbersome order. I have done this to win, if possible, the attention of those who believe that this principle—that everyone is bound to seek his own advantage—is the foundation, not of virtue and morality, but of immorality. Now that I have shown briefly that the contrary is true, I proceed to demonstrate this in the same way I have followed up to this point.

P19: *From the laws of his own nature, everyone necessarily wants, or is repelled by, what he judges to be good or evil.*

Dem.: Knowledge of good and evil (by P8) is itself an affect of joy or sadness, insofar as we are conscious of it. And therefore (by IIIP28), everyone necessarily wants what he judges to be good, and conversely, is repelled by what he judges to be evil. But this appetite is nothing but the very essence, *or* nature, of man (by the definition of appetite; see IIIP9S and Def. Aff. I). Therefore, everyone, from the laws of his own nature, necessarily, wants or is repelled by, and so on, q.e.d.

II/224

P20: *The more each one strives, and is able, to seek his own advantage, that is, to preserve his being, the more he is endowed with virtue; conversely, insofar as each one neglects his own advantage, that is, neglects to preserve his being, he lacks power.*

Dem.: Virtue is human power itself, which is defined by man's essence alone (by D8), that is (by IIIP7), solely by the striving by which man strives to persevere in his being. So the more each one strives, and is able, to preserve his being, the more he is endowed with virtue. And consequently (by IIIP4 and P6), insofar as someone neglects to preserve his being, he lacks power, q.e.d.

Schol: No one, therefore, unless he is defeated by causes external, and contrary, to his nature, neglects to seek his own advantage, *or* to preserve his being. No one, I say, avoids food or kills himself from the necessity of his own nature. Those who do such things are compelled by external causes, which can happen in many ways. Someone may kill himself because he is compelled by another, who twists his right hand (which happened to hold a sword) and forces him to direct the sword against his heart; or because he is forced by the command of a tyrant (as Seneca was) to open his veins, that is, he desires to avoid a greater evil by [submitting to] a lesser; or finally because hidden external causes so dispose his imagination, and so affect his body, that it takes on another nature, contrary to the former, a nature of which there cannot be an idea in the mind (by IIIP10). But that a man should, from the necessity of his own nature, strive not to exist, or to be changed into another form, is as impossible as that something should come from nothing. Anyone who gives this a little thought will see it.

II/225

P21: *No one can desire to be blessed, to act well and to live well, unless at the same time he desires to be, to act, and to live, that is, to actually exist.*

Dem.: The demonstration of this proposition, *or* rather the thing itself, is evident through itself, and also from the definition of desire. For the desire (by Def. Aff. I) to live blessedly, *or* well, to act, and so on, is the very essence of man, that is (by IIIP7), the striving by which each one strives to preserve his being. Therefore, no one can desire, and so on, q.e.d.

P22: *No virtue can be conceived prior to this [virtue] (viz. the striving to preserve oneself).*

Dem.: The striving to preserve itself is the very essence of a thing (by IIIP7). Therefore, if some virtue could be conceived prior to this [virtue], namely, to this striving, the very essence of the thing would be conceived prior to itself (by D8), which is absurd (as is known through itself). Therefore, no virtue, and so on, q.e.d.

Cor.: The striving to preserve oneself is the first and only foundation of virtue. For no other principle can be conceived prior to this one (by P22) and no virtue can be conceived without it (by P21).

P23: *A man cannot be said absolutely to act from virtue insofar as he is determined to do something because he has inadequate ideas, but only insofar as he is determined because he understands.*

Dem.: Insofar as a man is determined to act from the fact that he has inadequate ideas, he is acted on (by IIIP1), that is (by IIID1 and D2), he does something which cannot be perceived through his essence alone, that is (by D8), which does not follow from his virtue. But insofar as he is determined to do something from the fact that he understands, he acts (by IIIP1), that is (by IIID2), does something which is perceived through his essence alone, *or* (by D8) which follows adequately from his virtue, q.e.d.

II/226

P24: *Acting absolutely from virtue is nothing else in us but acting, living, and preserving our being (these three signify the same thing) by the guidance of reason, from the foundation of seeking one's own advantage.*

Dem.: Acting absolutely from virtue is nothing but acting from the laws of our own nature (by D8). But we act only insofar as we understand (by IIIP3). Therefore, acting from virtue is nothing else in us but acting, living, and preserving one's being by the guidance of reason, and doing this (by P22C) from the foundation of seeking one's own advantage, q.e.d.

P25: *No one strives to preserve his being for the sake of anything else.*

Dem.: The striving by which each thing strives to persevere in its being is defined by the thing's essence alone (by IIIP7). If this [essence] alone is given, then it follows necessarily that each one strives to preserve his being—but this does not follow necessarily from the essence of any other thing (by IIIP6).

II/227 This proposition, moreover, is evident from P22C. For if a man strove to preserve his being for the sake of something else, then that thing would be the first foundation of virtue (as is known through itself). But (by P22C) this is absurd. Therefore, no one strives, and so on, q.e.d.

P26: *What we strive for from reason is nothing but understanding; nor does the mind, insofar as it uses reason, judge anything else useful to itself except what leads to understanding.*

Dem.: The striving to preserve itself is nothing but the essence of the thing itself (by IIIP7), which, insofar as it exists as it does, is conceived to have a force for persevering in existing (by IIIP6) and for doing those things which necessarily follow from its given nature (see the definition of appetite in IIIP9S). But the essence of reason is nothing but our mind, insofar as it understands clearly and distinctly (see the definition of this in IIP40S2). Therefore (by IIP40) whatever we strive for from reason is nothing but understanding.

Next, since this striving of the mind, by which the mind, insofar as it reasons, strives to preserve its being, is nothing but understanding (by the first part of this demonstration), this striving for understanding (by P22C) is the first and only foundation of virtue, nor do we strive to understand things for the sake of some end (by P25). On the contrary, the mind, insofar as it reasons, cannot conceive anything to be good for itself except what leads to understanding (by D1), q.e.d.

P27: *We know nothing to be certainly good or evil, except what really leads to understanding or what can prevent us from understanding.*

Dem.: Insofar as the mind reasons, it wants nothing other than to understand, nor does it judge anything else to be useful to itself except what leads to understanding (by P26). But the mind (by IIP41, P43, and P43S) has certainty of things only insofar as it has adequate ideas, *or* (what is the same thing, by IIP40S) insofar as it reasons. Therefore, we know nothing to be certainly good except what really leads to understanding, and conversely, know nothing to be certainly evil except what can prevent us from understanding, q.e.d. II/228

P28: *Knowledge of God is the mind's greatest good; its greatest virtue is to know God.*

Dem.: The greatest thing the mind can understand is God, that is (by ID6), a being absolutely infinite, without which (by IP15) nothing can either be or be conceived. And so (by P26 and P27), the mind's greatest advantage, *or* (by D1) good, is knowledge of God.

Next, only insofar as the mind understands (by IIIP1 and P3), does it act, and can it be said absolutely to act from virtue (by P23). The absolute virtue of the mind, then, is understanding. But the greatest thing the mind can understand is God (as we have already demonstrated). Therefore, the greatest virtue of the mind is to understand, *or* know, God, q.e.d.

P29: *Any singular thing whose nature is entirely different from ours can neither aid nor restrain our power of acting, and absolutely, no thing can be either good or evil for us, unless it has something in common with us.*

Dem.: The power of each singular thing, and consequently (by IIP10C), man's power, by which he exists and produces an effect, is not determined except by another singular thing (by IP28), whose nature must be understood (by IIP6) through the same attribute through which human nature is conceived. Our power of acting, therefore, however it is conceived, can be determined, and hence aided or restrained, by the power of another singular thing which has something in common with us, and not by the power of a thing whose nature is completely different from ours. II/229

And because we call good or evil what is the cause of joy or sadness (by P8), that is (by IIIP11S), what increases or diminishes, aids or restrains, our power of acting, a thing whose nature is completely different from ours can be neither good nor evil for us, q.e.d.

P30: *No thing can be evil through what it has in common with our nature; but insofar as it is evil for us, it is contrary to us.*

Dem.: We call evil what is the cause of sadness (by P8), that is (by the definition of sadness, see IIIP11S), what diminishes or restrains our power of acting. So if a thing were evil for us through what it has in common with us, then the thing could diminish or restrain what it has in common with us. But (by IIIP4) this is absurd. Therefore, no thing can be evil for us through what it has in common with us. On the contrary, insofar as it is evil, that is (as we have already shown), insofar as it can diminish or restrain our power of acting, it is contrary to us (by IIIP5), q.e.d.

P31: *Insofar as a thing agrees with our nature, it is necessarily good.*

Dem.: Insofar as a thing agrees with our nature, it cannot be evil (by P30). So it must either be good or indifferent. If the latter is posited, namely, that it is neither good nor evil, then (by A3) nothing will follow from its nature which aids the preservation of our nature, that is (by hypothesis), which aids the preservation of the nature of the thing itself. But this is absurd (by IIIP6). Hence, insofar as it agrees with our nature, it must be good, q.e.d.

II/230

Cor.: From this it follows that the more a thing agrees with our nature, the more useful, *or* better, it is for us, and conversely, the more a thing is useful to us, the more it agrees with our nature.

For insofar as it does not agree with our nature, it will necessarily be different from it or contrary to it. If it is different from it, then (by P29) it can be neither good nor evil. And if it is contrary, then it will also be contrary to that which agrees with our nature, that is (by P31), contrary to the good, *or* evil. Nothing, therefore, can be good except insofar as it agrees with our nature. So the more a thing agrees with our nature, the more useful it is, and conversely, q.e.d.

P32: *Insofar as men are subject to passions, they cannot be said to agree in nature.*

Dem.: Things which are said to agree in nature are understood to agree in power (by IIIP7), but not in lack of power, *or* negation, and consequently (see IIIP3S) not in passion either. So insofar as men are subject to passions, they cannot be said to agree in nature, q.e.d.

Schol.: This matter is also evident through itself. If someone says that black and white agree only in this, that neither is red, he affirms absolutely that black and white agree in nothing. Similarly, if someone says that a stone and a man agree only in this, that each is finite, lacks power, does not exist from the necessity of its nature, or, finally, is indefinitely surpassed by the power of external causes, he affirms completely that a stone and a man do not agree in anything. For things which agree only in a negation, *or* in what they do not have, really agree in nothing.

II/231

P33: *Men can disagree in nature insofar as they are torn by affects which are passions; and to that extent also one and the same man is changeable and inconstant.*

Dem.: The nature, *or* essence, of the affects cannot be explained through our essence, *or* nature, alone (by IIID1 and D2), but must be defined by the power, that is (by IIIP7), by the nature of external causes compared with our own. That is why there are as many species of each affect as there are species of objects by which we are affected (see IIIP56); that is why men are affected differently by one and the same object (see IIIP51), and to that extent, disagree in nature. And finally, that is also why one and the same man (again, by IIIP51) is affected differently toward the same object, and to that extent is changeable, and so on, q.e.d.

P34: *Insofar as men are torn by affects which are passions, they can be contrary to one another.*

Dem.: A man—Peter, say—can be a cause of Paul's being saddened, because he has something like a thing Paul hates (by IIIP16), or because Peter alone possesses something which Paul also loves (see IIIP32 and P32S), or on account of other causes (for the main causes, see IIIP55S). And so it will happen, as a result (by Def. Aff. VII), that Paul hates Peter. Hence, it will easily happen (by IIIP40 and P40S) that Peter hates Paul in return, and so (by IIIP39) that they strive to harm one another; that is (by P30), that they are contrary to one another. But an affect of sadness is always a passion (by IIIP59). Therefore, men, insofar as they are torn by affects which are passions, can be contrary to one another, q.e.d. II/232

Schol.: I have said that Paul hates Peter because he imagines that Peter possesses what Paul himself also loves. At first glance it seems to follow from this that these two are injurious to one another because they love the same thing, and hence, because they agree in nature. If this were true, then P30 and P31 would be false.

But if we are willing to examine the matter fairly, we shall see that all these propositions are completely consistent. For these two are not troublesome to one another insofar as they agree in nature, that is, insofar as each loves the same thing, but insofar as they disagree with one another. For insofar as each loves the same thing, each one's love is thereby encouraged (by IIIP31). That is (by Def. Aff. VI), each one's joy is thereby encouraged. So it is far from true that they are troublesome to one another insofar as they love the same thing and agree in nature.

Instead, as I have said, the cause of [their enmity] is nothing but the fact that (as we suppose) they disagree in nature. For we suppose that

Peter has the idea of a thing he loves which is already possessed, whereas Paul has the idea of a thing he loves which is lost. That is why the one is affected with joy and the other with sadness, and to that extent they are contrary to one another.

In this way we can easily show that the other causes of hate depend only on the fact that men disagree in nature, not on that in which they agree.

P35: *Only insofar as men live according to the guidance of reason, must they always agree in nature.*

Dem.: Insofar as men are torn by affects which are passions, they can be different in nature (by P33), and contrary to one another (by P34). But insofar as men live according to the guidance of reason, they are said only to act (by IIIP3). Hence, whatever follows from human nature, insofar as it is defined by reason, must be understood through human nature alone (by IIID2), as through its proximate cause. But because each one, from the laws of his own nature, wants what he judges to be good, and strives to avert what he judges to be evil (by P19), and moreover, because what we judge to be good or evil when we follow the dictate of reason must be good or evil (by IIP41), it follows that insofar as men live according to the guidance of reason, they must do only those things which are good for human nature, and hence, for each man, that is (by P31C), those things which agree with the nature of each man. Hence, insofar as men live according to the guidance of reason, they must always agree among themselves, q.e.d.

Cor. 1: There is no singular thing in Nature which is more useful to man than a man who lives according to the guidance of reason.

For what is most useful to man is what most agrees with his nature (by P31C), that is (as is known through itself), man. But a man acts entirely from the laws of his own nature when he lives according to the guidance of reason (by IIID2), and only to that extent must he always agree with the nature of the other man (by P35). Therefore, among singular things there is nothing more useful to man than a man, and so on, q.e.d.

Cor. 2.: When each man most seeks his own advantage for himself, then men are most useful to one another.

For the more each one seeks his own advantage, and strives to preserve himself, the more he is endowed with virtue (by P20), *or* what is the same (by D8), the greater is his power of acting according to the laws of his own nature, that is (by IIIP3), of living from the guidance of reason. But men most agree in nature, when they live according to the guidance of reason (by P35). Therefore (by P35C1), men will be most useful to one another, when each one most seeks his own advantage, q.e.d.

Schol.: What we have just shown is also confirmed by daily experi- II/234
ence, which provides so much and such clear evidence that this saying is in almost everyone's mouth: man is a God to man.

Still, it rarely happens that men live according to the guidance of reason. Instead, their lives are so constituted that they are usually envious and burdensome to one another. They can hardly, however, live a solitary life; hence, that definition which makes man a social animal has been quite pleasing to most. And surely we do derive, from the society of our fellow men, many more advantages than disadvantages.

So let the satirists laugh as much as they like at human affairs, let the theologians curse them, let melancholics praise as much as they can a life that is uncultivated and wild, let them disdain men and admire the lower animals. Men still find from experience that by helping one another they can provide themselves much more easily with the things they require, and that only by joining forces can they avoid the dangers which threaten on all sides—not to mention that it is much preferable and more worthy of our knowledge to consider the deeds of men, rather than those of the lower animals. But I shall treat this topic more fully elsewhere.

P36: *The greatest good of those who seek virtue is common to all, and can be enjoyed by all equally.*

Dem.: To act from virtue is to act according to the guidance of reason (by P24), and whatever we strive for from reason is understanding (by P26). Hence (by P28), the greatest good of those who seek virtue is to know God, that is (by IIP47 and·P47S), a good that is common to all men, and can be possessed equally by all men insofar as they are of the same nature, q.e.d.

Schol.: But suppose someone should ask: what if the greatest good of those who seek virtue were not common to all? Would it not follow II/235
from that, as above (see P34), that men who live according to the guidance of reason, that is (by P35), men, insofar as they agree in nature, would be contrary to one another?

To this the answer is that it is not by accident that man's greatest good is common to all; rather, it arises from the very nature of reason, because it is deduced from the very essence of man, insofar as [that essence] is defined by reason, and because man could neither be nor be conceived if he did not have the power to enjoy this greatest good. For it pertains to the essence of the human mind (by IIP47) to have an adequate knowledge of God's eternal and infinite essence.

P37: *The good which everyone who seeks virtue wants for himself, he also desires for other men; and this desire is greater as his knowledge of God is greater.*

Dem.: Insofar as men live according to the guidance of reason, they are most useful to man (by P35C1); hence (by P19), according to the guidance of reason, we necessarily strive to bring it about that men live according to the guidance of reason. Now, the good which everyone who lives according to the dictate of reason (i.e., by P24, who seeks virtue) wants for himself is understanding (by P26). Therefore, the good which everyone who seeks virtue wants for himself, he also desires for other men.

Next, desire, insofar as it is related to the mind, is the very essence of the mind (by Def. Aff. I). Now the essence of the mind consists in knowledge (by IIP11), which involves knowledge of God (by IIP47). Without this [knowledge the mind] can neither be nor be conceived (by IP15). Hence, as the mind's essence involves a greater knowledge of God, so will the desire also be greater by which one who seeks virtue desires for another the good he wants for himself, q.e.d.

II/236 Alternative Dem.: The good which man wants for himself and loves, he will love more constantly if he sees that others love it (by IIIP31). So (by IIIP31C), he will strive to have the others love the same thing. And because this good is common to all (by P36), and all can enjoy it, he will therefore (by the same reason) strive that all may enjoy it. And this striving will be the greater, the more he enjoys this good (by IIIP37), q.e.d.

Schol. 1: He who strives, only because of an affect, that others should love what he loves, and live according to his temperament, acts only from impulse and is hateful—especially to those to whom other things are pleasing, and who also, therefore, strive eagerly, from the same impulse, to have other men live according to their own temperament. And since the greatest good men seek from an affect is often such that only one can possess it fully, those who love are not of one mind in their love—while they rejoice to sing the praises of the thing they love, they fear to be believed. But he who strives from reason to guide others acts not by impulse, but kindly, generously, and with the greatest steadfastness of mind.

Again, whatever we desire and do of which we are the cause insofar as we have the idea of God, *or* insofar as we know God, I relate to religion. The desire to do good generated in us by our living according to the guidance of reason, I call morality. The desire by which a man who lives according to the guidance of reason is bound to join others to himself in friendship, I call being honorable, and I call that honorable which men who live according to the guidance of reason praise; on the other hand, what is contrary to the formation of friendship, I call dishonorable.

In addition to this, I have also shown what the foundations of the state are.

Furthermore, from what has been said above, one can easily perceive the difference between true virtue and lack of power; true virtue is nothing but living according to the guidance of reason, and so lack of power consists only in this, that a man allows himself to be guided by things outside him, and to be determined by them to do what the common constitution of external things demands, not what his own nature, considered in itself, demands.

These are the things I promised, in P18S, to demonstrate. From them it is clear that the law against killing animals is based more on empty superstition and unmanly compassion than sound reason. The II/237 rational principle of seeking our own advantage teaches us to establish a bond with men, but not with the lower animals, or with things whose nature is different from human nature. We have the same right against them that they have against us. Indeed, because the right of each one is defined by his virtue, *or* power, men have a far greater right against the lower animals than they have against men. Not that I deny that the lower animals have sensations. But I do deny that we are therefore not permitted to consider our own advantage, use them at our pleasure, and treat them as is most convenient for us. For they do not agree in nature with us, and their affects are different in nature from human affects (see IIIP57S).

It remains now for me to explain what is just and what unjust, what sin is, and finally, what merit is. These matters will be taken up in the following scholium.

Schol. 2: In the Appendix of Part I, I promised to explain what praise and blame, merit and sin, and justice and injustice are. As far as praise and blame are concerned, I have explained them in IIIP29S. This will be the place to speak of the others. But first a few words must be said about man's natural state and his civil state.

Everyone exists by the highest right of Nature, and consequently everyone, by the highest right of Nature, does those things which follow from the necessity of his own nature. So everyone, by the highest right of Nature, judges what is good and what is evil, considers his own advantage according to his own temperament (see P19 and P20), avenges himself (see IIIP40C2), and strives to preserve what he loves and destroy what he hates (see IIIP28).

If men lived according to the guidance of reason, everyone would possess this right of his (by P35C1) without any injury to anyone else.

But because they are subject to the affects (by P4C), which far surpass man's power, *or* virtue (by P6), they are often drawn in different directions (by P33) and are contrary to one another (by P34), while they require one another's aid (by P35S).

In order, therefore, that men may be able to live harmoniously and be of assistance to one another, it is necessary for them to give up their natural right and to make one another confident that they will do nothing which could harm others. How it can happen that men who are necessarily subject to affects (by P4C), inconstant and changeable (by P33) should be able to make one another confident and have trust in one another, is clear from P7 and IIIP39. No affect can be restrained except by an affect stronger than and contrary to the affect to be restrained, and everyone refrains from doing harm out of timidity regarding a greater harm.

II/238

By this law, therefore, society can be maintained, provided it appropriates to itself the right everyone has of avenging himself, and of judging concerning good and evil. In this way society has the power to prescribe a common rule of life, to make laws, and to maintain them—not by reason, which cannot restrain the affects (by P17S), but by threats. This society, maintained by laws and the power it has of preserving itself, is called a state, and those who are defended by its law, citizens.

From this we easily understand that there is nothing in the state of nature which, by the agreement of all, is good or evil; for everyone who is in the state of nature considers only his own advantage, and decides what is good and what is evil from his own temperament, and only insofar as he takes account of his own advantage. He is not bound by any law to submit to anyone except himself. So in the state of nature no sin can be conceived.

But in the civil state, of course, it is decided by common agreement what is good or what is evil. And everyone is bound to submit to the state. Sin, therefore, is nothing but disobedience, which for that reason can be punished only by the law of the state. On the other hand, obedience is considered a merit in a citizen, because on that account he is judged worthy of enjoying the advantages of the state.

Again, in the state of nature there is no one who by common consent is Master of anything, nor is there anything in Nature which can be said to be this man's and not that man's. Instead, all things belong to all. So in the state of nature, there cannot be conceived any will to give to each his own, or to take away from someone what is his. That is, in the state of nature nothing is done which can be called just or unjust.

But in the civil state, of course, where it is decided by common consent what belongs to this man, and what to that [, things are done which can be called just or unjust]. II/239

From this it is clear that just and unjust, sin and merit, are extrinsic notions, not attributes which explain the nature of the mind. But enough of this.

P38: *Whatever so disposes the human body that it can be affected in a great many ways, or renders it capable of affecting external bodies in a great many ways, is useful to man; the more it renders the body capable of being affected in a great many ways, or of affecting other bodies, the more useful it is; on the other hand, what renders the body less capable of these things is harmful.*

Dem.: The more the body is rendered capable of these things, the more the mind is rendered capable of perceiving (by IIP14). And so what disposes the body in this way, and renders it capable of these things, is necessarily good, *or* useful (by P26 and P27), and the more useful the more capable of these things it renders the body. On the other hand (by the converse of IIP14, and by P26 and P27), it is harmful if it renders the body less capable of these things, q.e.d.

P39: *Those things are good which bring about the preservation of the proportion of motion and rest the human body's parts have to one another; on the other hand, those things are evil which bring it about that the parts of the human body have a different proportion of motion and rest to one another.*

Dem.: To be preserved, the human body requires a great many other bodies (by IIPost. 4). But what constitutes the form of the human body consists in this, that its parts communicate their motions to one another in a certain fixed proportion (by the definition [at II/99–100]). Therefore, things which bring it about that the parts of the human body preserve the same proportion of motion and rest to one another, preserve II/240
the human body's form. Hence, they bring it about that the human body can be affected in many ways, and that it can affect external bodies in many ways (by IIPost. 3 and Post. 6). So they are good (by P38).

Next, things which bring it about that the human body's parts acquire a different proportion of motion and rest to one another bring it about (by the same definition [at II/99–100]) that the human body takes on another form, that is (as is known through itself, and as I pointed out at the end of the preface of this part), that the human body is destroyed, and hence rendered completely incapable of being affected in many ways. So (by P38), they are evil, q.e.d.

Schol.: In Part V I shall explain how much these things can be harmful to or beneficial to the mind. But here it should be noted that I understand the body to die when its parts are so disposed that they acquire a different proportion of motion and rest to one another. For I dare not deny that—even though the circulation of the blood is maintained, as well as the other [signs] on account of which the body is thought to be alive—the human body can nevertheless be changed into another nature entirely different from its own. For no reason compels me to maintain that the body does not die unless it is changed into a corpse.

And, indeed, experience seems to urge a different conclusion. Sometimes a man undergoes such changes that I should hardly have said he was the same man. I have heard stories, for example, of a spanish poet who suffered an illness; though he recovered, he was left so oblivious to his past life that he did not believe the tales and tragedies he had written were his own. He could surely have been taken for a grown-up infant if he had also forgotten his native language.

If this seems incredible, what shall we say of infants? A man of advanced years believes their nature to be so different from his own that he could not be persuaded that he was ever an infant, if he did not make this conjecture concerning himself from [NS: the example of] others. But rather than provide the superstitious with material for raising new questions, I prefer to leave this discussion unfinished.

II/241   P40: *Things which are of assistance to the common society of men, or which bring it about that men live harmoniously, are useful; those, on the other hand, are evil which bring discord to the state.*

Dem.: For things which bring it about that men live harmoniously, at the same time bring it about that they live according to the guidance of reason (by P35). And so (by P26 and P27) they are good.

And on the other hand (by the same reasoning), those are evil which arouse discord, q.e.d.

P41: *Joy is not directly evil, but good; sadness, on the other hand, is directly evil.*

Dem.: Joy (by IIIP11 and P11S) is an affect by which the body's power of acting is increased or aided. Sadness, on the other hand, is an affect by which the body's power of acting is diminished or restrained. And so (by P38) joy is directly good, and so on, q.e.d.

P42: *Cheerfulness cannot be excessive, but is always good; melancholy, on the other hand, is always evil.*

Dem.: Cheerfulness (see its Def. in IIIP11S) is a joy which, insofar as it is related to the body, consists in this, that all parts of the body are equally affected. That is (by IIIP11), the body's power of acting is increased or aided, so that all of its parts maintain the same proportion of motion and rest to one another. And so (by P39), cheerfulness is always good, and cannot be excessive.

But melancholy (see its Def., also in IIIP11S) is a sadness, which, insofar as it is related to the body, consists in this, that the body's power of acting is absolutely diminished or restrained. And so (by P38) it is always evil, q.e.d.

P43: *Pleasure can be excessive and evil, whereas pain can be good insofar as the pleasure, or joy, is evil.*

Dem.: Pleasure is a joy which, insofar as it is related to the body, consists in this, that one (or several) of its parts are affected more than the others (see its Def. in IIIP11S). The power of this affect can be so great that it surpasses the other actions of the body (by P6), remains stubbornly fixed in the body, and so prevents the body from being capable of being affected in a great many other ways. Hence (by P38), it can be evil.

Pain, on the other hand, which is a sadness, cannot be good, considered in itself alone (by P41). But because its force and growth are defined by the power of an external cause compared with our power (by P5), we can conceive infinite degrees and modes of the powers of this affect (by P3). And so we can conceive it to be such that it can restrain pleasure, so that it is not excessive, and thereby prevent the body from being rendered less capable (by the first part of this proposition). To that extent, therefore, it will be good, q.e.d.

P44: *Love and desire can be excessive.*

Dem.: Love is joy, accompanied by the idea of an external cause (by Def. Aff. VI). Pleasure, therefore (by IIIP11S), accompanied by the idea of an external cause, is love. And so, love (by P43) can be excessive.

Again, desire is greater as the affect from which it arises is greater (by IIIP37). Hence, as an affect (by P6) can surpass the rest of man's actions, so also the desire which arises from that affect can surpass the rest of his desires. It can therefore be excessive in the same way we have shown pleasure can be (in P43), q.e.d.

Schol.: Cheerfulness, which I have said is good, is more easily conceived than observed. For the affects by which we are daily torn are generally related to a part of the body which is affected more than the others. Generally, then, the affects are excessive, and occupy the mind in the consideration of only one object so much that it cannot think of others. And though men are liable to a great many affects, so that one rarely finds them to be always agitated by one and the same affect, still there are those in whom one affect is stubbornly fixed. For we sometimes see that men are so affected by one object that, although it is not present, they still believe they have it with them.

When this happens to a man who is not asleep, we say that he is mad or insane. Nor are they thought to be less mad who burn with love, and dream, both night and day, only of a lover or a courtesan. For they usually provoke laughter. But when a greedy man thinks of nothing else but profit, or money, and an ambitious man of esteem, they are not thought to be mad, because they are usually troublesome and are considered worthy of hate. But greed, ambition, and lust really are species of madness, even though they are not numbered among the diseases.

P45: *Hate can never be good.*

Dem.: We strive to destroy the man we hate (by IIIP39), that is (by P37), we strive for something which is evil. Therefore, and so on, q.e.d.

II/244   Schol.: Note that here and in what follows I understand by hate only hate toward men.

Cor. 1: Envy, mockery, disdain, anger, vengeance, and the rest of the affects which are related to hate or arise from it, are evil. This too is evident from P37 and IIIP39.

Cor. 2: Whatever we want because we have been affected with hate is dishonorable; and [if we live] in a state, it is unjust. This too is evident from IIIP39, and from the definitions of dishonorable and unjust (see P37S).

Schol.: I recognize a great difference between mockery (which, in Cor. 1, I said was evil) and laughter. For laughter and joking are pure joy. And so, provided they are not excessive, they are good through themselves (by P41). Nothing forbids our pleasure except a savage and sad superstition. For why is it more proper to relieve our hunger and thirst than to rid ourselves of melancholy?

My account of the matter, the view I have arrived at, is this: no deity, nor anyone else, unless he is envious, takes pleasure in my lack of power and my misfortune; nor does he ascribe to virtue our tears, sighs, fear, and other things of that kind, which are signs of a weak mind. On the contrary, the greater the joy with which we are affected, the greater the perfection to which we pass, that is, the more we must participate in the divine nature. To use things, therefore, and take pleasure in them as far as possible—not, of course, to the point where we are disgusted with them, for there is no pleasure in that—this is the part of a wise man.

It is the part of a wise man, I say, to refresh and restore himself in moderation with pleasant food and drink, with scents, with the beauty of green plants, with decoration, music, sports, the theater, and other things of this kind, which anyone can use without injury to another. For the human body is composed of a great many parts of different natures, which constantly require new and varied nourishment, so that the whole body may be equally capable of all the things which can follow from its nature, and hence, so that the mind also may be equally capable of understanding many things at once. II/245

This plan of living, then, agrees best both with our principles and with common practice. So, if any other way of living [is to be commended], this one is best, and to be commended in every way. Nor is it necessary for me to treat these matters more clearly or more fully.

P46: *He who lives according to the guidance of reason strives, as far as he can, to repay the other's hate, anger, and disdain toward him, with love, or nobility.*

Dem.: All affects of hate are evil (by P45C1). So he who lives according to the guidance of reason will strive, as far as he can, to bring it about that he is not troubled with affects of hate (by P19), and consequently (by P37), will strive that the other also should not undergo those affects. Now hate is increased by being returned, and on the other hand, can be destroyed by love (by IIIP43), so that the hate passes into love (by IIIP44). Therefore, one who lives according to the guidance of reason will strive to repay the other's hate, and so on, with love, and so on, with nobility (see its Def. in IIIP59S), q.e.d.

Schol.: He who wishes to avenge wrongs by hating in return surely lives miserably. On the other hand, one who is eager to overcome hate by love, strives joyously and confidently, resists many men as easily as one, and requires the least help from fortune. Those whom he conquers yield joyously, not from a lack of strength, but from an increase in their powers. All these things follow so clearly simply from the definitions of love and of intellect, that there is no need to demonstrate them separately.

P47: *Affects of hope and fear cannot be good of themselves.*

Dem.: There are no affects of hope or fear without sadness. For fear II/246
is a sadness (by Def. Aff. XIII), and there is no hope without fear (see the explanation following Def. Aff. XII and XIII). Therefore (by P41) these affects cannot be good of themselves, but only insofar as they can restrain an excess of joy (by P43), q.e.d.

Schol.: We may add to this that these affects show a defect of knowledge and a lack of power in the mind. For this reason also confidence and despair, gladness and remorse are signs of a mind lacking in power. For though confidence and gladness are affects of joy, they still presuppose that a sadness has preceded them, namely, hope and fear. Therefore, the more we strive to live according to the guidance of reason, the more we strive to depend less on hope, to free ourselves from fear, to conquer fortune as much as we can, and to direct our actions by the certain counsel of reason.

P48: *Affects of overestimation and scorn are always evil.*

Dem.: These affects are contrary to reason (by Def. Aff. XXI and XXII). So (by P26 and P27) they are evil, q.e.d.

P49: *Overestimation easily makes the man who is overestimated proud.*

Dem.: If we see that someone, out of love, thinks more highly of us than is just, we shall easily exult at being esteemed (by IIIP41S), *or* be affected with joy (by Def. Aff. XXX), and we shall easily believe the good we hear predicated of us (by IIIP25). And so, out of love of ourselves, we shall think more highly of ourselves than is just, that is (by Def. Aff. XXVIII), we shall easily become proud, q.e.d.

II/247 P50: *Pity, in a man who lives according to the guidance of reason, is evil of itself and useless.*

Dem.: For pity (by Def. Aff. XVIII) is a sadness, and therefore (by P41), of itself, evil.

Moreover, the good which follows from it, namely, that we strive to free the man we pity from his suffering (by IIIP27C3), we desire to do from the dictate of reason alone (by P37), and we can only do from the dictate of reason alone something which we know certainly to be good (by P27).

Hence, pity, in a man who lives according to the guidance of reason, is both evil of itself and useless, q.e.d.

Cor.: From this it follows that a man who lives according to the dictate of reason, strives, as far as he can, not to be touched by pity.

Schol.: He who rightly knows that all things follow from the necessity of the divine nature, and happen according to the eternal laws and rules of Nature, will surely find nothing worthy of hate, mockery, or disdain, nor anyone whom he will pity. Instead he will strive, as far as human virtue allows, to act well, as they say, and rejoice.

To this we may add that he who is easily touched by the affect of pity, and moved by another's suffering or tears, often does something he later repents—both because, from an affect, we do nothing which we certainly know to be good, and because we are easily deceived by false tears.

Here I am speaking expressly of a man who lives according to the guidance of reason. For one who is moved to aid others neither by reason nor by pity is rightly called inhuman. For (by IIIP27) he seems to be unlike a man.

P51: *Favor is not contrary to reason, but can agree with it and arise from it.*   II/248

Dem.: For favor is a love toward him who has benefited another (by Def. Aff. XIX), and so can be related to the mind insofar as it is said to act (by IIIP59), that is (by IIIP3), insofar as it understands. Therefore, it agrees with reason, and so on, q.e.d.

Alternate Dem.: He who lives according to the guidance of reason, desires for the other, too, the good he wants for himself (by P37). So because he sees someone benefiting another, his own striving to do good is aided, that is (by IIIP11S), he will rejoice. And this joy (by hypothesis) will be accompanied by the idea of him who has benefited another. He will, therefore (by Def. Aff. XIX), favor him, q.e.d.

Schol.: Indignation, as we define it (see Def. Aff. XX), is necessarily evil (by P45). But it should be noted that when the supreme power, bound by its desire to preserve peace, punishes a citizen who has wronged another, I do not say that it is indignant toward the citizen. For it punishes him, not because it has been aroused by hate to destroy him, but because it is moved by duty.

P52: *Self-esteem can arise from reason, and only that self-esteem which does arise from reason is the greatest there can be.*

Dem.: Self-esteem is a joy born of the fact that man considers himself and his power of acting (by Def. Aff. XXV). But man's true power of acting, *or* virtue, is reason itself (by IIIP3), which man considers clearly and distinctly (by IIP40 and P43). Therefore, self-esteem arises from   II/249
reason.

Next, while a man considers himself, he perceives nothing clearly and distinctly, *or* adequately, except those things which follow from his power of acting (by IIID2), that is (by IIIP3), which follow from his power of understanding. And so the greatest self-esteem there can be arises only from this reflection, q.e.d.

Schol.: Self-esteem is really the highest thing we can hope for. For (as we have shown in P25) no one strives to preserve his being for the sake of any end. And because this self-esteem is more and more encouraged and strengthened by praise (by IIIP53C), and on the other hand, more and more upset by blame (by IIIP55C), we are guided most by love of esteem and can hardly bear a life in disgrace.

P53: *Humility is not a virtue, or does not arise from reason.*

Dem.: Humility is a sadness which arises from the fact that a man considers his own lack of power (by Def. Aff. XXVI). Moreover, insofar as a man knows himself by true reason, it is supposed that he understands his own essence, that is (by IIIP7), his own power. So if a man, in considering himself, perceives some lack of power of his, this is not because he understands himself, but because his power of acting is restrained (as we have shown in IIIP55). But if we suppose that the man conceives his lack of power because he understands something more powerful than himself, by the knowledge of which he determines his power of acting, then we conceive nothing but that the man understands himself distinctly *or* (by P26) that his power of acting is aided. So humility, *or* the sadness which arises from the fact that a man reflects on his own lack of power, does not arise from a true reflection, *or* reason, and is a passion, not a virtue, q.e.d.

II/250   P54: *Repentance is not a virtue,* or *does not arise from reason; instead, he who repents what he has done is twice wretched,* or *lacking in power.*

Dem.: The first part of this is demonstrated as P53 was. The second is evident simply from the definition of this affect (see Def. Aff. XXVII). For first he suffers himself to be conquered by an evil desire, and then by sadness.

Schol.: Because men rarely live from the dictate of reason, these two affects, humility and repentance, and in addition, hope and fear, bring more advantage than disadvantage. So since men must sin, they ought rather to sin in that direction. If weak-minded men were all equally proud, ashamed of nothing, and afraid of nothing, how could they be united or restrained by any bonds?

The mob is terrifying, if unafraid. So it is no wonder that the prophets, who considered the common advantage, not that of the few, commended humility, repentance, and reverence so greatly. Really, those who are subject to these affects can be guided far more easily than others, so that in the end they may live from the guidance of reason, that is, may be free and enjoy the life of the blessed.

P55: *Either very great pride or very great despondency is very great ignorance of oneself.*

Dem.: This is evident from Defs. Aff. XXVIII and XXIX.

P56: *Either very great pride or very great despondency indicates very great weakness of mind.*

II/251   Dem.: The first foundation of virtue is preserving one's being (by P22C) and doing this from the guidance of reason (by P24). Therefore, he who is ignorant of himself is ignorant of the foundation of all the virtues, and consequently, ignorant of all the virtues. Next, acting from virtue is nothing but acting from the guidance of reason (by P24), and he who acts from the guidance of reason must know that he acts from the guidance of reason (by IIP43). Therefore, he who is ignorant of himself, and consequently (as we have just now shown) of all the virtues, does not act from virtue at all, that is (as is evident from D8), is extremely weak-minded. And so (by P55) either very great pride or very great despondency indicate very great weakness of mind, q.e.d.

Cor.: From this it follows very clearly that the proud and the despondent are highly liable to affects.

Schol.: Nevertheless, despondency can be corrected more easily than pride, since pride is an affect of joy, whereas despondency is an affect of sadness. And so (by P18), pride is stronger than despondency.

P57: *The proud man loves the presence of parasites, or flatterers, but hates the presence of the noble.*

Dem.: Pride is a joy born of the fact that man thinks more highly of himself than is just (see Defs. Aff. XXVIII and VI). The proud man will strive as far as he can to encourage this opinion (see IIIP13S). And so the proud will love the presence of parasites or flatterers (I have omitted the definitions of these because they are too well known) and will flee the presence of the noble, who think of them as is appropriate, q.e.d.

Schol.: It would take too long to enumerate all the evils of pride here, since the proud are subject to all the affects (though they are least subject to affects of love and compassion). But we ought not to pass over in silence here the fact that he also is called proud who thinks less highly of others than is just. So in this sense pride should be defined as a joy born of a man's false opinion that he is above others. And the despondency contrary to this pride would need to be defined as a sadness born of a man's false opinion that he is below others.

But this being posited, we easily conceive that the proud man must be envious (see IIIP55S) and hate those most who are most praised for their virtues, that his hatred of them is not easily conquered by love or benefits (see IIIP41S), and that he takes pleasure only in the presence of those who humor his weakness of mind and make a madman of a fool.

Although despondency is contrary to pride, the despondent man is still very near the proud one. For since his sadness arises from the fact that he judges his own lack of power from the power, *or* virtue, of others, his sadness will be relieved, that is, he will rejoice, if his imagination is occupied in considering the vices of others. Hence the proverb: *misery loves company*.

On the other hand, the more he believes himself to be below others, the more he will be saddened. That is why no one is more prone to envy than the despondent man is, and why they strive especially to observe men's deeds, more for the sake of finding fault than to improve them,

II/252

and why, finally, they praise only despondency, and exult over it—but in such a way that they still seem despondent.

These things follow from this affect as necessarily as it follows from the nature of a triangle that its three angles are equal to two right angles. I have already said that I call these, and like affects, evil insofar as I attend only to human advantage. But the laws of Nature concern the common order of Nature, of which man is a part. I wished to remind my readers of this here, in passing, in case anyone thought my purpose was only to tell about men's vices and their absurd deeds, and not to demonstrate the nature and properties of things. For as I said in the Preface of Part III, I consider men's affects and properties just like other natural things. And of course human affects, if they do not indicate man's power, at least indicate the power and skill of Nature, no less than many other things we wonder at and take pleasure in contemplating. But I continue to note, concerning the affects, those things which bring advantage to men, and those which bring them harm.

II/253

P58: *Love of esteem is not contrary to reason, but can arise from it.*

Dem.: This is evident from Def. Aff. XXX, and from the definition of what is honorable (see P37S1).

Schol.: The love of esteem which is called empty is a self-esteem that is encouraged only by the opinion of the multitude. When that ceases, the self-esteem ceases, that is (by P52S), the highest good that each one loves. That is why he who exults at being esteemed by the multitude is made anxious daily, strives, acts, and schemes, in order to preserve his reputation. For the multitude is fickle and inconstant; unless one's reputation is guarded, it is quickly destroyed. Indeed, because everyone desires to secure the applause of the multitude, each one willingly puts down the reputation of the other. And since the struggle is over a good thought to be the highest, this gives rise to a monstrous lust of each to crush the other in any way possible. The one who at last emerges as victor exults more in having harmed the other than in having benefited himself. This love of esteem, *or* self-esteem, then, is really empty, because it is nothing.

The things which must be noted about shame are easily inferred from what we said about compassion and repentance. I add only this, that like pity, shame, though not a virtue, is still good insofar as it indicates, in the man who blushes with shame, a desire to live honorably. In the same way pain is said to be good insofar as it indicates that the injured part is not yet decayed. So though a man who is ashamed of some deed is really sad, he is still more perfect than one who is shameless, who has no desire to live honorably.

II/254

These are the things I undertook to note concerning the affects of joy and sadness. As far as desires are concerned, they, of course, are good or evil insofar as they arise from good or evil affects. But all of them, really, insofar as they are generated in us from affects which are passions, are blind (as may easily be inferred from what we said in P44S), and would be of no use if men could easily be led to live according to the dictate of reason alone. I shall now show this concisely.

P59: *To every action to which we are determined from an affect which is a passion, we can be determined by reason, without that affect.*

Dem.: Acting from reason is nothing but doing those things which follow from the necessity of our nature, considered in itself alone (by IIIP3 and D2). But sadness is evil insofar as it decreases or restrains this power of acting (by P41). Therefore, from this affect we cannot be determined to any action which we could not do if we were led by reason.

Furthermore, joy is bad [only] insofar as it prevents man from being capable of acting (by P41 and P43), and so to that extent also, we cannot be determined to any action which we could not do if we were guided by reason.

Finally, insofar as joy is good, it agrees with reason (for it consists in this, that a man's power of acting is increased or aided), and is not a passion except insofar as the man's power of acting is not increased to the point where he conceives himself and his actions adequately. So if a man affected with joy were led to such a great perfection that he conceived himself and his actions adequately, he would be capable—indeed more capable—of the same actions to which he is now determined from affects which are passions.

But all affects are related to joy, sadness, or desire (see the explanation of Def. Aff. IV), and desire (by Def. Aff. I) is nothing but the striving to act itself. Therefore, to every action to which we are determined from an affect which is a passion, we can be led by reason alone, without the affect, q.e.d. II/255

Alternate Dem.: Any action is called evil insofar as it arises from the fact that we have been affected with hate or with some evil affect (see P45C1). But no action, considered in itself, is good or evil (as we have shown in the Preface of this Part); instead, one and the same action is now good, now evil. Therefore, to the same action which is now evil, *or* which arises from some evil affect, we can (by P19) be led by reason, q.e.d.

Schol.: These things are more clearly explained by an example. The act of beating, insofar as it is considered physically, and insofar as we attend only to the fact that the man raises his arm, closes his fist, and moves his whole arm forcefully up and down, is a virtue, which is conceived from the structure of the human body. Therefore, if a man moved by anger or hate is determined to close his fist or move his arm, that (as we have shown in Part II) happens because one and the same action can be joined to any images of things whatever. And so we can be determined to one and the same action both from those images of things which we conceive confusedly and [from those images of things?] we conceive clearly and distinctly.

It is evident, therefore, that every desire which arises from an affect which is a passion would be of no use if men could be guided by reason. Let us see now why we call a desire blind which arises from an affect which is a passion.

P60: *A desire arising from either a joy or a sadness related to one, or several, but not to all parts of the body, has no regard for the advantage of the whole man.*

II/256   Dem.: Suppose, for example, that part A of the body is so strengthened by the force of some external cause that it prevails over the others (by P6). This part will not, on that account, strive to lose its powers so that the other parts of the body may fulfill their function. For [if it did], it would have to have a force, *or* power, of losing its own powers, which (by IIIP6) is absurd. Therefore, that part will strive, and consequently (by IIIP7 and P12), the mind also will strive, to preserve that state. And so the desire which arises from such an affect of joy does not have regard to the whole.

If, on the other hand, it is supposed that part A is restrained so that the others prevail, it is demonstrated in the same way that the desire which arises from sadness also does not have regard to the whole, q.e.d.

Schol.: Therefore, since joy is generally (by P44S) related to one part of the body, for the most part we desire to preserve our being without regard to our health as a whole. To this we may add that the desires by which we are most bound (by P9C) have regard only to the present and not to the future.

P61: *A desire which arises from reason cannot be excessive.*

Dem.: Desire, considered absolutely, is the very essence of man (by Def. Aff. I), insofar as it is conceived to be determined in any way to doing something. And so a desire which arises from reason, that is (by IIIP3), which is generated in us insofar as we act is the very essence, *or* nature, of man, insofar as it is conceived to be determined to doing those things which are conceived adequately through man's essence alone (by IIID2). So if this desire could be excessive, then human nature, considered in itself alone, could exceed itself, *or* could do more than it can. This is a manifest contradiction. Therefore, this desire cannot be excessive, q.e.d.

P62: *Insofar as the mind conceives things from the dictate of reason, it is affected equally, whether the idea is of a future or past thing, or of a present one.* II/257

Dem.: Whatever the mind conceives under the guidance of reason, it conceives under the same species of eternity, *or* necessity (by IIP44C2) and is affected with the same certainty (by IIP43 and P43S). So whether the idea is of a future or a past thing, or of a present one, the mind conceives the thing with the same necessity and is affected with the same certainty. And whether the idea is of a future or a past thing or of a present one, it will nevertheless be equally true (by IIP41), that is (by IID4), it will nevertheless always have the same properties of an adequate idea. And so, insofar as the mind conceives things from the dictate of reason, it is affected in the same way, whether the idea is of a future or a past thing, or of a present one, q.e.d.

Schol.: If we could have adequate knowledge of the duration of things, and determine by reason their times of existing, we would regard future things with the same affect as present ones, and the mind would want the good it conceived as future just as it wants the good it conceives as present. Hence, it would necessarily neglect a lesser present good for a greater future one, and what would be good in the present, but the cause of some future ill, it would not want at all, as we shall soon demonstrate.

But we can have only a quite inadequate knowledge of the duration of things (by IIP31), and we determine their times of existing only by the imagination (by IIP44S), which is not equally affected by the image of a present thing and the image of a future one. That is why the true knowledge we have of good and evil is only abstract, *or* universal, and the judgment we make concerning the order of things and the connection of causes, so that we may be able to determine what in the present is good or evil for us, is imaginary, rather than real. And so it is no wonder if the desire which arises from a knowledge of good and evil, insofar as this looks to the future, can be rather easily restrained by a desire for the pleasures of the moment. On this, see P16. II/258

P63: *He who is guided by fear, and does good to avoid evil, is not guided by reason.*

Dem.: The only affects which are related to the mind insofar as it acts, that is (by IIIP3), which are related to reason, are affects of joy and desire (by IIIP59). And so (by Def. Aff. XIII) one who is guided by fear, and does good from timidity regarding an evil, is not guided by reason, q.e.d.

Schol.: The superstitious know how to reproach people for their vices better than they know how to teach them virtues, and they strive, not to guide men by reason, but to restrain them by fear, so that they flee the evil rather than love virtues. Such people aim only to make others as wretched as they themselves are, so it is no wonder that they are generally burdensome and hateful to men.

Cor.: By a desire arising from reason, we directly follow the good, and indirectly flee the evil.

Dem.: For a desire which arises from reason can arise solely from an affect of joy which is not a passion (by IIIP59), that is, from a joy which cannot be excessive (by P61). But it cannot arise from sadness, and therefore this desire (by P8) arises from knowledge of the good, not knowledge of the evil. And so from the guidance of reason we want the good directly, and to that extent only, we flee the evil, q.e.d.

Schol.: This corollary may be illustrated by the example of the sick and the healthy. The sick man, from timidity regarding death, eats what he is repelled by, whereas the healthy man enjoys his food, and in this way enjoys life better than if he feared death, and directly desired to avoid it. Similarly, a judge who condemns a guilty man to death—not from hate or anger, and the like, but only from a love of the general welfare—is guided only by reason.

P64: *Knowledge of evil is an inadequate knowledge.*

Dem.: Knowledge of evil (by P8) is sadness itself, insofar as we are conscious of it. But sadness is a passage to a lesser perfection (by Def. Aff. III), which therefore cannot be understood through man's essence itself (by IIIP6 and P7). Hence (by IIID2), it is a passion, which (by IIIP3) depends on inadequate ideas. Therefore (by IIP29), knowledge of this, namely, knowledge of evil, is inadequate, q.e.d.

Cor.: From this it follows that if the human mind had only adequate ideas, it would form no notion of evil.

P65: *From the guidance of reason, we shall follow the greater of two goods or the lesser of two evils.*

Dem.: A good which prevents us from enjoying a greater good is really an evil. For good and evil (as we have shown in the Preface of this Part) are said of things insofar as we compare them to one another. By the same reasoning, a lesser evil is really a good, so (by P63C) from the guidance of reason we want, *or* follow, only the greater good and the lesser evil, q.e.d.

Cor.: From the guidance of reason, we shall follow a lesser evil as a greater good, and pass over a lesser good which is the cause of a greater evil. For the evil which is here called lesser is really good, and the good which is here called lesser, on the other hand, is evil. So (by P63C) we want the [lesser evil] and pass over the [lesser good], q.e.d.

II/260

P66: *From the guidance of reason we want a greater future good in preference to a lesser present one, and a lesser present evil in preference to a greater future one.*

Dem.: If the mind could have an adequate knowledge of a future thing, it would be affected toward it with the same affect as it is toward a present one (by P62). So insofar as we attend to reason itself, as in this proposition we suppose ourselves to do, the thing will be the same, whether the greater good or evil is supposed to be future or present. And therefore (by P65), we want the greater future good in preference to the lesser present one, and so on, q.e.d.

Cor.: From the guidance of reason, we shall want a lesser present evil which is the cause of a greater future good, and pass over a lesser present good which is the cause of a greater future evil. This corollary stands to P66 as P65C does to P65.

Schol.: If these things are compared with those we have shown in this Part up to P18, concerning the powers of the affects, we shall easily see what the difference is between a man who is led only by an affect, *or* by opinion, and one who is led by reason. For the former, whether he will or not, does those things he is most ignorant of, whereas the latter complies with no one's wishes but his own, and does only those things he knows to be the most important in life, and therefore desires very greatly. Hence, I call the former a slave, but the latter, a free man.

I wish now to note a few more things concerning the free man's temperament and manner of living.

P67: *A free man thinks of nothing less than of death, and his wisdom is a meditation on life, not on death.*

II/261

Dem.: A free man, that is, one who lives according to the dictate of reason alone, is not led by fear (by P63), but desires the good directly (by P63C), that is (by P24), acts, lives, and preserves his being from the foundation of seeking his own advantage. And so he thinks of nothing less than of death. Instead his wisdom is a meditation on life, q.e.d.

P68: *If men were born free, they would form no concept of good and evil so long as they remained free.*

Dem.: I call him free who is led by reason alone. Therefore, he who is born free, and remains free, has only adequate ideas, and so has no concept of evil (by P64C). And since good and evil are correlates, he also has no concept of good, q.e.d.

Schol.: It is evident from P4 that the hypothesis of this proposition is false, and cannot be conceived unless we attend only to human nature, *or* rather to God, not insofar as he is infinite, but insofar only as he is the cause of man's existence.

This and the other things I have now demonstrated seem to have been indicated by Moses in that story of the first man. For in it the only power of God conceived is that by which he created man, that is, the power by which he consulted only man's advantage. And so we are told that God prohibited a free man from eating of the tree of knowledge of good and evil, and that as soon as he should eat of it, he would immediately fear death, rather than desiring to live; and then, that, the man having found a wife who agreed completely with his nature, he knew that there could be nothing in Nature more useful to him than she was; but that after he believed the lower animals to be like himself, he immediately began to imitate their affects (see IIIP27) and to lose his freedom; and that afterwards this freedom was recovered by the patriarchs, guided by the Spirit of Christ, that is, by the idea of God, on which alone it depends that man should be free, and desire for other men the good he desires for himself (as we have demonstrated above, by P37).

P69: *The virtue of a free man is seen to be as great in avoiding dangers as in overcoming them.*

Dem.: An affect can be neither restrained nor removed except by an affect contrary to and stronger than the affect to be restrained (by P7). But blind daring and fear are affects which can be conceived to be equally great (by P3 and P5). Therefore, an equally great virtue of the mind, *or* strength of character (for the definition of this, see IIIP59S) is required to restrain daring as to restrain fear, that is (by Defs. Aff. XL and XLI), a free man avoids dangers by the same virtue of the mind by which he tries to overcome them, q.e.d.

Cor.: In a free man, a timely flight is considered to show as much tenacity as fighting; or a free man chooses flight with the same tenacity, *or* presence of mind, as he chooses a contest.

Schol.: I have explained in IIIP59S what tenacity is, or what I understand by it. And by danger I understand whatever can be the cause of some evil, such as sadness, hate, discord, and the like.

P70: *A free man who lives among the ignorant strives, as far as he can, to avoid their favors.*

Dem.: Everyone judges according to his own temperament what is good (see IIIP39). Someone who is ignorant, therefore, and who has

II/262

II/263

conferred a favor on someone else, will value it according to his own temperament, and will be saddened if he sees it valued less by him to whom it was given (by IIIP42). But a free man strives to join other men to him in friendship (by P37), not to repay men with benefits which are equivalent in their eyes, but to lead himself and the others by the free judgment of reason, and to do only those things which he himself knows to be most excellent. Therefore, a free man will strive, as far as he can, to avoid the favors of the ignorant, so as not to be hated by them, and at the same time to yield only to reason, not to their appetite, q.e.d.

Schol.: I say *as far as he can*. For though men may be ignorant, they are still men, who in situations of need can bring human aid. And there is no better aid than that. So it often happens that it is necessary to accept favors from them, and hence to return thanks to them according to their temperament [i.e., in a way they will appreciate].

To this we may add that we must be careful in declining favors, so that we do not seem to disdain them, or out of greed to be afraid of repayment. For in that way, in the very act of avoiding their hate, we would incur it. So in declining favors we must take account both of what is useful and of what is honorable.

P71: *Only free men are very thankful to one another.*

Dem.: Only free men are very useful to one another, are joined to one another by the closest bond of friendship (by P35 and P35C1), and strive to benefit one another with equal eagerness for love (by P37). So (by Def. Aff. XXXIV) only free men are very thankful to one another, q.e.d.

Schol.: The thankfulness which men are led by blind desire to display toward one another is for the most part a business transaction *or* an entrapment, rather than thankfulness.

II/264

Again, ingratitude is not an affect. Nevertheless, ingratitude is dishonorable because it generally indicates that the man is affected with too much hate, anger, pride, greed, and so on. For one who, out of foolishness, does not know how to reckon one gift against another, is not ungrateful; much less one who is not moved by the gifts of a courtesan to assist her lust, nor by those of a thief to conceal his thefts, nor by those of anyone else like that. On the contrary, he shows firmness of mind who does not allow any gifts to corrupt him, to his or to the general ruin.

P72: *A free man always acts honestly, not deceptively.*

Dem.: If a free man, insofar as he is free, did anything by deception, he would do it from the dictate of reason (for so far only do we call him free). And so it would be a virtue to act deceptively (by P24), and hence (by the same Prop.), everyone would be better advised to act deceptively to preserve his being. That is (as is known through itself), men would be better advised to agree only in words, and be contrary to one another in fact. But this is absurd (by P31C). Therefore, a free man and so on, q.e.d.

Schol.: Suppose someone now asks: What if a man could save himself from the present danger of death by treachery? Would not the principle of preserving his own being recommend, without qualification, that he be treacherous?

The reply to this is the same. If reason should recommend that, it would recommend it to all men. And so reason would recommend, without qualification, that men should make agreements to join forces and to have common laws only by deception—that is, that really they should have no common laws. This is absurd.

P73: *A man who is guided by reason is more free in a state, where he lives according to a common decision, than in solitude, where he obeys only himself.*

Dem.: A man who is guided by reason is not led to obey by fear (by P63), but insofar as he strives to preserve his being from the dictate of reason, that is (by P66S), insofar as he strives to live freely, desires to maintain the principle of common life and common advantage (by P37). Consequently (as we have shown in P37S2), he desires to live according to the common decision of the state. Therefore, a man who is guided by reason desires, in order to live more freely, to keep the common laws of the state, q.e.d.

Schol.: These and similar things which we have shown concerning the true freedom of man are related to strength of character, that is (by IIIP59S), to tenacity and nobility. I do not consider it worthwhile to demonstrate separately here all the properties of strength of character, much less that a man strong in character hates no one, is angry with no one, envies no one, is indignant with no one, scorns no one, and is not at all proud. For these and all things which relate to true life and religion are easily proven from P37 and P46, namely, that hate is to be conquered by returning love, and that everyone who is led by reason desires for others also the good he wants for himself.

To this we may add what we have noted in P50S and in other places: a man strong in character considers this most of all, that all things follow from the necessity of the divine nature, and hence, that whatever he thinks is troublesome and evil, and moreover, whatever seems immoral, dreadful, unjust, and dishonorable, arises from the fact that he conceives the things themselves in a way which is disordered, mutilated, and confused. For this reason, he strives most of all to conceive things as they are in themselves, and to remove the obstacles to true knowledge, like hate, anger, envy, mockery, pride, and the rest of the things we have noted in the preceding pages.

And so, as we have said [II/47/21], he strives, as far as he can, to act well and rejoice. In the following part, I shall demonstrate how far human virtue can go in the attainment of these things, and what it is capable of.

APPENDIX

The things I have taught in this part concerning the right way of living have not been so arranged that they could be seen at a glance. Instead, I have demonstrated them at one place or another, as I could more easily deduce one from another. So I have undertaken to collect them here and bring them under main headings.

I. All our strivings, *or* desires, follow from the necessity of our nature in such a way that they can be understood either through it alone, as through their proximate cause, or insofar as we are a part of Nature, which cannot be conceived adequately through itself without other individuals.

II. The desires which follow from our nature in such a way that they can be understood through it alone are those which are related to the mind insofar as it is conceived to consist of adequate ideas. The remaining desires are not related to the mind except insofar as it conceives things inadequately, and their force and growth must be defined not by human power, but by the power of things which are outside us. The former, therefore, are rightly called actions, while the latter are rightly called passions. For the former always indicate our power, whereas the latter indicate our lack of power and mutilated knowledge.

III. Our actions—that is, those desires which are defined by man's power, *or* reason—are always good; but the other [desires] can be both good and evil.

IV. In life, therefore, it is especially useful to perfect, as far as we can, our intellect, *or* reason. In this one thing consists man's highest happiness, *or* blessedness. Indeed, blessedness is nothing but that satisfaction of mind which stems from the intuitive knowledge of God. But perfecting the intellect is nothing but understanding God, his attributes, and his actions, which follow from the necessity of his nature. So the ultimate end of the man who is led by reason, that is, his highest desire, by which he strives to moderate all the others, is that by which he is led to conceive adequately both himself and all things which can fall under his understanding.

V. No life, then, is rational without understanding, and things are good only insofar as they aid man to enjoy the life of the mind, which is defined by understanding. On the other hand, those which prevent man from being able to perfect his reason and enjoy the rational life, those only we say are evil.

VI. But because all those things of which man is the efficient cause must be good, nothing evil can happen to a man except by external causes, namely, insofar as he is a part of the whole of Nature, whose laws human nature is compelled to obey, and to which it is forced to accommodate itself in ways nearly infinite.

II/268   VII. It is impossible for man not to be a part of Nature and not to follow the common order of Nature. But if he lives among such individuals as agree with his nature, his power of acting will thereby be aided and encouraged. On the other hand, if he is among men who do not agree at all with his nature, he will hardly be able to accommodate himself to them without greatly changing himself.

VIII. It is permissible for us to avert, in the way which seems safest, whatever there is in Nature which we judge to be evil, *or* able to prevent us from being able to exist and enjoy a rational life. On the other hand, we may take for our own use, and use in any way, whatever there is which we judge to be good, *or* useful for preserving our being and enjoying a rational life. And absolutely, it is permissible for everyone to do, by the highest right of Nature, what he judges will contribute to his advantage.

IX. Nothing can agree more with the nature of any thing than other individuals of the same species. And so (by VII) nothing is more useful to man in preserving his being and enjoying a rational life than a man who is guided by reason. Again, because, among singular things, we know nothing more excellent than a man who is guided by reason, we

II/269   can show best how much our skill and understanding are worth by educating men so that at last they live according to the command of their own reason.

X. Insofar as men are moved against one another by envy or some [NS: other] affect of hate, they are contrary to one another, and consequently are the more to be feared, as they can do more than other individuals in Nature.

XI. Minds, however, are conquered not by arms, but by love and nobility.

XII. It is especially useful to men to form associations, to bind themselves by those bonds most apt to make one people of them, and absolutely, to do those things which serve to strengthen friendships.

XIII. But skill and alertness are required for this. For men vary—there being few who live according to the rule of reason—and yet generally they are envious, and more inclined to vengeance than to compassion. So it requires a singular power of mind to bear with each one according to his understanding, and to restrain oneself from imitating their affects.

But those who know how to find fault with men, to castigate vices rather than teach virtues, and to break men's minds rather than strengthen them—they are burdensome both to themselves and to others. That is why many, from too great an impatience of mind, and a false zeal for religion, have preferred to live among the lower animals rather than among men. They are like boys or young men who cannot bear calmly the scolding of their parents, and take refuge in the army. They choose the inconveniences of war and the discipline of an absolute commander in preference to the conveniences of home and the admonitions of a father; and while they take vengeance on their parents, they allow all sorts of burdens to be placed on them.

II/270

XIV. Though men, therefore, generally direct everything according to their own lust, nevertheless, more advantages than disadvantages follow from their forming a common society. So it is better to bear men's wrongs calmly, and apply one's zeal to those things which help to bring men together in harmony and friendship.

XV. The things which beget harmony are those which are related to justice, fairness, and being honorable. For men find it difficult to bear, not only what *is* unjust and unfair, but also what *is thought* dishonorable, *or* that someone rejects the accepted practices of the state. But especially necessary to bring people together in love, are the things which concern religion and morality. On this, see P37S1 and S2, P46S, and P73S.

XVI. Harmony is also commonly born of fear, but then it is without trust. Add to this that fear arises from weakness of mind, and therefore does not pertain to the exercise of reason. Nor does pity, though it seems to present the appearance of morality.

II/271

XVII. Men are also won over by generosity, especially those who do not have the means of acquiring the things they require to sustain life. But to bring aid to everyone in need far surpasses the powers and advantage of a private person. For his riches are quite unequal to the task. Moreover the capacity of one man is too limited for him to be able to unite all men to him in friendship. So the care of the poor falls upon society as a whole, and concerns only the general advantage.

XVIII. In accepting favors and returning thanks an altogether different care must be taken. See P70S and P71S.

XIX. A purely sensual love, moreover, that is, a lust to procreate which arises from external appearance, and absolutely, all love which has a cause other than freedom of mind, easily passes into hate—unless (which is worse) it is a species of madness. And then it is encouraged more by discord than by harmony. See IIIP31.

XX. As for marriage, it certainly agrees with reason, if the desire for II/272 physical union is not generated only by external appearance but also by a love of begetting children and educating them wisely, and moreover, if the love of each, of both the man and the woman, is caused not by external appearance only, but mainly by freedom of mind.

XXI. Flattery also gives rise to harmony, but by the foul crime of bondage, or by treachery. No one is more taken in by flattery than the proud, who wish to be first and are not.

XXII. In despondency, there is a false appearance of morality and religion. And though despondency is the opposite of pride, still the despondent man is very near the proud. See P57S.

XXIII. Shame, moreover, contributes to harmony only in those things which cannot be hidden. Again, because shame itself is a species of sadness, it does not belong to the exercise of reason.

XXIV. The other affects of sadness toward men are directly opposed to justice, fairness, being honorable, morality, and religion. And though indignation seems to present an appearance of fairness, nevertheless, when each one is allowed to pass judgment on another's deeds, and to enforce either his own or another's right, we live without a law.

XXV. Courtesy, that is, the desire to please men which is determined II/273 by reason, is related to morality (as we said in P37S1). But if it arises from an affect, it is ambition, *or* a desire by which men generally arouse discord and seditions, from a false appearance of morality. For one who desires to aid others by advice or by action, so that they may enjoy the highest good together, will aim chiefly at arousing their love for him, but not at leading them into admiration so that his teaching will be called after his name. Nor will he give any cause for envy. Again, in common conversations he will beware of relating men's vices, and will take care to speak only sparingly of a man's lack of power, but generously of the man's virtue, *or* power, and how it can be perfected, so that men, moved not by fear or aversion, but only by an affect of Joy, may strive to live as far as they can according to the rule of reason.

XXVI. Apart from men we know no singular thing in Nature whose mind we can enjoy, and which we can join to ourselves in friendship, or some kind of association. And so whatever there is in Nature apart from men, the principle of seeking our own advantage does not demand that we preserve it. Instead, it teaches us to preserve or destroy it according to its use, or to adapt it to our use in any way whatever.

XXVII. The principal advantage we derive from things outside us— apart from the experience and knowledge we acquire from observing them and changing them from one form into another—lies in the preservation of our body. That is why those things are most useful to us II/274 which can feed and maintain it, so that all its parts can perform their function properly. For the more the body is capable of affecting, and being affected by, external bodies in a great many ways, the more the mind is capable of thinking (see P38 and P39).

But there seem to be very few things of this kind in Nature. So to nourish the body in the way required, it is necessary to use many different kinds of food. Indeed, the human body is composed of a great many parts of different natures, which require continuous and varied food so that the whole body may be equally capable of doing everything which can follow from its nature, and consequently, so that the mind may also be equally capable of conceiving many things.

XXVIII. Now to achieve these things the powers of each man would hardly be sufficient if men did not help one another. But money has provided a convenient instrument for acquiring all these aids. That is why its image usually occupies the mind of the multitude more than anything else. For they can imagine hardly any species of joy without the accompanying idea of money as its cause.

XXIX. But this is a vice only in those who seek money neither from need nor on account of necessities, but because they have learned the art of making money and pride themselves on it very much. As for the body, they feed it according to custom, but sparingly, because they believe they lose as much of their goods as they devote to the preservation II/275 of their body. Those, however, who know the true use of money, and set bounds to their wealth according to need, live contentedly with little.

XXX. Since those things are good which assist the parts of the body to perform their function, and joy consists in the fact that man's power, insofar as he consists of mind and body, is aided or increased, all things which bring joy are good. Nevertheless, since things do not act in order to affect us with joy, and their power of acting is not regulated by our advantage, and finally, since joy is generally related particularly to one part of the body, most affects of joy are excessive (unless reason and alertness are present). Hence, the desires generated by them are also excessive. To this we may add that when we follow our affects, we value most the pleasures of the moment, and cannot appraise future things with an equal affect of mind. See P44S and P60S.

XXXI. Superstition, on the other hand, seems to maintain that the good is what brings sadness, and the evil, what brings joy. But as we have already said (see P45S), no one, unless he is envious, takes pleasure in my lack of power and misfortune. For as we are affected with a greater joy, we pass to a greater perfection, and consequently participate more

II/276 in the divine nature. Nor can joy which is governed by the true principle of our advantage ever be evil. On the other hand, he who is led by fear, and does the good only to avoid evil, is not governed by reason.

XXXII. But human power is very limited and infinitely surpassed by the power of external causes. So we do not have an absolute power to adapt things outside us to our use. Nevertheless, we shall bear calmly those things which happen to us contrary to what the principle of our advantage demands, if we are conscious that we have done our duty, that the power we have could not have extended itself to the point where we could have avoided those things, and that we are a part of the whole of Nature, whose order we follow. If we understand this clearly and distinctly, that part of us which is defined by understanding, that is, the better part of us, will be entirely satisfied with this, and will strive to persevere in that satisfaction. For insofar as we understand, we can want nothing except what is necessary, nor absolutely be satisfied with anything except what is true. Hence, insofar as we understand these things rightly, the striving of the better part of us agrees with the order of the whole of Nature.

II/277
FIFTH PART OF THE ETHICS
OF THE POWER OF THE INTELLECT, *OR* ON
HUMAN FREEDOM

PREFACE

I pass, finally, to the remaining part of the Ethics, *which concerns the means, or way, leading to freedom. Here, then, I shall treat of the power of reason, showing what it can do against the affects, and what freedom of mind, or blessedness, is. From this we shall see how much more the wise man can do than the ignorant. But it does not pertain to this investigation to show how the intellect must be perfected, or in what way the body must be cared for, so that it can perform its function properly. The former is the concern of logic, and the latter of medicine.*

Here, then, as I have said, I shall treat only of the power of the mind, or of reason, and shall show, above all, how great its dominion over the affects is, and what kind of dominion it has for restraining and moderating them. For we have already demonstrated above that it does not have an absolute dominion over them. Nevertheless, the Stoics thought that they depend entirely on our will, and that we can command them absolutely. But experience cries out against this, and has forced them, in spite of their principles, to confess that much practice and application are required to restrain and moderate them. If I remember rightly, someone tried to show this by the example of two dogs, one
II/278 *a house dog, the other a hunting dog. For by practice he was finally able to bring*

it about that the house dog was accustomed to hunt, and the hunting dog to refrain from chasing hares.

Descartes was rather inclined to this opinion. For he maintained that the soul, or mind, was especially united to a certain part of the brain, called the pineal gland, by whose aid the mind is aware of all the motions aroused in the body and of external objects, and which the mind can move in various ways simply by willing. He contended that this gland was suspended in the middle of the brain in such a way that it could be moved by the least motion of the animal spirits. He maintained further that this gland is suspended in the middle of the brain in as many varying ways as there are varying ways that the animal spirits strike against it, and moreover, that as many varying traces are impressed upon it as there are varying external objects which drive the animal spirits against it. That is why, if the soul's will afterwards moves the gland so that it is suspended as it once was by the motion of the animal spirits, the gland will drive and determine the animal spirits in the same way as when they were driven back before by a similar placement of the gland.

Furthermore, he maintained that each will of the mind is united by nature to a certain fixed motion of this gland. For example, if someone has a will to look at a distant object, this will brings it about that the pupil is dilated. But if he thinks only of the pupil which is to be dilated, nothing will be accomplished by having a will for this, because Nature has not joined the motion of the gland which serves to drive the animal spirits against the optic nerve in a way suitable for dilating or contracting the pupil with the will to dilate or contract it. Instead, it has joined that motion with the will to look at distant or near objects.

Finally, he maintained that even though each motion of this gland seems to have been connected by nature from the beginning of our life with a particular one of our thoughts, they can still be joined by habit to others. He tries to prove this in The Passions of the Soul I, 50. *From these claims, he infers that there is no soul so weak that it cannot—when it is well directed—acquire an absolute power over its passions. For as he defines them, these are*

II/279

> perceptions, or feelings, or emotions of the soul, which are particularly related to the soul, and which [NB] are produced, preserved, and strengthened by some motion of the spirits (see *The Passions of the Soul I, 27*).

But since to any will we can join any motion of the gland (and consequently any motion of the spirits), and since the determination of the will depends only on our power, we shall acquire an absolute dominion over our passions, if we determine our will by firm and certain judgments according to which we will to direct the actions of our life, and if we join to these judgments the motions of the passions we will to have.

Such is the opinion of that most distinguished man—as far as I can gather

*it from his words. I would hardly have believed it had been propounded by so
great a man, had it not been so subtle. Indeed, I cannot wonder enough that a
philosopher of his caliber—one who had firmly decided to deduce nothing except
from principles known through themselves, and to affirm nothing which he did
not perceive clearly and distinctly, one who had so often censured the Scholastics
for wishing to explain obscure things by occult qualities—that such a philosopher should assume a hypothesis more occult than any occult quality.*

*What, I ask, does he understand by the union of mind and body? What clear
and distinct concept does he have of a thought so closely united to some little
portion of quantity? Indeed, I wish he had explained this union by its proximate
cause. But he had conceived the mind to be so distinct from the body that he
could not assign any singular cause, either of this union or of the mind itself.
Instead, it was necessary for him to have recourse to the cause of the whole
Universe, that is, to God.*

II/280

*Again, I should like very much to know how many degrees of motion the
mind can give to that pineal gland, and how great a force is required to hold
it in suspense. For I do not know whether this gland is driven about more slowly
by the mind than by the animal spirits, or more quickly; nor do I know whether
the motions of the passions which we have joined closely to firm judgments can
be separated from them again by corporeal causes. If so, it would follow that
although the mind had firmly resolved to face dangers, and had joined the
motions of daring to this decision, nevertheless, once the danger had been seen,
the gland might be so suspended that the mind could think only of flight. And
of course, since there is no common measure between the will and motion, there
is also no comparison between the power, or forces, of the mind and those of the
body. Consequently, the forces of the body cannot in any way be determined by
those of the mind. To this we may add that this gland is not found to be so placed
in the middle of the brain that it can be driven about so easily and in so many
ways, and that not all the nerves extend to the cavities of the brain. Finally, I
pass over all those things he claimed about the will and its freedom, since I have
already shown, more than adequately, that they are false.*

*Therefore, because the power of the mind is defined only by understanding,
as I have shown above, we shall determine, by the mind's knowledge alone, the
remedies for the affects. I believe everyone in fact knows them by experience,
though they neither observe them accurately, nor see them distinctly. From that
we shall deduce all those things which concern the mind's blessedness.*

II/281

AXIOMS

A1: If two contrary actions are aroused in the same subject, a change will
have to occur, either in both of them, or in one only, until they cease to
be contrary.

A2: The power of an effect is defined by the power of its cause, insofar as its essence is explained or defined by the essence of its cause.

This axiom is evident from IIIP7.

P1: *In just the same way as thoughts and ideas of things are ordered and connected in the mind, so the affections of the body, or images of things are ordered and connected in the body.*

Dem.: The order and connection of ideas is the same as the order and connection of things (by IIP7), and vice versa, the order and connection of things is the same as the order and connection of ideas (by IIP6C and P7). So just as the order and connection of ideas happens in the mind according to the order and connection of affections of the body (by IIP18), so vice versa (by IIIP2), the order and connection of affections of the body happens as thoughts and ideas of things are ordered and connected in the mind, q.e.d.

P2: *If we separate emotions, or affects, from the thought of an external cause, and join them to other thoughts, then the love, or hate, toward the external cause is destroyed, as are the vacillations of mind arising from these affects.*

Dem.: For what constitutes the form of love, or hate, is joy, or sadness, accompanied by the idea of an external cause (by Defs. Aff. VI, VII). So if this is taken away, the form of love or hate is taken away at the same time. Hence, these affects, and those arising from them, are destroyed, q.e.d.

P3: *An affect which is a passion ceases to be a passion as soon as we form a clear and distinct idea of it.*

Dem.: An affect which is a passion is a confused idea (by Gen. Def. Aff.). Therefore, if we should form a clear and distinct idea of the affect itself, this idea will only be distinguished by reason from the affect itself, insofar as it is related only to the mind (by IIP21 and P21S). Therefore (by IIIP3), the affect will cease to be a passion, q.e.d.

Cor.: The more an affect is known to us, then, the more it is in our power, and the less the mind is acted on by it.

P4: *There is no affection of the body of which we cannot form a clear and distinct concept.*

Dem.: Those things which are common to all can only be conceived adequately (by IIP38), and so (by IIP12 and L2 [II/98]) there is no affection of the body of which we cannot form some clear and distinct concept, q.e.d.

Cor.: From this it follows that there is no affect of which we cannot form some clear and distinct concept. For an affect is an idea of an

II/282

II/283

affection of the body (by Gen. Def. Aff.), which therefore (by P4) must involve some clear and distinct concept.

Schol.: There is nothing from which some effect does not follow (by IP36), and we understand clearly and distinctly whatever follows from an idea which is adequate in us (by IIP40); hence, each of us has—in part, at least, if not absolutely—the power to understand himself and his affects, and consequently, the power to bring it about that he is less acted on by them.

We must, therefore, take special care to know each affect clearly and distinctly (as far as this is possible), so that in this way the mind may be determined from an affect to thinking those things which it perceives clearly and distinctly, and with which it is fully satisfied, and so that the affect itself may be separated from the thought of an external cause and joined to true thoughts. The result will be not only that love, hate, and the like, are destroyed (by P2), but also that the appetites, *or* desires, which usually arise from such an affect, cannot be excessive (by IVP61).

For it must particularly be noted that the appetite by which a man is said to act, and that by which he is said to be acted on, are one and the same. For example, we have shown that human nature is so constituted that each of us wants the others to live according to his temperament (see IIIP31S). And indeed, in a man who is not led by reason this appetite is the passion called ambition, which does not differ much from pride. On the other hand, in a man who lives according to the dictate of reason it is the action, *or* virtue, called morality (see IVP37S1 and P37 Alternate Dem.).

In this way, all the appetites, *or* desires, are passions only insofar as they arise from inadequate ideas, and are counted as virtues when they are aroused or generated by adequate ideas. For all the desires by which we are determined to do something can arise as much from adequate ideas as from inadequate ones (by IVP59). And—to return to the point from which I have digressed—we can devise no other remedy for the affects which depends on our power and is more excellent than this, which consists in a true knowledge of them. For the mind has no other power than that of thinking and forming adequate ideas, as we have shown (by IIIP3) above.

II/284

P5: *The greatest affect of all, other things equal, is one toward a thing we imagine simply, and neither as necessary, nor as possible, nor as contingent.*

Dem.: An affect toward a thing we imagine to be free is greater than that toward a thing we imagine to be necessary (by IIIP49), and consequently is still greater than that toward a thing we imagine as possible or contingent (by IVP11). But imagining a thing as free can be nothing but simply imagining it while we are ignorant of the causes by which it has been determined to act (by what we have shown in IIP35S). Therefore, an affect toward a thing we imagine simply is, other things equal, greater than that toward a thing we imagine as necessary, possible, or contingent. Hence, it is the greatest of all, q.e.d.

P6: *Insofar as the mind understands all things as necessary, it has a greater power over the affects, or is less acted on by them.*

Dem.: The mind understands all things to be necessary (by IP29), and to be determined by an infinite connection of causes to exist and produce effects (by IP28). And so (by P5) to that extent [the mind] brings it about that it is less acted on by the affects springing from these things, and (by IIIP48) is less affected toward them, q.e.d.

Schol.: The more this knowledge that things are necessary is concerned with singular things, which we imagine more distinctly and vividly, the greater is this power of the mind over the affects, as experience itself also testifies. For we see that sadness over some good which has perished is lessened as soon as the man who has lost it realizes that this good could not, in any way, have been kept. Similarly, we see that no one pities infants because of their inability to speak, to walk, or to reason, or because they live so many years, as it were, unconscious of themselves. But if most people were born grown up, and only one or two were born infants, then everyone would pity the infants, because they would regard infancy itself, not as a natural and necessary thing, but as a vice of nature, *or* a sin. We could point out many other things along this line.

II/285

P7: *Affects arising from or aroused by reason are, if we take account of time, more powerful than those related to singular things we regard as absent.*

Dem.: We regard a thing as absent, not because of the affect by which we imagine it, but because the body is affected by another affect which excludes the thing's existence (by IIP17). So an affect related to a thing we regard as absent is not of such a nature that it surpasses men's other actions and power (see IVP6); on the contrary, its nature is such that it can, in some measure, be restrained by those affections which exclude the existence of its external cause (by IVP9). But an affect arising from reason is necessarily related to the common properties of things (see the Def. of reason in IIP40S2), which we always regard as present (for there can be nothing which excludes their present existence) and which we always imagine in the same way (by IIP38). So such an affect will always remain the same, and hence (by A1), the affects which are contrary to it and are not encouraged by their external causes will have to accommodate themselves to it more and more, until they are no longer contrary to it. To that extent, an affect arising from reason is more powerful, q.e.d.

II/286

P8: *The more an affect arises from a number of causes concurring together, the greater it is.*

Dem.: A number of causes together can do more than if they were fewer (by IIIP7). And so (by IVP5), the more an affect is aroused by a number of causes together, the stronger it is, q.e.d.

Schol.: This proposition is also evident from A2.

P9: *If an affect is related to more and different causes which the mind considers together with the affect itself, it is less harmful, we are less acted on by it, and we are affected less toward each cause, than is the case with another, equally great affect, which is related only to one cause, or to fewer causes.*

Dem.: An affect is only evil, *or* harmful, insofar as it prevents the mind from being able to think (by IVP26 and P27). And so that affect which determines the mind to consider many objects together is less harmful than another, equally great affect which engages the mind solely in considering one, or a few objects, so that it cannot think of others. This was the first point.

Next, because the mind's essence, that is, power (by IIIP7), consists only in thought (by IIP11), the mind is less acted on by an affect which determines it to consider many things together than by an equally great affect which keeps the mind engaged solely in considering one or a few objects. This was the second point.

II/287   Finally (by IIIP48), insofar as this affect is related to many external causes, it is also less toward each one, q.e.d.

P10: *So long as we are not torn by affects contrary to our nature, we have the power of ordering and connecting the affections of the body according to the order of the intellect.*

Dem.: Affects which are contrary to our nature, that is (by IVP30), which are evil, are evil insofar as they prevent the mind from understanding (by IVP27). Therefore, so long as we are not torn by affects contrary to our nature, the power of the mind by which it strives to understand things (by IVP26) is not hindered. So long, then, the mind has the power of forming clear and distinct ideas, and of deducing some from others (see IIP40S2 and P47S). And hence, so long do we have (by P1) the power of ordering and connecting the affections of the body according to the order of the intellect, q.e.d.

Schol.: By this power of rightly ordering and connecting the affections of the body, we can bring it about that we are not easily affected with evil affects. For (by P7) a greater force is required for restraining affects ordered and connected according to the order of the intellect than for restraining those which are uncertain and random. The best thing, then, that we can do, so long as we do not have perfect knowledge of our affects, is to conceive a correct principle of living, *or* sure maxims of life, to commit them to memory, and to apply them constantly to the particular cases frequently encountered in life. In this way our imagination will be extensively affected by them, and we shall always have them ready.

For example, we have laid it down as a maxim of life (see IVP46 and P46S) that hate is to be conquered by love, *or* nobility, not by repaying it with hate in return. But in order that we may always have this rule of reason ready when it is needed, we ought to think about and meditate frequently on the common wrongs of men, and how they may be warded off best by nobility. For if we join the image of a wrong to the imagination of this maxim, it will always be ready for us (by IIP18) when a wrong is done to us. If we have ready also the principle of our own true advantage, and also of the good which follows from mutual friendship and common society, and keep in mind, moreover, that the highest satisfaction of mind stems from the right principle of living (by IVP52), and that men, like other things, act from the necessity of nature, then the wrong, *or* the hate usually arising from it, will occupy a very small part of the imagination, and will easily be overcome.

II/288

Or if the anger which usually arises from the greatest wrongs is not so easily overcome, it will still be overcome, though not without some vacillation. And it will be overcome in far less time than if we had not considered these things beforehand in this way (as is evident from P6, P7, and P8).

To put aside fear, we must think in the same way of tenacity: that is, we must recount and frequently imagine the common dangers of life, and how they can be best avoided and overcome by presence of mind and strength of character.

But it should be noted that in ordering our thoughts and images, we must always (by IVP63C and IIIP59) attend to those things which are good in each thing so that in this way we are always determined to acting from an affect of joy. For example, if someone sees that he pursues esteem too much, he should think of its correct use, the end for which it ought be pursued, and the means by which it can be acquired, not of its misuse and emptiness, and men's inconstancy, or other things of this kind, which only someone sick of mind thinks of. For those who are most ambitious are most upset by such thoughts when they despair of attaining the honor they strive for; while they spew forth their anger, they wish to seem wise. So it is certain that they most desire esteem who cry out most against its misuse, and the emptiness of the world.

Nor is this peculiar to the ambitious—it is common to everyone whose luck is bad and whose mind is weak. For the poor man, when he is also greedy, will not stop talking about the misuse of money and the vices of the rich. In doing this he only distresses himself, and shows others that he cannot bear calmly either his own poverty, or the wealth of others.

So also, one who has been badly received by a lover thinks of nothing but the inconstancy and deceptiveness of women, and their other, often sung vices. All of these he immediately forgets as soon as his lover receives him again.

One, therefore, who is anxious to moderate his affects and appetites from the love of freedom alone will strive, as far as he can, to come to know the virtues and their causes, and to fill his mind with the gladness which arises from the true knowledge of them, but not at all to consider men's vices, or to disparage men, or to enjoy a false appearance of freedom. And he who will observe these [rules] carefully—for they are not difficult—and practice them, will soon be able to direct most of his actions according to the command of reason.

P11: *As an image is related to more things, the more frequent it is, or the more often it flourishes, and the more it engages the mind.*

Dem.: For as an image, *or* affect, is related to more things, there are more causes by which it can be aroused and encouraged, all of which the mind (by hypothesis) considers together as a result of the affect itself. And so the affect is the more frequent, *or* flourishes more often, and (by P8) engages the mind more, q.e.d.

P12: *The images of things are more easily joined to images related to things we understand clearly and distinctly than to other images.*

Dem.: Things we understand clearly and distinctly are either common properties of things or deduced from them (see the Def. of reason in IIP40S2), and consequently (by P11) are aroused in us more often. And so it can more easily happen that we consider other things together with them rather than with [things we do not understand clearly and distinctly]. Hence (by IIP18), [images of things] are more easily joined with [things we understand clearly and distinctly] than with others, q.e.d.

P13: *The more an image is joined with other images, the more often it flourishes.*

Dem.: For the more an image is joined with other images, the more causes there are (by IIP18) by which it can be aroused, q.e.d.

P14: *The mind can bring it about that all the body's affections, or images of things, are related to the idea of God.*

Dem.: There is no affection of the body of which the mind cannot form some clear and distinct concept (by P4). And so it can bring it about (by IP15) that they are related to the idea of God, q.e.d.

P15: *He who understands himself and his affects clearly and distinctly loves God, and does so the more, the more he understands himself and his affects.*

Dem.: He who understands himself and his affects clearly and distinctly rejoices (by IIIP53), and this joy is accompanied by the idea of God (by P14). Hence (by Def. Aff. VI), he loves God, and (by the same reasoning) does so the more, the more he understands himself and his affects, q.e.d.

P16: *This love toward God must engage the mind most.*

Dem.: For this love is joined to all the affections of the body (by P14), which all encourage it (by P15). And so (by P11), it must engage the mind most, q.e.d.

II/291

P17: *God is without passions, and is not affected with any affect of joy or sadness.*

Dem.: All ideas, insofar as they are related to God, are true (by IIP32), that is (by IID4), adequate. And so (by Gen. Def. Aff.), God is without passions.

Next, God can pass neither to a greater nor a lesser perfection (by IP20C2); hence (by Defs. Aff. II, III) he is not affected with any affect of joy or sadness, q.e.d.

Cor.: Strictly speaking, God loves no one, and hates no one. For God (by P17) is not affected with any affect of joy or sadness. Consequently (by Defs. Aff. VI, VII), he also loves no one and hates no one.

P18: *No one can hate God.*

Dem.: The idea of God which is in us is adequate and perfect (by IIP46, P47). So insofar as we consider God, we act (by IIIP3). Consequently (by IIIP59), there can be no sadness accompanied by the idea of God, that is (by Def. Aff. VII), no one can hate God, q.e.d.

Cor.: Love toward God cannot be turned into hate.

Schol.: But, it can be objected, while we understand God to be the cause of all things, we thereby consider God to be the cause of sadness. To this I reply that insofar as we understand the causes of sadness, it ceases (by P3) to be a passion, that is (by IIIP59), to that extent it ceases to be sadness. And so, insofar as we understand God to be the cause of sadness, we rejoice.

II/292

P19: *He who loves God cannot strive that God should love him in return.*

Dem.: If a man were to strive for this, he would desire (by P17C) that God, whom he loves, not be God. Consequently (by IIIP19), he would desire to be saddened, which is absurd (by IIIP28). Therefore, he who loves God, and so on, q.e.d.

P20: *This love toward God cannot be tainted by an affect of envy or jealousy: instead, the more men we imagine to be joined to God by the same bond of love, the more it is encouraged.*

Dem.: This love toward God is the highest good which we can want from the dictate of reason (by IVP28), and is common to all men (by IVP36); we desire that all should enjoy it (by IVP37). And so (by Def. Aff. XXIII), it cannot be stained by an affect of envy, nor (by P18 and the Def. of jealousy, see IIIP35S) by an affect of jealousy. On the contrary (by IIIP31), the more men we imagine to enjoy it, the more it must be encouraged, q.e.d.

Schol.: Similarly we can show that there is no affect which is directly contrary to this love and by which it can be destroyed. So we can conclude that this love is the most constant of all the affects, and insofar as it is related to the body, cannot be destroyed, unless it is destroyed with the body itself. What the nature of this love is insofar as it is related only to the mind, we shall see later.

II/293

And with this, I have covered all the remedies for the affects, *or* all that the mind, considered only in itself, can do against the affects. From this it is clear that the power of the mind over the affects consists:

I. In the knowledge itself of the affects (see P4S);

II. In the fact that it separates the affects from the thought of an external cause, which we imagine confusedly (see P2 and P4S);

III. In the time by which the affections related to things we understand surpass those related to things we conceive confusedly, *or* in a mutilated way (see P7);

IV. In the multiplicity of causes by which affections related to common properties or to God are encouraged (see P9 and P11);

V. Finally, in the order by which the mind can order its affects and connect them to one another (see P10, and in addition, P12, P13, and P14).

But to understand better this power of the mind over the affects, the most important thing to note is that we call affects great when we compare the affect of one man with that of another, and see that the same affect troubles one more than the other, or when we compare the affects of one and the same man with each other, and find that he is affected, *or* moved, more by one affect than by another. For (by IVP5) the force of each affect is defined by the power of the external cause compared with our own. But the power of the mind is defined by knowledge alone, whereas lack of power, *or* passion, is judged solely by the privation of knowledge, that is, by that through which ideas are called inadequate.

From this it follows that that mind is most acted on, of which inadequate ideas constitute the greatest part, so that it is distinguished more by what it undergoes than by what it does. On the other hand, that mind acts most, of which adequate ideas constitute the greatest part, so that though it may have as many inadequate ideas as the other, it is still distinguished more by those which are attributed to human virtue than by those which betray man's lack of power.

Next, it should be noted that sickness of the mind and misfortunes take their origin especially from too much love toward a thing which is liable to many variations and which we can never fully possess. For no one is disturbed or anxious concerning anything unless he loves it, nor do wrongs, suspicions, and enmities arise except from love for a thing which no one can really fully possess.

II/294

From what we have said, we easily conceive what clear and distinct knowledge—and especially that third kind of knowledge (see IIP47S), whose foundation is the knowledge of God itself—can accomplish against the affects. Insofar as the affects are passions, if clear and distinct knowledge does not absolutely remove them (see P3 and P4S), at least it brings it about that they constitute the smallest part of the mind (see P14). And then it begets a love toward a thing immutable and eternal (see P15), which we really fully possess (see IIP45), and which therefore cannot be tainted by any of the vices which are in ordinary love, but can always be greater and greater (by P15), and occupy the greatest part of the mind (by P16), and affect it extensively.

With this I have completed everything which concerns this present life. Anyone who attends to what we have said in this scholium, and at the same time, to the definitions of the mind and its affects, and finally to IIIP1 and P3, will easily be able to see what I said at the beginning of this scholium, namely, that in these few words I have covered all the remedies for the affects. So it is time now to pass to those things which pertain to the mind's duration without relation to the body.

P21: *The mind can neither imagine anything, nor recollect past things, except while the body endures.*

Dem.: The mind neither expresses the actual existence of its body, nor conceives the body's affections as actual, except while the body endures (by IIP8C); consequently (by IIP26), it conceives no body as actually existing except while its body endures. Therefore, it can neither imagine anything (see the Def. of imagination in IIP17S) nor recollect past things (see the Def. of Memory in IIP18S) except while the body endures, q.e.d.

P22: *Nevertheless, in God there is necessarily an idea that expresses the essence of this or that human body, under a species of eternity.*

Dem.: God is the cause, not only of the existence of this or that human body, but also of its essence (by IP25), which therefore must be conceived through the very essence of God (by IA4), by a certain eternal necessity (by IP16), and this concept must be in God (by IIP3), q.e.d.

P23: *The human mind cannot be absolutely destroyed with the body, but something of it remains which is eternal.*

Dem.: In God there is necessarily a concept, *or* idea, which expresses the essence of the human body (by P22), an idea, therefore, which is necessarily something that pertains to the essence of the human mind (by IIP13). But we do not attribute to the human mind any duration that can be defined by time, except insofar as it expresses the actual existence of the body, which is explained by duration, and can be defined by time, that is (by IIP8C), we do not attribute duration to it except while the body endures. However, since what is conceived, with a certain eternal necessity, through God's essence itself (by P22) is nevertheless something, this something that pertains to the essence of the mind will necessarily be eternal, q.e.d.

Schol.: As we have said, this idea, which expresses the essence of the body under a species of eternity, is a certain mode of thinking, which pertains to the essence of the mind, and which is necessarily eternal.

And though it is impossible that we should recollect that we existed before the body—since there cannot be any traces of this in the body, and eternity can neither be defined by time nor have any relation to time—still, we feel and know by experience that we are eternal. For the mind feels those things that it conceives in understanding no less than those it has in the memory. For the eyes of the mind, by which it sees and observes things, are the demonstrations themselves.

Therefore, though we do not recollect that we existed before the body, we nevertheless feel that our mind, insofar as it involves the essence of the body under a species of eternity, is eternal, and that this existence it has cannot be defined by time *or* explained through duration. Our mind, therefore, can be said to endure, and its existence can be defined by a certain time, only insofar as it involves the actual existence of the body, and to that extent only does it have the power of determining the existence of things by time, and of conceiving them under duration.

172

P24: *The more we understand singular things, the more we understand God.*
Dem.: This is evident from IP25C.

P25: *The greatest striving of the mind, and its greatest virtue is understanding things by the third kind of knowledge.*
Dem.: The third kind of knowledge proceeds from an adequate idea of certain attributes of God to an adequate knowledge of the essence of things (see its Def. in IIP40S2), and the more we understand things in this way, the more we understand God (by P24). Therefore (by IVP28), the greatest virtue of the mind, that is (by IVD8), the mind's power, *or* nature, *or* (by IIIP7) its greatest striving, is to understand things by the third kind of knowledge, q.e.d.

P26: *The more the mind is capable of understanding things by the third kind*   II/297
of knowledge, the more it desires to understand them by this kind of knowledge.
Dem.: This is evident. For insofar as we conceive the mind to be capable of understanding things by this kind of knowledge, we conceive it as determined to understand things by the same kind of knowledge. Consequently (by Def. Aff. I), the more the mind is capable of this, the more it desires it, q.e.d.

P27: *The greatest satisfaction of mind there can be arises from this third kind of knowledge.*
Dem.: The greatest virtue of the mind is to know God (by IVP28), *or* to understand things by the third kind of knowledge (by P25). Indeed, this virtue is the greater, the more the mind knows things by this kind of knowledge (by P24). So he who knows things by this kind of knowledge passes to the greatest human perfection, and consequently (by Def. Aff. II), is affected with the greatest joy, accompanied (by IIP43) by the idea of himself and his virtue. Therefore (by Def. Aff. XXV), the greatest satisfaction there can be arises from this kind of knowledge, q.e.d.

P28: *The striving, or desire, to know things by the third kind of knowledge cannot arise from the first kind of knowledge, but can indeed arise from the second.*
Dem.: This proposition is evident through itself. For whatever we understand clearly and distinctly, we understand either through itself,   II/298
or through something else which is conceived through itself; that is, the ideas which are clear and distinct in us, *or* which are related to the third kind of knowledge (see IIP40S2), cannot follow from mutilated and confused ideas, which (by IIP40S2) are related to the first kind of knowledge; but they can follow from adequate ideas, *or* (by IIP40S2) from the second and third kind of knowledge. Therefore (by Def.

Aff. I), the desire to know things by the third kind of knowledge cannot arise from the first kind of knowledge, but can from the second, q.e.d.

P29: *Whatever the mind understands under a species of eternity, it understands not from the fact that it conceives the body's present actual existence, but from the fact that it conceives the body's essence under a species of eternity.*

Dem.: Insofar as the mind conceives the present existence of its body, it conceives duration, which can be determined by time, and to that extent only it has the power of conceiving things in relation to time (by P21 and IIP26). But eternity cannot be explained by duration (by ID8 and its explanation). Therefore, to that extent the mind does not have the power of conceiving things under a species of eternity.

But because it is of the nature of reason to conceive things under a species of eternity (by IIP44C2), and it also pertains to the nature of the mind to conceive the body's essence under a species of eternity (by P23), and beyond these two, nothing else pertains to the mind's essence (by IIP13), this power of conceiving things under a species of eternity pertains to the mind only insofar as it conceives the body's essence under a species of eternity, q.e.d.

Schol.: We conceive things as actual in two ways: either insofar as we conceive them to exist in relation to a certain time and place, or insofar II/299 as we conceive them to be contained in God and to follow from the necessity of the divine nature. But the things we conceive in this second way as true, *or* real, we conceive under a species of eternity, and their ideas involve the eternal and infinite essence of God (as we have shown in IIP45 and P45S).

P30: *Insofar as our mind knows itself and the body under a species of eternity, it necessarily has knowledge of God, and knows that it is in God and is conceived through God.*

Dem.: Eternity is the very essence of God insofar as this involves necessary existence (by ID8). To conceive things under a species of eternity, therefore, is to conceive things insofar as they are conceived through God's essence, as real beings, *or* insofar as through God's essence they involve existence. Hence, insofar as our mind conceives itself and the body under a species of eternity, it necessarily has knowledge of God, and knows, and so on, q.e.d.

P31: *The third kind of knowledge depends on the mind, as on a formal cause, insofar as the mind itself is eternal.*

Dem.: The mind conceives nothing under a species of eternity except insofar as it conceives its body's essence under a species of eternity (by P29), that is, (by P21 and P23), except insofar as it is eternal. So (by P30)

174

insofar as it is eternal, it has knowledge of God, knowledge which is necessarily adequate (by IIP46). And therefore, the mind, insofar as it is eternal, is capable of knowing all those things which can follow from this given knowledge of God (by IIP40), that is, of knowing things by the third kind of knowledge (see the Def. of this in IIP40S2); therefore, the mind, insofar as it is eternal, is the adequate, *or* formal, cause of the third kind of knowledge (by IIID1), q.e.d.

Schol.: Therefore, the more each of us is able to achieve in this kind   II/300
of knowledge, the more he is conscious of himself and of God, that is, the more perfect and blessed he is. This will be even clearer from what follows.

But here it should be noted that although we are already certain that the mind is eternal, insofar as it conceives things under a species of eternity, nevertheless, for an easier explanation and better understanding of the things we wish to show, we shall consider it as if it were now beginning to be, and were now beginning to understand things under a species of eternity, as we have done up to this point. We may do this without danger of error, provided we are careful to draw our conclusions only from evident premises.

P32: *Whatever we understand by the third kind of knowledge we take pleasure in, and our pleasure is accompanied by the idea of God as a cause.*

Dem.: From this kind of knowledge there arises the greatest satisfaction of mind there can be (by P27), that is (by Def. Aff. XXV), joy; this joy is accompanied by the idea of oneself, and consequently (by P30) it is also accompanied by the idea of God, as its cause, q.e.d.

Cor.: From the third kind of knowledge, there necessarily arises an intellectual love of God. For from this kind of knowledge there arises (by P32) joy, accompanied by the idea of God as its cause, that is (by Def. Aff. VI), love of God, not insofar as we imagine him as present (by P29), but insofar as we understand God to be eternal. And this is what I call intellectual love of God.

P33: *The intellectual love of God, which arises from the third kind of knowledge, is eternal.*

Dem.: For the third kind of knowledge (by P31 and by IA3) is eternal.   II/301
And so (by IA3), the love that arises from it must also be eternal, q.e.d.

Schol.: Although this love toward God has had no beginning (by P33), it still has all the perfections of love, just as if it had come to be (as we have feigned in P32C). There is no difference here, except that the mind has had eternally the same perfections which, in our fiction, now come to it, and that it is accompanied by the idea of God as an eternal cause. If joy, then, consists in the passage to a greater perfection, bless-

175

edness must surely consist in the fact that the mind is endowed with perfection itself.

P34: *Only while the body endures is the mind subject to affects which are related to the passions.*

Dem.: An imagination is an idea by which the mind considers a thing as present (see its Def. in IIP17S), which nevertheless indicates the present constitution of the human body more than the nature of the external thing (by IIP16C2). An affect, then, (by the Gen. Def. Aff.) is an imagination, insofar as it indicates the present constitution of the body. So (by P21) only while the body endures is the mind subject to affects which are related to passions, q.e.d.

Cor.: From this it follows that no love except intellectual love is eternal.

Schol.: If we attend to the common opinion of men, we shall see that they are indeed conscious of the eternity of their mind, but that they confuse it with duration, and attribute it to the imagination, *or* memory, which they believe remains after death.

II/302

P35: *God loves himself with an infinite intellectual love.*

Dem.: God is absolutely infinite (by ID6), that is (by IID6), the nature of God enjoys infinite perfection, accompanied (by IIP3) by the idea of himself, that is (by IP11 and D1), by the idea of his cause. And this is what we said (P32C) intellectual love is.

P36: *The mind's intellectual love of God is the very love of God by which God loves himself, not insofar as he is infinite, but insofar as he can be explained by the human mind's essence, considered under a species of eternity; that is, the mind's intellectual love of God is part of the infinite love by which God loves himself.*

Dem.: This love the mind has must be related to its actions (by P32C and IIIP3); it is, then, an action by which the mind contemplates itself, with the accompanying idea of God as its cause (by P32 and P32C), that is (by IP25C and IIP11C), an action by which God, insofar as he can be explained through the human mind, contemplates himself, with the accompanying idea of himself [as the cause]; so (by P35), this love the mind has is part of the infinite love by which God loves himself, q.e.d.

Cor.: From this it follows that insofar as God loves himself, he loves men, and consequently that God's love of men and the mind's intellectual love of God are one and the same.

II/303

Schol.: From this we clearly understand wherein our salvation, *or* blessedness, *or* freedom, consists, namely, in a constant and eternal love of God, *or* in God's love for men. And this love, *or* blessedness, is called glory in the Sacred Scriptures—not without reason. For whether this love is related to God or to the mind, it can rightly be called satisfaction of mind, which is really not distinguished from glory (by Defs. Aff. XXV and XXX). For insofar as it is related to God (by P35), it is joy (if I may still be permitted to use this term), accompanied by the idea of himself [as its cause]. And similarly insofar as it is related to the mind (by P27).

Again, because the essence of our mind consists only in knowledge, of which God is the beginning and foundation (by IP15 and IIP47S), it is clear to us how our mind, with respect both to essence and existence, follows from the divine nature, and continually depends on God.

I thought this worth the trouble of noting here, in order to show by this example how much the knowledge of singular things I have called intuitive, *or* knowledge of the third kind (see IIP40S2), can accomplish, and how much more powerful it is than the universal knowledge I have called knowledge of the second kind. For although I have shown generally in Part I that all things (and consequently the human mind also) depend on God both for their essence and their existence, nevertheless, that demonstration, though legitimate and put beyond all chance of doubt, still does not affect our mind as much as when this is inferred from the very essence of any singular thing which we say depends on God.

P37: *There is nothing in Nature which is contrary to this intellectual love, or which can take it away.*

Dem.: This intellectual love follows necessarily from the nature of the mind insofar as it is considered as an eternal truth, through God's nature (by P33 and P29). So if there were something contrary to this love, it would be contrary to the true; consequently, what could remove this love would bring it about that what is true would be false. This (as is known through itself) is absurd. Therefore, there is nothing in Nature, and so on, q.e.d.

Schol.: IVA1 concerns singular things insofar as they are considered in relation to a certain time and place. I believe no one doubts this.

P38: *The more the mind understands things by the second and third kind of knowledge, the less it is acted on by affects which are evil, and the less it fears death.*

Dem.: The mind's essence consists in knowledge (by IIP11); therefore, the more the mind knows things by the second and third kind of knowledge, the greater the part of it that remains (by P23 and P29), and consequently (by P37), the greater the part of it that is not touched by affects which are contrary to our nature, that is, which (by IVP30) are

II/304

evil. Therefore, the more the mind understands things by the second and third kind of knowledge, the greater the part of it that remains unharmed, and hence, the less it is acted on by affects, and so on, q.e.d.

Schol.: From this we understand what I touched on in IVP39S, and what I promised to explain in this part, namely, that death is less harmful to us, the greater the mind's clear and distinct knowledge, and hence, the more the mind loves God.

Next, because (by P27) the highest satisfaction there can be arises from the third kind of knowledge, it follows from this that the human mind can be of such a nature that the part of the mind which we have shown perishes with the body (see P21) is of no moment in relation to what remains. But I shall soon treat this more fully.

P39: *He who has a body capable of a great many things has a mind whose greatest part is eternal.*

II/305

Dem.: He who has a body capable of doing a great many things is least troubled by evil affects (by IVP38), that is (by IVP30), by affects contrary to our nature. So (by P10) he has a power of ordering and connecting the affections of his body according to the order of the intellect, and consequently (by P14), of bringing it about that all the affections of the body are related to the idea of God. The result (by P15) is that it is affected with a love of God, which (by P16) must occupy, *or* constitute the greatest part of the mind. Therefore (by P33), he has a mind whose greatest part is eternal, q.e.d.

Schol.: Because human bodies are capable of a great many things, there is no doubt but what they can be of such a nature that they are related to minds which have a great knowledge of themselves and of God, and of which the greatest, *or* chief, part is eternal. So they hardly fear death.

But for a clearer understanding of these things, we must note here that we live in continuous change, and that as we change for the better or worse, we are called happy or unhappy. For he who has passed from being an infant or child to being a corpse is called unhappy. On the other hand, if we pass the whole length of our life with a sound mind in a sound body, that is considered happiness. And really, he who, like an infant or child, has a body capable of very few things, and very heavily dependent on external causes, has a mind which considered solely in itself is conscious of almost nothing of itself, or of God, or of things. On the other hand, he who has a body capable of a great many things, has a mind which considered only in itself is very much conscious of itself, and of God, and of things.

In this life, then, we strive especially that the infant's body may change (as much as its nature allows and assists) into another, capable of a great many things and related to a mind very much conscious of itself, of God, and of things. We strive, that is, that whatever is related to its memory or imagination is of hardly any moment in relation to the intellect (as I have already said in P38S).

P40: *The more perfection each thing has, the more it acts and the less it is acted* II/306 *on; and conversely, the more it acts, the more perfect it is.*

Dem.: The more each thing is perfect, the more reality it has (by IID6), and consequently (by IIIP3 and P3S), the more it acts and the less it is acted on. This demonstration indeed proceeds in the same way in reverse, from which it follows that the more a thing acts, the more perfect it is, q.e.d.

Cor.: From this it follows that the part of the mind that remains, however great it is, is more perfect than the rest.

For the eternal part of the mind (by P23 and P29) is the intellect, through which alone we are said to act (by IIIP3). But what we have shown to perish is the imagination (by P21), through which alone we are said to be acted on (by IIIP3 and the Gen. Def. Aff.). So (by P40), the intellect, however extensive it is, is more perfect than the imagination, q.e.d.

Schol.: These are the things I have decided to show concerning the mind, insofar as it is considered without relation to the body's existence. From them—and at the same time from IP21 and other things—it is clear that our mind, insofar as it understands, is an eternal mode of thinking, which is determined by another eternal mode of thinking, and this again by another, and so on, to infinity; so that together, they all constitute God's eternal and infinite intellect.

P41: *Even if we did not know that our mind is eternal, we would still regard as of the first importance morality, religion, and absolutely all the things we have shown (in Part IV) to be related to tenacity and nobility.*

Dem.: The first and only foundation of virtue, *or* of the method of living rightly (by IVP22C and P24) is the seeking of our own advantage. But to determine what reason prescribes as useful, we took no account of the eternity of the mind, which we only came to know in the Fifth Part. Therefore, though we did not know then that the mind is eternal, II/307 we still regarded as of the first importance the things we showed to be related to tenacity and nobility. And so, even if we also did not know this now, we would still regard as of the first importance the same rules of reason, q.e.d.

Schol.: The usual conviction of the multitude seems to be different. For most people apparently believe that they are free to the extent that they are permitted to yield to their lust, and that they give up their right to the extent that they are bound to live according to the rule of the divine law. Morality, then, and religion, and absolutely everything related to strength of character, they believe to be burdens, which they hope to put down after death, when they also hope to receive a reward for their bondage, that is, for their morality and religion. They are induced to live according to the rule of the divine law (as far as their weakness and lack of character allows) not only by this hope, but also, and especially, by the fear that they may be punished horribly after death. If men did not have this hope and fear, but believed instead that minds die with the body, and that the wretched, exhausted with the burden of morality, cannot look forward to a life to come, they would return to their natural disposition, and would prefer to govern all their actions according to lust, and to obey fortune rather than themselves.

These opinions seem no less absurd to me than if someone, because he does not believe he can nourish his body with good food to eternity, should prefer to fill himself with poisons and other deadly things, or because he sees that the mind is not eternal, *or* immortal, should prefer to be mindless, and to live without reason. These [common beliefs] are so absurd they are hardly worth mentioning.

P42: *Blessedness is not the reward of virtue, but virtue itself; nor do we enjoy it because we restrain our lusts; on the contrary, because we enjoy it, we are able to restrain them.*

II/308 Dem.: Blessedness consists in love of God (by P36 and P36S), a love which arises from the third kind of knowledge (by P32C). So this love (by IIIP59 and P3) must be related to the mind insofar as it acts. Therefore (by IVD8), it is virtue itself. This was the first point.

Next, the more the mind enjoys this divine love, *or* blessedness, the more it understands (by P32), that is (by P3C), the greater the power it has over the affects, and (by P38) the less it is acted on by evil affects. So because the mind enjoys this divine love *or* blessedness, it has the power of restraining lusts. And because human power to restrain the affects consists only in the intellect, no one enjoys blessedness because he has restrained the affects. Instead, the power to restrain lusts arises from blessedness itself, q.e.d.

Schol.: With this I have finished all the things I wished to show concerning the mind's power over the affects and its freedom. From what has been shown, it is clear how much the wise man is capable of, and how much more powerful he is than one who is ignorant and is driven only by lust. For not only is the ignorant man troubled in many ways by external causes, and unable ever to possess true peace of mind, but he also lives as if he knew neither himself, nor God, nor things; and as soon as he ceases to be acted on, he ceases to be. On the other hand, the wise man, insofar as he is considered as such, is hardly troubled in spirit, but being, by a certain eternal necessity, conscious of himself, and of God, and of things, he never ceases to be, but always possesses true peace of mind.

If the way I have shown to lead to these things now seems very hard, still, it can be found. And of course, what is found so rarely must be hard. For if salvation were at hand, and could be found without great effort, how could nearly everyone neglect it? But all things excellent are as difficult as they are rare.

INDEX

This index[1] is intended to provide a basic guide to the key concepts of Spinoza's philosophy, as represented by this volume. The construction of an index for a translated text presents formidable problems, arising mainly from the frequent lack of a one-to-one correspondence between the terms of the original text and those of the translation. I have discussed and attempted to deal with those problems in the glossary-index of volume 1 of the *Collected Works of Spinoza* (Princeton University Press, 1985), but cannot undertake anything so complex here. Students who may want to undertake a more comprehensive investigation of Spinoza's terminology, can consult the glossary-index of that volume.[2]

Page numbers marked with an asterisk contain definitions.

---

1. I am very much indebted to my wife Ruth for her work on the construction of this index, as well as for her help with the proof-reading of the text.

2. The electronic version of that volume is available now with a very fast and powerful search program from InteLex Corp., P.O. Box 859, Charlottesville, VA, 22902–0859. (This provides, in effect, a complete concordance to the text.)

THE STORY OF PENGUIN CLASSICS

Before 1946 ...'Classics' are mainly the domain of academics and students, without readable editions for everyone else. This all changes when a little-known classicist, E. V. Rieu, presents Penguin founder Allen Lane with the translation of Homer's *Odyssey* that he has been working on and reading to his wife Nelly in his spare time.

1946 *The Odyssey* becomes the first Penguin Classic published, and promptly sells three million copies. Suddenly, classic books are no longer for the privileged few.

1950s Rieu, now series editor, turns to professional writers for the best modern, readable translations, including Dorothy L. Sayers's *Inferno* and Robert Graves's *The Twelve Caesars*, which revives the salacious original.

1960s The Classics are given the distinctive black jackets that have remained a constant throughout the series's various looks. Rieu retires in 1964, hailing the Penguin Classics list as 'the greatest educative force of the 20th century'.

1970s A new generation of translators arrives to swell the Penguin Classics ranks, and the list grows to encompass more philosophy, religion, science, history and politics.

1980s The Penguin American Library joins the Classics stable, with titles such as *The Last of the Mohicans* safeguarded. Penguin Classics now offers the most comprehensive library of world literature available.

1990s The launch of Penguin Audiobooks brings the classics to a listening audience for the first time, and in 1999 the launch of the Penguin Classics website takes them online to a larger global readership than ever before.

The 21st Century Penguin Classics are rejacketed for the first time in nearly twenty years. This world famous series now consists of more than 1300 titles, making the widest range of the best books ever written available to millions – and constantly redefining the meaning of what makes a 'classic'.

The Odyssey continues ...

The best books ever written

PENGUIN (🐧) CLASSICS

SINCE 1946